Claims and Speculations

Claims and Speculations
Mining and Writing in the Gilded Age

∞

JANET FLOYD

University of New Mexico Press ❦ Albuquerque

© 2012 by the University of New Mexico Press
All rights reserved. Published 2012
Printed in the United States of America

First paperback edition, 2020
Paperback ISBN: 978-0-8263-5140-1

LIBRARY OF CONGRESS CATALOGING-IN-PUBLICATION DATA
Floyd, Janet.
Claims and speculations : mining and writing in the Gilded Age / Janet Floyd.
p. cm.
Includes bibliographical references and index.
ISBN 978-0-8263-5139-5 (cloth : alk. paper) — ISBN 978-0-8263-5141-8 (electronic)
1. American literature—History and criticism. 2. Mines and mineral resources in literature. 3. Mineralogy in literature. 4. Miners in literature. I. Title.
PS169.M56F56 2012
810'.9'355—dc23   2012014861

For Molly Clark and Carl Schwarcz

Contents

Illustrations
ix

Acknowledgments
xi

Introduction
"Hard Places"
1

CHAPTER ONE
Claims and Speculations
13

CHAPTER TWO
Mining and Writing
32

CHAPTER THREE

Knowing the Mines "Interiorly"

54

CHAPTER FOUR

The Romance of Mining

74

CHAPTER FIVE

Sex Work

91

CHAPTER SIX

"Talking Klondike"

110

Afterword

129

Notes

135

Selected Bibliography

160

Index

180

Illustrations

FIGURES

1. "Overcome by gas, the recusitation" (1899) — xii
2. *Miners: A Moment at Rest (Gold Rush Camp)* (1882) — 106
3. *Sunday Morning in the Mines* (1872) — 107
4. *Packers ascending summit of Chilkoot Pass* (1898) — 115

Acknowledgments

☙

✣ THIS PROJECT BEGAN WITH MY INTEREST IN THE MINING FICTIONS of Mary Hallock Foote, and I would like to thank Paul and Marian Brewin for feeding that interest with questions and gifts of editions of Foote's work. I am very glad that Marian was able, before she died, to listen to some of this outcome of her inquiring spirit.

I want to acknowledge the wealth of assistance I have received in the writing of this book: encouragement from colleagues in the American Studies Department at King's College London, as well as funding from the College's School of Arts and Humanities; great patience on the part of the staff at the British Library and the Bancroft Library at the University of California; the companionable hospitality of June Menzies. I have also enjoyed, and depended on, the help and advice of Laurel Forster, Richard Thompson, Jane Seymour, and Sue Sissling. The enthusiasm of W. Clark Whitehorn at the University of New Mexico Press was a major spur to complete the final draft. I am also grateful to the Press's readers for their advice, and to Nicole Schlutt for her help with the editing the manuscript. *Claims and Speculations* is dedicated to Molly Clark and Carl Schwarcz of Sausalito, California. My happiest experiences in writing this book have derived from their hospitality and friendship.

Figure 1: Kinsey & Kinsey. "Overcome by gas, the recusitation" (1899). University of Washington Libraries, Special Collections, UW12490.

Introduction

"Hard Places"

⁓

❧ I WANT TO BEGIN WITH AN IMAGE OF MINING. OPPOSITE IS A PHOTOGRAPH taken in 1899 during the Klondike Gold Rush, captioned "Overcome by gas, the recusitation [sic]." The place is remote and the landscape forbidding; it might be located anywhere in the western regions of North America or indeed in other isolated, mountainous regions of the world. These men seem unlikely to make either a lasting impact on the landscape or their own fortunes with their flimsy operation and simple technologies; it is doubtful if even the detritus of the mine will leave much of a mark. Yet this disordered mining scene exemplifies what was long thought of—and in some contexts is still thought of—as an extraordinary mid- and late nineteenth-century democratic adventure. The particular adventure of these men occurred during the last rush in a series of gold and silver rushes that, for the half century after the Californian Gold Rush of 1849, took disparate populations to a succession of far-flung sites. These rushes began as new technologies of communication spread news of the strikes internationally.[1] They ended once mining became comprehensively technologized, corporate, professionalized, and operated by workers who were characteristically settled in one place.[2] Over the intervening half century, gold and silver mining proved preoccupying and full of imaginative interest to participants and observers alike. It is with this late nineteenth-century response that this book is concerned.

This photograph does not depict such excitements, however. Its focus is the grim scene of an accident. But it is an image that is no less easily inhabited than the portrait of a Gold Rush Argonaut, or a scene of striking gold. Certain disasters at work, as Archie Green (1972) points out, have become "fully vivid and present to the public mind," and Green includes mining accidents in this category (75). Understandings of mining have become suffused with visions of the dreadful damage done to human bodies in mines and especially with the ever-present threat of death stalking underground workings. Mines are invisible to most people until disaster strikes, at which point they are transformed into scenes of terror: the terror of entrapment underground, certainly, and also perhaps terror at the specter of corporate indifference to workers' safety. As I write this introduction in September 2010, there are daily, even at times hourly, reports on the situation of thirty-three miners who have been trapped in the San José Mine in northern Chile for almost two months. In July the death of forty-six men caught in an explosion in a coal mine in Pingdingshan City in Henan Province, China, was in the news. In April, twenty-five miners were killed in an explosion at the Upper Big Branch Mine in West Virginia, and this, too, was internationally reported. In March there was news that thirty-eight miners had been drowned in the Wangjialing Mine in northern China, a mine that was still being built.

The accident that this Klondike photograph represents is on a much smaller scale, of course. This is low-technology mining, where the men have been digging a few feet through the permafrost to excavate gold-bearing gravel. A man has collapsed as a result of inhaling the poisonous gas produced when the frozen remains of underground vegetation thaw.[3] He has been dragged up, his blood polluted by gas, and his rescuers face the challenge of resuscitating him. In the context of an industry blighted, if not defined, by human carnage, this is a minor incident. But images of injury, mutilation, and destruction dominate the representation of mining to the point where mining seems constituted of these disasters, and not from the excitements of finding precious metals or the skill of extracting precious metal from earth and rock. Mines are, in Richard V. Francaviglia's (1991) words, "hard places": hard to work certainly, and hard to contemplate, too.[4]

The use of mining as a literary subject is difficult as well. Langston Hughes (1928), writing about the racialized industrial complex of mining in Johannesburg, worked by "240,000 natives," asks: "What kind of poem would you make out of that?"[5] Poetic writing can scarcely do justice to such a scene, much less extend support to the miners. These mines refute poetry's power to transform the world for its readers. In resorting instead to the power of numbers and of the word "natives" with all its historical and political freight, Hughes is in accord with a longstanding view that the representation of mining should be documentary in style and reformist in purpose. This point is sometimes made in more positive terms. Michael Kowalewski (2000), for example, has argued that "the true imaginative wealth of the Gold Rush resides in its non-fictional prose" and in its response to the "demands of everyday life" in the diggings and mining towns (214). The claim is often made that writing that takes the least distance on experience does greatest justice to mining events.

This Klondike image—and I hope this book—takes up Hughes's challenge as to how, or indeed whether, mining should be represented, unless by miners. Without question mines were, and have always been, hard and dangerous places, but they have also been as productive of thought as of precious materials. Miners have certainly suffered and struggled, but they have also written, painted, and made photographs. The photograph we are considering here is not the work of fearful or intrusive observers or documentary journalists, but of miners, and it forms part of an extraordinary outpouring of images of the Klondike Gold Rush made by participants. The Klondike Rush produced miners who wanted to represent themselves and to be represented by others, and who generated a body of vernacular expression with its own distinctive typologies of shared experience. There was not as substantial or as coherent a response as this to every rush, but throughout the late nineteenth century, gold and silver mines, mining, and miners generated a mass of expressive material. The miners, amateur and experienced, who followed the strikes and rushes of the period did not wait for professional writers to undertake the task of evoking their experience. They developed a lore, literature, photography, and art of their own, for a range of audiences. Indeed, most of the representation of gold and silver mining during this period was the work of people who were drawing on a range of engagements with the industry, and it is this engaged creative work that has generated the questions about mining and writing that I consider in this study.

It was not just that miners were keen to represent their participation in rushes and strikes to "outsiders" and families left behind, but that mining and its representation were tightly entwined. "Overcome by gas" depicts the staging of an accident for the camera. The men who took photographs and made art were also digging mines. The image was produced by Kinsey and Kinsey, a firm belonging to two brothers, both of whom were involved in mining as well as in taking pictures commercially.[6] Clarke Kinsey, who took the picture, may have taken some degree of responsibility for proposing the subject and posing the men because he was the most experienced photographer. Although he invested in the mines, he shifted from mining to photography quite soon after his arrival in the Klondike.[7] Clarke's brother Clarence joined in the performance by squatting on the right of the "patient." He also took photographs to make a living, but became increasingly involved in working his mining claims, staying, in the end, for over a decade in the area—an unusually long stay for a small-time claim owner. Meanwhile, the man performing the process of resuscitation, Asa Thurston Hayden, combined mining and selling delicate etchings of the natural landscapes of the Klondike to the local press.[8] George Archer, to the left of the group, was the only one of the four with substantial mining experience at this point. He may have been one of those newcomers to the region who had spent years migrating from one metal strike to another, or someone who had been prospecting in the Klondike in the 1880s and early 1890s, before the rush began. Here he acted out an event of which he may or may not have had experience. What this photograph reminds us, in short, is that while onlookers may, like Langston Hughes, sense that the work of mining—dreadful, toilsome, dangerous, physical work—and the work of cultural production have a troubling relationship ("What kind of poem would you make out of that?"), for those involved, mining inspired a profusion of cultural projects with various aesthetic and economic agendas, and diverse audiences, too.

Such a band of miners as this raises questions, though, about whom we are going to call a miner and how a miner might be defined in the era of gold and silver rushes and strikes. What claims, for example, might Clarke or Clarence Kinsey make to be considered "real" miners as opposed to transient fortune seekers? This has been a significant question in the scholarship about writing and mining in the American West. Scholars have tended to evaluate the worth of a text's response to the industry in some part on the grounds of length of experience of mining, so that to be in some sense an insider to the industry has been a critically important marker for the integrity of a writer's or artist's work. As a consequence, Bret Harte's writing about mining cultures in California has been seen as compromised by his scant experience of working in the mines himself. Mary Hallock Foote, as a middle-class female, seems unlikely, to her critics, to have much of worth to say about mining in Leadville, Colorado, in her novels. A key difficulty with this measurement of worth lies in its vision of mining as a stable form of work involving experienced miners as, say, in coal mining. But gold and silver mining in this late nineteenth-century context involved both experienced and inexperienced actors as well as dramatically different types of activity above and below ground. There was a major disparity in the form and routines of work between the placer miner who panned alluvial deposits or mines close to the surface in California and the Klondike and the hard rock miner working in deep shafts in Virginia City and Leadville. In the late nineteenth century, the former might be skilled or unskilled, working seasonally and likely to mine in informal or familial groups. The latter was generally a skilled, hierarchized, full-time worker, in some cases intensely aware of craft traditions in the industry.[9] At the same time, though, individual workers during this period might move between hard rock sites operating at different levels of technological complexity, as well as between working deep shaft mines for mining companies and prospecting and panning for themselves. So, for example, it was common for hard rock miners who worked as waged employees to prospect in their spare time in the hope of a strike.[10] It was also common for people to work in mines temporarily or to become involved in the industry in other ways for short or extended periods. For many, mining was, as Susan Lawrence (1998) puts it, "only one part of a broader subsistence strategy" (48).

Given this fluid and intricately variable scene, it is difficult to evaluate the worth of any kind of mining text against length or type of experience, or to favor the insights of professionals rather than amateurs, underground rather than placer miners. Instead, in this book, I have embraced Bryan Pfaffenberger's (1998) wonderful description of mining as "fabulously complex": a dynamic, volatile scene that was experienced in a mass of ways. Pfaffenberger uses the phrase to evoke mining's ability to generate "vast hinterland supply regions, transportation systems . . . manufacturers and distributors of mining equipment, political arrangements . . . laws and regulations, labor unions, management styles and much more" (296). Looked at in this way, mining always encompasses different forms and intensities of involvement. I take Pfaffenberger's expression more literally, too. Mining seems to me peculiarly writable—actually "fabulous"—and as likely to generate stories and images as to produce transportation networks and new technologies. It is indeed "complex" in the prospects and problems it offers to those who strive to evoke its qualities and significance. Mining has been well served in the forms of documentary, social criticism, and political activism. It is, as we shall see, equally hospitable to folklore, legend, novels, poetry, and romance.

It comes as something of a surprise, then, to find that the scholarly study of American writing about the gold and silver rushes is quite scarce. Wallace Stegner's (1969) salty suggestion that "readers panning the tailings and gravel heaps of these old literary placers [of the Gold Rush] sometimes find more gold than the original Argonauts found" has not been taken up, for all the literary, historical, and cultural interest in the writing of the West (233). Even historians preoccupied with the mining West, though they may draw on certain writers,[11] have argued that the whole scene has failed to attract the cultural attention enjoyed by homesteading or the cattle industry.[12] The acknowledgment of all that was published about the gold and silver strikes now resides, in fact, in the work of very few literary historians to whom this study is much indebted, most notably Lawrence I. Berkove and Michael Kowalewski.[13] True, the Sagebrush writers of Nevada's silver mining era have remained visible (though this is largely due to Mark Twain's involvement with Virginia City journalism), but with the exception of Bret Harte, a writer in whom few scholars take pleasure, and Jack London, most of the published writers of the rushes are rarely more than thinly anthologized. Miners' folklore briefly attracted scholarly attention during the 1940s and 1950s: a number of articles were published collating mining lore in the West and noted how the work lore of miners surfaced in the work of Harte, Twain, and others. But that interest in mining's complex world of lore and its relationship with published texts in the nineteenth century has not been sustained.[14]

Some explanation for this may be found in the cultural antipathy to mining that I discussed at the start of this introduction and to the preference for documentary and historical representations of mining that address all that is most oppressive in the industry.[15] The representation of mining in lore, texts, and images during the gold and silver rushes is not generally documentary in style or intention, and much of it has become obscure as a result. At the same time, there is an implicit preference for realism in the scholarship of literary western writing. It is generally the case that those writers who worked outside the realist tradition have been valued less. Some part of the explanation for the disappearance of writing about mining as a category, then, lies in the critical tendency to argue that human experiences of the nineteenth-century American West were susceptible to certain kinds of literary treatment and resistant to others.

Perhaps another reason for the neglect of writing about mining lies in the industry's role within worldwide imperial and capitalistic projects rather than a local and regional history. Events in California in 1849 coincided with strikes in Australia and British Columbia in the early 1850s, and the gold rushes in Colorado in the 1860s and early 1870s took place alongside similar events in New Zealand. It has always been clear that mining rushes and their outcomes operate in a world system and that this might be a matter for disapproving comment. Mark Twain's portrait of his journey to make his fortune in Nevada and his sojourn in Virginia City in *Roughing It* (1872), for example, inspired a review in the English *Manchester Guardian* that reflected on "that frenzied lust for gain and universal spirit of gambling" that succeeded all metal strikes. This reviewer went on to comment that "Mr. Charles Reade's description of the Australian goldfields... would hold equally good for California or the diamond miners of the Cape," and doubtless for Nevada, too. Twain's portrait had little "local" interest for this reviewer, and it is perhaps the transnational logic and the cosmopolitanism of the mining industry that has made the writing of mining difficult to contain in the fields of regional and national literary analysis (7).[16]

In this study, I have drawn together a diverse range of responses to mining in generic and stylistic terms, tracing links between texts about mining generated in different late nineteenth-century settings within and beyond the American West. The imaginative response to mines, mining, and miners has surfaced in the sometimes separate, sometimes overlapping, fields of folklore and labor lore, popular culture and working-class writing, as well as in literary writing and journalism. My interest here, however, is not primarily in comparing sources, or in considering different expressive or generic practices, but rather in trying tentatively to uncover different strands of the late nineteenth-century engagement with an activity loaded with significance. This has involved traversing some rather treacherous ground between vernacular and print cultural forms, labor lore and literary writing, and mining legend and romance—ground that is fraught with difficulties of definition and unclear relationships. For some scholars, the relationship of literary writing to work lore and folklore must always be compromised.[17] Here, I have chosen to address mining matters on which different modes of expression converge. In doing so, I will, if nothing else, have gathered a body of responses to a critically important late nineteenth-century industry. I leave it to others to grapple with some of the methodological problems created by showing different expressive forms in conversation with one another.

Equally, I have tried to address mining's transnational reach. Where studies have appeared (for example, discussions of H. Rider Haggard's

King Solomon's Mines [1885]), their arguments have focused upon the justifications and anxieties of the late nineteenth-century Anglo-European imperial project. This is a mode of response that is engaged in this study, too; however, in focusing on the experience of miners and the representation of that experience, I have also thought in terms of what David Thelan (1992) has called "transnationalism from below" (438). As energetic as the mining companies were in delivering precious metals to metropolitan economies and imperial centers, so were miners equally dynamic as they congregated at the sites of strikes. And as indifferent as those economies and centers may have been to spaces perceived as empty and featureless margins, so were the circumstances of those sites nonetheless specific and highly variable. This study takes as its focus a series of American episodes, moving into Canada in the final chapter. It discusses writing in English or translated into English. There is no temptation to treat these episodes solely as part of a trajectory of national and imperial history or as anything less than distinct from one another, although transnational comparisons between like mining cultures have proved surprisingly enlightening.

But I want also to make some broader claims than this for mining texts produced during this extraordinary period of activity. The gold and silver rushes and the mining industry and cultures that they created were harbingers of new conditions: they drove migration and created new cosmopolitan camps, towns, and cities; they made fortunes for companies and speculators; they had profound effects on the development and the demise of nations and communities; they supported new technologies; they promoted unionization; they revolutionized finance; they wrecked landscapes. My argument in this study is that the representation of mining, since the 1850s, addressed the unfolding forms of a new industrial experience. Writing about mining, as I have acknowledged, is always hard, but these gold and silver rushes and strikes, created and sustained by print, faced those engaged in them with unfamiliar challenges. How, for example, should experiences created by speculation be written? How could the social, sexual, and psychic fallout of fast industrialization be handled? How might one write an industrial American "frontier"? How could the instant cities created by strikes be situated in space and time? The paucity of scholarly interest in mining writing has made the dynamic, diverse response made by a range of writers obscure, but their varying reactions to industrialism, their engagements with modernity, and their readings of the locations of the strikes deserve to be enfolded in the literary history of the period. This is a time, after all, that we frequently name by reference to precious metals and their troubling cultural impact: the Gilded Age.

Scholarly enterprises often begin with statements of what the writer or speaker is not going to do, and this is no exception. In striving to explore the ground shared between the rich, imaginative world of miners and the writing of those who engaged variously with mines, I have worked at a distance from the particular historical episodes in which miners battled against the conditions imposed on them, though such conditions are described throughout this study. Another absence in this study is the discussion of mined materials other than gold and silver. The American West of the late nineteenth century was identified with metal mining, but coal mining has often been seen as mining's definitive form. Readers of Owen Wister's *The Virginian* (1902), for example, will recall how the ranch workers' rush to find gold, read by the Virginian as a threat to paternalistic labor relations, is trumped by his adoption of coal mining. But coal mining is both different from metal mining and constitutes a literary subject in its own right. For that reason, and notwithstanding the links between different forms of mining and the people involved, I have set aside coal mining in this study.

No cultural study of mining, however, can ignore the grand narratives that the industry has generated. In the opening chapter of this study, I look at some of the forms that such narratives have taken and consider a late nineteenth-century novel that took up the explanations of mining produced at the time: Frank Norris's *McTeague* (1899). Important and deeply compelling as these totalizing analyses have been, however, they have not organized my own approach to the representation of mining. On the contrary, my impulse has been to take the understandings of mining that arise from the work culture of mining and the folklore of miners as my starting point and to see how those understandings surface in texts such as Ambrose Bierce's "The Night-Doings at 'Deadman's'" (1877). Chapter two returns to the project of representing mining in language and to arguments about representing and misrepresenting the world of the rushes. My focus here is on Gold Rush writing and, in particular, the case of Bret Harte. The criticism of his mining of California (in particular the comparison with the work of Alonso Delano and "Dame Shirley") brings me to the mining metaphors that have suffused the discussion of writing since the Renaissance: the mining of subjects, the following of seams, the writing in veins, the issue of depth.

Chapter three moves to the setting of Comstock Lode, Nevada, and to the writing of silver mining by journalists who were indubitably industry insiders: the Sagebrush writers. Here I explore the implications of reporting on the mines for mining newspapers and for the journalists involved, particularly Dan De Quille, Fred H. Hart, and Mark Twain. Chapter four deals with mining's affinity with legend and romance, not only in terms of its hospitality to mythical, magical stories charged with moral significance, but also in its use of legend's play on space and time. In this chapter I consider the difficulties of handling the spaces and places of mining and in particular the tactics used by journalists and visitors to deal with instant cities. I then look at what writers of romance—Hamlin Garland and Mary Hallock Foote in particular—achieve in their portraits of mining. Mines teem with gendered and sexual meaning, and in chapter five I address traditions of understanding mining as an arena for the performance of aggressive masculinity, and more recent claims that the late nineteenth-century rushes proved to be episodes within which non-normative relationships might be developed. The thematic slippages of David Belasco's *Girl of the Golden West* (1905) and Delano's *Live Woman in the Mines* (1857) and the eroticism of Harte's work are key points of reference in a chapter dealing with a complex scene of sexual behavior in the mines and its representation. Finally, returning to the Klondike in chapter six, I look at the writing of the "poor man's rush." Here, the experience of the poor miner occupies center stage and is explored and appropriated in a range of writing for local, North American, and international readerships. Much of the writing under discussion in the previous chapters has engaged with mining's radically new circumstances during this period. Writers of the Klondike, especially Robert Service and Jack London, were dealing with what was always clearly the last rush of the era.

In this study, I have thought of mining as a challenge to understanding and summary, a dynamic, volatile scene that generated and inspired a broad range of imaginative responses. Mining has always forced human beings to imagine new dimensions of experience and shaped thought.[18] Stories of all types have long crystallized around the figure of the miner and the depths of the mine, as well as around precious metals. Small wonder, then, that in the late nineteenth century, the strikes and rushes, the movement of money, the mines, the camps, and the boomtowns demanded attention. The fate of any and all of these was unpredictable and difficult to grasp. What follows is an exploration of the attempts, as diverse as the strikes themselves, to grasp the essence of gold and silver mining during this period.

CHAPTER ONE

Claims and Speculations

❦ THE GOLD AND SILVER STRIKES OF THE LATE NINETEENTH CENTURY generated a mass of claims and counterclaims about how the rushes could be positioned within grand narratives of human behavior and history. H. H. Bancroft (1888) wrote of an unstoppable natural force: the forty-niners were like "inland streams and ocean currents, social tricklings and oozings from scattered and far distant homes, gathering into rivulets, and expanding into human rivers" (83); and Emerson (1860) referred grandly to "Sabine rapes" leading to "real Romes" as he speculated about the "malfaisance" of the Gold Rush turning to social "good" (224). These rushes were extraordinary events by any measure, of course, and likely to inspire a range of attempts to position them in broad histories of human activity. And in any case, one expects these panoramic, transhistorical perspectives from nineteenth-century commentators entranced by Anglo-American and European expansionism and keen to talk up America's position in world history and the new nation's prospects as a world power. What is perhaps more surprising is to find much the same kinds of explanations of mining rushes now. Peter Bell (1998), for example, describes participants as "like a cloud of insects, apparently formless, but with a single purpose" (28), while Eugene P. Moehring (2004) refers to San Francisco, a hub of late nineteenth-century American mining, as "much like Athens" (xviii). However, the conception of mining as the discharge of irresistible human energies across a series of repeating episodes has a dominant presence in writing about mining in general. Whether the writer is examining a particular case or a regional mining scene over time, recourse to these forms of rhetoric has been absolutely routine. The triumphal narrative sweep from ancient history to the present still appears in modern histories. Marvin D. Bernstein (1965), for example, writing about the Mexican mining industry after 1890, begins with "the ancient conquests of the Pharaohs for the copper mines of Sinai and the silver and gold mines of Nubia" and the "fabled expedition of Jason for the Golden Fleece, which symbolized the gold of the Crimea," before tackling human history:

> Man's interest and stake in mining is enormous. The drive to discover mines; the struggle of individuals and governments to control mines; the fixing of relationships between the State and the miners . . . the development of world metal markets; and the modern industrial system dependent on international lines of commerce—all are part of the prodigious influence of mining upon history and the economic structure of the world. (xv)

This chapter begins with a look at these kinds of broad analysis, not only because they have been so seminal to the intellectual engagement with mining and mining's outcomes, but because they have had such a marked impact on what we recognize as writing about mining. My response to these narratives is twofold. First, it seems to me that the magisterial analyses of mining come close to erasing the agency, work, and culture of miners. If we take on that agency, work, and culture, we can construct a very different and much less determined mining. My second argument builds on this point. For the nineteenth century, certainly, mining was far from being "singularly tellable," to use John Law's (1999) phrase, and certainly not in the late nineteenth-century world of gold and silver mining (8). I have already discussed the difficulty of defining mining and miners during this period, but I shall return to these points later in the chapter.

The examples of grand mining narratives that I have quoted so far are, of course, too brief to give a sense of the complexity of the kinds of overarching analysis of mining and its impact that I want to discuss. Certainly, some nineteenth-century commentaries were nationalistic, congratulatory, and sweeping in their triumphalism. Others, though, strove to find a multidimensional significance to the strikes and rushes of gold and silver mining. At the opening of Dan De Quille's history of the Comstock Lode, *The Big Bonanza* (1876), for instance, there is the immediate address to a familiar narrative—a narrative that the writer assumes will be shared—of transformation through discovery. Here is the appeal to multiple histories in different temporal registers: the famous silver strike in Potosi, Peru, with its associations with Spanish imperialism and its geography of the Americas, and the broader European vision of the Americas as an El Dorado; we catch a glimpse, too, of the history of the first English settlers on the Atlantic seaboard and their relations with "Indians," a group whom the reader is able to link with this "Indian hunter" in Potosi. These are, of course, the coordinates of an imperial history.

> The bare mention of a mine of silver calls up in most minds visions of glittering wealth and a world of romantic situations and associations. All no doubt have read the story of the Indian hunter Diego Hualca, who, in the year 1545, discovered the world-famous silver mine of Potosí, Peru. How, while climbing up the face of a steep mountain in pursuit of a wild goat, this fortunate hunter laid hold upon a bush in order to pull himself up over a steep ledge of rocks, and how the bush was torn out by the roots, when lo! wonderful store of wealth was laid bare. . . . Having all our lives had in mind this romantic story, and having a thousand times pictured to ourselves the great shining lumps of native silver as they lay exposed in the black soil before that Indian, who stood alone in a far-away place on the wild mountain, we are able to imagine something of the same kind is to be seen wherever a silver mine exists. Besides, we have all heard the stories told by the old settlers of the Atlantic states in regard to the wonderful mines of silver known to the Indians in early days. (3)

In charging the everyday landscape of Diego Hualca's discovery with the resonances of destiny and the iconography of myth—the mountain, the bush, the hoard of glowing treasure—De Quille achieves the effect of releasing the event of mining silver in Nevada from its actual context of economic depression in California, national and regional war, and legal wrangling. He calls up instead the "world of romantic situations and associations" that "the bare mention of a mine of silver" arouses: the world of fantasy that is broken open when, as the ordinary human struggles through the daily round, a heap of treasure appears.

Arguments about mining's social and environmental fallout have, however, been quite as powerful and penetrating as the consensual fantasies of progress and individual fulfillment. A touchstone for this debate is the sixteenth-century mining treatise of Georgius Agricola, *De Re Metallica* (1555), a work apparently so learned and authoritative as to have shaped mining practice for some generations after its publication.[1] Agricola famously begins his work by describing his contemporaries' bitter objections to the industry: the arguments that mining is "an occupation of sordid toil" (1), dangerous and morally corrupting; it is neither profitable to those who practice it nor useful to society generally (4); it is unstable and inferior to farming (5); and the strongest argument, mining causes the devastation of the landscape (8). Ironically, Agricola's sarcastic account of his opponents' anxiety and disgust has retained an impact his learned and detailed rebuttals have not. As he writes:

> It is almost our daily experience to learn that, for the sake of obtaining gold and silver, doors are burst open, walls are pierced, wretched travelers are struck down by rapacious and cruel men born to theft, sacrilege, invasion and robbery. We see thieves seized and strung up before us, sacrilegious persons buried alive, the limbs of robbers broken on the wheel, wars waged for the same reason.... Nay, but they say that precious metals foster all manner of vice, such as the seduction of women, adultery and unchastity, in short, crimes of violence against the person.... Moreover, the fidelity of many men is overthrown by the love of gold and silver, judicial sentences are bought, and innumerable crimes perpetuated. (10)

Hundreds of years later we find Gary Brechin (2006), a journalist and scholar writing at the intersection of polemic and environmental history, turning back, in his study of California's "urban power and earthly ruin," to engage Agricola's mid-sixteenth-century argument (25–29). Allan Sekula (1983), in a famous essay on traditions of representation under industrial capitalism, uses the illustrations in Agricola's text to show the beginnings of the desire to normalize the power relations of an industrial machine (194).

In our own time, though, it is Lewis Mumford's condemnation in *Technics and Civilization* (1934) that has achieved canonical status in cultural arguments about mining. Mumford reaches back to ancient industry and finds incontrovertible evidence that this has always been a "primitive" occupation, the "lowest on the human scale," "a form of punishment" dealt out "in the bowels of the earth" (67). The mine offers no "environment of life" (69), but "the very image of backwardness, isolation, raw animosities and lethal struggles" (73). Mining, Mumford insists, forms the worst possible local base for a civilized social world: when mines fail, they are abandoned and only debris and ruin are left behind (157). It exists at the very core of war, with its "premium on brute force," and "its unflinching assault upon the physical environment" (69). Beyond this though, and more importantly for Mumford's analysis, is his systematic argument that mining "set the pattern for capitalist exploitation," in its emphasis on technologization at the expense of the worker and for the benefit of the owner, in its "heaping up of fortunes" for the benefit of bankers and in the service of the nefarious works of the ruling classes (74). Mining and all of its works have created, in short, a human nightmare that is escalating under industrial capitalism.

Cultural critics return to Mumford's painful discussions of mining as assiduously as they do to Agricola's defense to elaborate on this tradition of horrified condemnation. Zygmunt Baumann (2004), for example, in mounting a critique of modernity's routines of waste, goes back to Mumford's comparison between the restorative cycles of farming and the damaging extraction of mining. He describes the destruction of woodland, the removal of soil to access ore with all of Mumford's passion: "Each point through which mining proceeds is a point of no return. Mining is a one-way movement, irreversible and irrevocable. The chronicle of mining is a graveyard of used up, repudiated and abandoned lodes and shafts" (21).

We can find something very similar in recent histories dealing with mining in the American West during the late nineteenth century. The New Western historians, in particular, have found in mining a focus for their interests in environmental damage, imperialism, and war. In 1987, for example, one of the earliest texts in this vein, Patricia Limerick's *The Legacy of Conquest* (1987), used as its frontispiece a photograph that shows a group of miners surrounded by trash.[2] Elliott West (2001), adding, in a revised edition, to Rodman Paul's 1963 frontier history of western mining, imports the language of war and injury, colonialism, and racism. "A mining camp," he writes, "was like an artillery shell lobbed into the outback. Its concussion spread outward and rolled over native peoples who would never see a sluice or mine" (231). Richard White's (1991) mining industry is catastrophic in its impact on human bodies and landscape alike. It generates a "half-world" of violent, racially divided urban communities (304).[3]

These twin traditions of progress and degeneration inform Frank Norris's late nineteenth-century portrait of mining in *McTeague* (1899). Other texts of the period produced more triumphalist narratives: H. Rider Haggard's *King Solomon's Mines* (1885), for instance, or Richard Harding Davis's *Soldiers of Fortune* (1897). A few used mining to critique industrial capitalism: Émile Zola's *Germinal* (1885) is the obvious example. Norris regards mining as an industry of ancient lineage, and one that exemplifies, too, the forces driving modernity: the domination of nature, the impulse to accumulate, the recasting of the structures of human relations. The California of *McTeague* has been profoundly shaped by mining, and Norris's eponymous protagonist, a miner, has to adapt himself to a working and domestic existence in a city permeated by gold seeking.

In developing a panoramic vision of mining at the intersection of forces, Norris had at his shoulder the model of Émile Zola and the most famous mining novel of the nineteenth century, *Germinal*.[4] Zola's sociological Naturalism impelled him to research the coal mining of northern France carefully and, in consequence, *Germinal* displays a much more vivid and forensic interest than *McTeague* in the detail of the miners' work and the social relations of the coal-mining community.[5] For all the attention and respect he accords the miners, however, Zola goes to great trouble to show how the prejudices and attitudes of managers and shareholders, along with shifting and unpredictable economic conditions, dominate mining. In a comparable way, Norris, who wrote his novel after his journalistic trip to the mines in the Transvaal and a working holiday at Iowa Hill, California, found different but, for him, no less irresistible forces and agents determining the shape of mining: competition for precious metals, corporate clout, and violent conflict in the service of Anglo-Saxon imperial expansion. Though not given to the kind of research undertaken by Zola, Norris did observe the geopolitics of mining at first hand at the Witwatersrand mines of southern Africa. Not only did he spend time in the company of John Hays Hammond, a mining engineer with an international portfolio who took as read the rights of Anglo-Saxon nations to imperial supremacy, he also supported, as actively as he was allowed, the British attempt to annex the Witwatersrand.[6] Norris plainly thrilled to the project of imperial mastery of the mines.

Zola's coal miners are physically, intellectually, and emotionally crushed by the work of mining and their grinding poverty; a limited range of instinctual feelings and pleasures survive. Norris's McTeague is a blond giant, but his deficiencies are no less evident. He cannot express himself in words, often repeating the simple utterance "I don' know" (132). Some of his thinking has been assimilated from mining forbears: he has "the old-time miner's idea of wealth easily gained" (132). Much of his behavior is inherited: the legacy of McTeague's mining forbears is "a foul stream of hereditary evil," as well as the tendency to become violent when drunk (32).

McTeague's other inheritance derives from Norris's encounters in southern Africa with the African men who came to the mines as temporary workers from the surrounding areas, and who, by the time Norris observed them, were restricted to the most dangerous work and living in appalling conditions.[7] Here, portraying an African miner's response to an injury (his flesh has been gouged to the bone in the mine) Norris uses precisely the terms that he later employs to describe McTeague's response to events—stupefaction, passivity, rolling eyes, vagueness, stupidity:

> Did you ever notice how a shot bird or a rabbit will be, as it were, struck dumb by the wound, will suddenly become passive, inert, stupefied? So it was with the Kaffir: he made no sound, he hardly moved, merely turning his head from side to side, rolling his eyes about vaguely, now staring at the bandaged arm, now looking stupidly into the circle of faces around him.[8]

Elsewhere, in descriptions of the Dutch inhabitants of the Transvaal, Norris uses some similar terms: "sluggish, unambitious, unenergetic, unspeakably stupid," "slow, placid, content, stupid," "ox-like."[9] Again, McTeague is described using all these words, and Norris makes the link between the determinisms of occupation and "race."

The outcome of mining for Norris, and this too is similar to Zola, inspires horror:

> In some place east of the Mississippi, nature is cosey [sic], intimate, small and homelike, like a good-natured housewife. In Placer County, California, she is a vast unconquered brute of the Pliocene epoch, savage, sullen and magnificently indifferent to man. But there were men in these mountains, like lice on a mammoth's hides, fighting them stubbornly, now with hydraulic "monitors," now with drill and

dynamite, boring into the vitals of them, or tearing away great yellow gravelly scars in the flanks of them, sucking their blood, extracting gold. (379–80)

This is a vision of shocking, and shockingly sexualized, violence. The landscape of Placer County is an "unconquered brute" of a Mother Earth toward which the miners direct a frenzy of vicious attacks. Norris sets the scene in such a way as to emphasize mining's dreadful heritage in violent aggression, as well as its modern manifestations in monitors, drills, and dynamite. One can scarcely imagine a view of mining that exhibits a stronger sense of the squalor of the work and its dreadfully destructive impact.

Yet Norris's text makes an opposing argument about mining, too. For much of the novel McTeague is alienated from the mines that have formed him. The tough, energetic, masculinized work of mining is reduced to clumsily executed dentistry; the underground of the mine morphs into dingy city basements. Gold is not extracted but horribly fetishized. Consequently, once back in the gold mine in the final section of the novel, McTeague seems finally released into a working world that fulfills him, with its "play of crude and simple forces—the powerful attacks of the Burly drills; the great exertions of bared bent backs overlaid with muscle; the brusque, resistless expansion of dynamite; the silent, vast, Titanic force, mysterious and slow, that cracked the timbers supporting the roof of the tunnel" (387). These forces, unmediated by urban culture, have a sublime as well as a monstrous power: the stamp-mill, for example is "the crusher, the insatiable monster, gnashing the rocks to powder with its long iron teeth, vomiting them out again in a thin stream of wet gray mud"; it is "glutted . . . with the very entrails of the earth and growling over its endless meal, like some savage animal, some legendary dragon, some fabulous beast" (380). Crushing is a dominant and productive activity of the mines. Transported to the city, it is transformed into cruelty and murder. So McTeague instinctively looks to "crush down" those who thwart him: when his wife Trina defies him, he tries to "crush her struggle with his immense strength" (85), "to crush down her struggle with his enormous strength, to subdue her, conquer her by sheer brute force" (87). This behavior is savage, clearly, but, in the terms of the novel, it is understood as a "real" response undistorted by the urban consciousness epitomized in the neurotic parsimony of Trina, the madness of Maria Macapa, the perversions of Zerkow, or the pinched social miseries of the rest of the San Francisco dramatis personae. Norris makes it possible, then, to imagine the mine as a place of direct engagement with a range of natural and economic forces.

He reinforces the point by decorating the novel with the tropes of epic. McTeague and others are constantly referred to as if they were the characters of epic, using an identifying epithet. McTeague, for example, is "ox-eyed." Clearly this is ironic given that this is a descriptor given in Homer to the crafty, intelligent, and hyper-feminine Juno, yet Norris is also offering the reader a way to imagine McTeague as the mythical stumbling giant. Such epithets, along with the recreation of a desert landscape as a setting for battle rather than a localized space, and of course the emphasis on fate: all these facets of epic lend a sense of profound importance to the figure of the miner.

To sum up, then, Norris's portrait of mining, in all its dimensions, offers a vision of the industry that may be recognized, as Mumford's portrait or Zola's may be recognized, as an irreversible blight, as well as a drama of human history. This kind of analysis sometimes situates mining in a tradition of slavery, a tradition that certainly survives: some mines in countries that are poor or made dangerous by war are still worked by enslaved and indentured people, including children.[10] But the recognition of this terrible circumstance cannot suffuse our vision of all mining without erasing the very different ways in which mining may be understood, particularly by participants in the industry. It has been possible to approach mining from a different direction, to examine and imagine it in other ways to those that I have been describing, by considering the experience and the culture of the miner. It is to this different tradition that I want to turn now.

It is perhaps worth remembering that mining is an extraordinary form of work. It has the kind of uniqueness that is more readily attributed to the equally brutal work of seafaring.[11] It is not only that, uniquely, the miner works in the ground, but also that, like the sailor, the miner works in a space that is peculiarly inaccessible, not to say intimidating, to those outside the industry. Mines are, like ships at sea, characteristically isolated. Both are subject to the kinds of arcane rules, traditions, and hierarchies generated by the especially difficult conditions in which the workforce performs its work. The work in both cases is tremendously demanding physically.

Yet the strains that mining places on the worker have produced a strong tradition of mine workers' independence. As mining historian Klaus Tenfelde

(1992) points out, the miners of popular imagination, the "exploited, emaciated mining proletariat, often apparently vegetating on the edge of existence," is in fact usually a "lively, self-confident" body of workers; miners are willing "to assert themselves in their environs, to fight back, and in fact to be rebellious" (1202). The miner is associated with stroppiness and an ever-present threat of rebellion against the impositions of mine owners. Mining and slavery are linked, without doubt. But so are mining and protest. In the first modern mining operation in Freiberg, miners were able to insist upon special work conditions, as well as high pay, in which they were exempted from taxes, and were able to develop a highly independent work culture.[12] Subsequently, miners have been able, at times, to insist, in this same tradition, on their own working practices (especially their practices with respect to hours of work).[13]

In the nineteenth century, while slavery and forced labor were used to mine in some countries, the gold and silver strikes and rushes created episodes of work interspersed with independent movement from site to site, and indeed made movement in and out of mining easy. Duane A. Smith (1971) cites the experience of Richard Irwin, who, "in the 20 years after 1860 . . . lived and worked in Central City, Buckskin Joe, Tarryall, Georgia Gulch, Gold Run, Empire, Georgetown, Rosita, the San Juans and the Gunnison country." Irwin also made "excursions" in search of work to New Mexico, Utah, and South Dakota (307). For some historians, this continual movement signifies insecurity rather than independence: it speaks to instability in mining communities, to hyper-individualism, or seems likely to cause fragile psychological states and aggressive behavior, especially between different ethnic groups.[14] Mining camps, where they were not actually situated in areas of fighting amongst indigenous and immigrant populations and soldiers, were certainly violent places. Yet when Elliott West writes so evocatively of mining's effect of "toss[ing] [strangers] together with a rare suddenness face-to-face and thought-to-thought," he evokes new possibilities as well as confusion and ferocity (281). The varying makeup of mining communities offered opportunities for self-identification as well as the threat of violent exclusion, subjection, or anomie.

Alongside this independence and disposition for movement rests the pride of experienced miners in undertaking difficult work. Even Mumford, who can find no more than a "simple animal poise" in the miner, still balances "the brutalization [that is] . . . inevitably there" with the miner's "profound personal pride and self-respect" (62). This is the dignity of the miner's skill in sensing "the vein and cleavage in the very guts of rock" that Gary Snyder catches in "Milton by Firelight, Piute Creek" (1955). There is much more here than the grit involved in doing work that most would find toilsome: knowledge, skill, dedication to the task, attentiveness to the earth. Miners' autobiographies are few and far between, but looking at, for example, Frank A. Crampton's (1956) autobiography of "a working stiff in the Western mine camps"—Crampton mined in Cripple Creek and then Gold Field, Nevada, in 1904, and spent his life in the industry—there is evidence everywhere of the pride he took in becoming a skilled worker. Crampton gives list after list to demonstrate the range of skills he learned as a young miner:

> I was taught to lay track, test the roof and walls for loose ground, and to stand clear of rock falls while I was doing it. After I had learned the things needed to hold a job . . . there came a course in timbering, cutting hitches for stulls, framing for chutes and raises, and putting in tunnel or drift sets with room behind the posts and caps for lagging.

He learns "the things needed to hold a job," and the skills "to keep alive while doing it," his work-worn hands "so hard from callouses that a nail couldn't be driven into them" (28). At the same time, he records his intense satisfaction in the acquisition of skills to a level that enables him to win lucrative contracts to work particular drifts independently, as well as the status he enjoys amongst his peers as a result of winning drilling contests.

Crampton describes too an "atmosphere tense with mining tradition" as a new strike is made (29). Of course, a rich lore surrounds any descent underground, a drama with a dense and complex literary, mythological, and mystical meaning. As Rosalind Williams (1990) writes, this "metaphorical journey of discovery through descent" is "one of the most enduring and powerful cultural traditions of humankind" (8).[15] But mining has its own lore and its particular and traditional preoccupations. As seamen are able to draw a wealth of seafaring and whaling associations and stories in the Bible (*Moby-Dick* comes irresistibly to mind), so the miner may call on the association between the Almighty and rock, between the wisdom of Solomon and his amassing of precious metals and gemstones, as well as on the book most closely involved with mining, the Book of Job. Wolfgang Paul (1970), in his eccentric storehouse of mining lore, makes much of the link between mining and religious debate. The association between the religious revolution of the Reformation and the independence of the German miners (whose society world produced Martin Luther after all) is suggestive of a tradition of freedom and self-determination in spiritual matters and a rebellious approach to the hierarchies of institutionalized religious practice and belief.[16] The practices around "the last shift," for example, which are particular to the mining communities in the American West, address death's nature and meaning. In believing that working the last shift of a contract is courting death (and should be skipped), miners attribute multiple meanings to death: that it may be likened to forces of authority and defied accordingly or that death is like a "last shift."[17]

A working life shaped by danger is one that gives a fine concentration to surroundings. Mining lore is full of signs, sounds, and attention to the behavior of other creatures believed to be more sensitive to danger than human beings. Folklorist Wayland D. Hand (1942) evokes a mysterious and even enervating world of a "myriad sizes, shapes, and colors of rocks" becoming "visible in the flickering light," and "the dripping of water on rocks, metal surfaces and the like, the creaking of the timbers as they 'take weight.'" He also describes the ways in which sounds and signs have been orchestrated by miners, sometimes as a prank ("tapping on walls to frighten greenhorns"), sometimes "to rid the mine of certain undesirable workmen." But equally, he describes a world in which miners were alarmed or terrified by apparently inexplicable noises:

> At a mine near Nevada City in the early days someone conceived the idea of unloosing a flood of gibberish into the airline to rid the mine of Chinese.... At the Mayflower Mine east of Nevada City there was long tunnel from which strange noises were said to emanate... Italians at the Black Oak Mine near Soulsbyville interpreted the periodic ringing of a bell in a certain part of the mine as being caused in some manner by a man who had died. (131)

Finally, the lore of miners has populated the mine with another level of beings whose relationship to the miner is mischievous and uncertain. Hand describes western American miners' stories about "the spirits of dead miners entombed in the bowels of the earth," or about Tommy Knockers, the "little elf men, bewhiskered and wizened" acting, by means of tapping, as "messengers" of the threat of death, or Blind Dave appearing in native peoples' dress, whose presence signals "dynamic forces which cause ground to shift" (128–30). Ronald C. Brown (1979) describes the belief of Mexican and native miners in a "step devil," a dwarf with abnormally long arms striking in times of disaster: "It climbed the underground ladders ahead of the frightened miners and pulled itself upward with its hands while stamping off the lower ladder rungs with its feet"; "The spirit of the step devil was perpetuated in other myths of ghosts thought to destroy the miners' means of escape in times of crisis" (96–97). As Poggie and Gersuny (1972) argue, "situations of uncertainty and risk foster magic and ritual," though there are arguments in folkloristics as to whether magic and ritual expresses or alleviates anxiety (137). Clearly, though, miners have inherited and generated a body of live and usable lore.

A student of miners' lore with no direct experience either of the industry or of collecting the lore itself is in no position, of course, to make claims about the significance given to lore either by experienced miners or by men working temporarily in the mines; nor can such a reader know how far beliefs crossed over between ethnic communities at work in mines. How might such beliefs have been articulated? C. Grant Loomis (1956) has argued that much of the mining lore of the American West was imported by the international population that swept into the region, mingling with the lore of the indigenous Mexican and native populations (19). Such arguments render the uses of lore more impenetrable: what impact might Mexican lore have had on Cornish miners, and how easily might, say, European mining lore have become part of Anglo-American belief. What is surely indisputable, however, is that this lore of mining was extraordinarily elaborate: crammed with material for the imaginative representation of mines and mining, and of the worlds that formed around them. It is quite clear, too, that the forms and subject matter of miners' lore appear in multiple ways and in different intensities in the writing of mining. It is sometimes argued that lore and writing, including literary writing, are always in communication. De Caro and Jordan (2004), for example, suggest that lore, "rich and ripe with meaning," is always a fertile source for writing (15). Writers appropriate material they have heard and seen, certainly, taking to their work what, in multiple metaphors, Albert B. Friedman (1979) describes as the "savor," the "suggestiveness," the "glazes," and the "subterranean presence" of lore (145–46).[18]

A text that seems to me to have the "savor" of miners' lore, and also to draw deeply on the multiple mining cultures of the American West during this period, is Ambrose Bierce's short story, "The Night-Doings at 'Deadman's'" (1877).[19] Bierce was publishing about mines at a time when audience interest was, as with Norris, focused as much on the battles over land in which precious metals had been "discovered" as on the strikes themselves: there was a high pitch of interest in the rush for gold in the Black Hills and the wars with the Sioux that American incursion into the Hills had produced.[20] Bierce, like Norris, had connections in the field of mining: in his job in the Assay Office of the Mint in San Francisco, and through his father-in-law, apparently "a famous mining expert of long experience in California and Nevada."[21] Later he proved willing to put writing to one side, when an opportunity to become involved more closely in the industry presented itself. In 1880, Bierce took off for the Black Hills, taking a mining management job that he found through a friend.[22]

Here, though, the likeness to Norris ends because Bierce approached the representation of mining in stories that drew strongly on the cultures and lore of miners. "The Night-Doings at 'Deadman's'" presents the figure of an Anglo-American miner, Hiram Beeson, who has returned alone to a deserted mining camp. Isolated in his former cabin, he watches, night after night, for the Chinese "domestic" whom he and his erstwhile companions have buried under the floorboards. At the time of the domestic's death, his queue has been cut off, and this loss is preventing him from resting quietly in his grave—or such is the belief attributed to him.[23] The dead man has been striving to regain his hair, but Beeson has nailed it to a beam and has barricaded the body beneath the floor boards. The sleepless, melancholy miner, who has aged decades in the two years that he has watched, is visited first by a silent stranger—Death—and then by a spruce, "swarthy little man" ("from San Francisco evidently") who waits impatiently for the events of the story to conclude (206). As the three are watching together, the Chinese domestic bursts through the floorboards to claim his hair, and then disappears when the queue is released by a gunshot. The gun has been fired by Death, who has simultaneously allowed the domestic to rest in peace and killed Beeson. The San Franciscan, having looked on, makes his speedy exit up the chimney (208).

"The Night-Doings" makes a very explicit engagement with contemporary mining culture's anti-Chinese sentiment.[24] It was published at the height of a storm of hostile feeling toward Chinese workers on the part of miners and other working people, which focused, with all of Beeson's peculiar intensity, on such signs of foreignness as wearing a pigtail. At this point, Bierce was de facto editor of the San Francisco *Argonaut*, an organ set up specifically to drown out the views of the Workingman's Party and the local trades unions, including their desire to drive out the Chinese population they claimed were taking scarce jobs.[25] In "The Night-Doings," Bierce, who had no sympathy for anti-Chinese activism, evokes the quality of anti-Chinese feeling in his portrait of Beeson's obsessive, paranoid watching for signs of a Chinese domestic whom he has already murdered. Beeson's half-conscious utterance, as he allows himself, finally, to sleep, is "They are swiping my dust!" (204), a reference to the intense rivalry that Chinese miners aroused in American and other miners. Most notably, though, Beeson fetishizes the domestic's queue as a sign of Chinese superstition. The taunting of Chinese men by cutting off their queues as well as by hair pulling was a common feature within a repertoire of anti-Chinese activity that included lynching as well as the destruction of Chinese businesses.[26] Beeson is, in effect, torturing the murdered Chinese domestic by barricading him from his pigtail.

The racialized violence of Californian mining culture surfaces repeatedly in the tale. As Beeson asks Death, "'Do you play me for a Modoc?'"("'Do you think I'm a coward?'"), referring of course to a native Modoc nation, Bierce glosses the term as interchangeable with "Do you play me for a Chinaman?" (203). If the destruction of Chinese men obsesses and haunts the miners who taunt and murder them, so too, it seems, does the hostile activity against native nations. Even in naming his setting Deadman's Gulch, Bierce recalls mining stories that centered on native nations' hostility to incoming miners, as well as, in an ironic twist, stories of abandoned underground treasure.[27] Deadman's Gulch, Colorado, was the focus of multiple stories of fighting over access to gold. In 1859, prospectors were ambushed and killed by Utes and their bones discovered—hence the gulch's name; and then in 1863, two Germans claimed to have found $7,000 worth of gold, after which one died and the other left.

Alongside this engagement with Anglo-American mining culture's beliefs about the Chinese and popular tales of lost mines stands Bierce's use of a more mediated strain of miners' culture: the lore of the Harz miners. This was a body of lore originating in the Middle Ages amongst the miners of the Harz Mountains in Germany. Collected during the late eighteenth and early nineteenth century, it entered the bloodstream of American culture through the tales of the Brothers Grimm and their imitators, as well as through the writing of authors such as Washington Irving. Harz tales were still in print in the late nineteenth century and presented an obvious point of reference for writers of mining. So, when, for example, Helen Hunt Jackson describes the environs of Georgetown, Colorado, in *Bits of Travel at Home* (1878), she refers straightaway to the Harz miners:

> It might have been just such a nook in the Hartz [sic] mountains to which the genii of gold and silver led the favored mortals to whom they elected to open the doors of their treasure house. (19)

Here Hunt Jackson is using what amounted to a kind of popular shorthand to evoke a particular landscape: the exciting prospect of a glittering legendary landscape set in an old world. When she describes the miners she observes at Georgetown as growing "more and more unhuman, less and less friendly" as they work deeper and deeper in the mine, she is turning to the tales of devils, dwarves, and imps of the type familiar from the Harz stories (297). In "The Night-Doings," Bierce also catches some of the distinctive flavor of these tales in the "cold sparkle" of the landscape, the depiction of a scene of a lonely miner in his cabin, inaccessible to the mass of humankind, literally spellbound by his compulsion to wait on the reappearance of a dead man (194). The story's movement between the everyday and the wildly magical is also in Harz mode: from the grubby bedding of the cabin to Death's green cowboy boots, from the miner's paltry meal to the sudden appearance and disappearance of grotesque supernatural figures.

Finally, "The Night-Doings" seems to bring a less literary strain of miner's lore into the tale. Beeson's lonely isolation in the dark, the impenetrable ground beneath him, the movement that the Chinese man's body makes as if it were "convulsed by a galvanic battery," and the chimney shaft that sucks the swarthy San Franciscan away (207): all of these details recall the emphasis, in many miners' tales, on the lone miner experiencing the sudden presence and absence of a mysterious figure. We are reminded, too, of the sounds and silences that are the staple of mining lore: the knocking at the door that Beeson ignores, the tapping of the San Franciscan's foot, the long silences and then the succession of worrying sounds. The sudden appearance of supernatural beings and especially small magical men (the small, contorted body of the domestic and the "swarthy little man") are just the kinds of figures that populate mining lore. Above all, there is the emphasis on the necessity to avoid and exclude dangers and the closeness of death through ritualized activity. Death and its rituals suffuse "The Night-Doings": starting with miners' euphemisms for death ("He has gone up the flume" [195]), and spreading to a plethora of references to the handling of dead bodies: the work of undertakers, body language at funerals, words uttered in the ear of those who have suddenly died, and the moment of covering the face of a dead body with a sheet. All of these act as accompaniments to story's elaborations on the grave of the murdered domestic in the center of the cabin, the appearance of Death himself, and, finally, Beeson's own death in Deadman's Gulch.

What we have here, then, is Bierce's dynamic engagement, hostile as well as receptive, with mining cultures, and an engagement that brings into the foreground the intricacy of miners' lore and the mysteriousness of the lived experience of mining. This is not to raise a text such as Bierce's to a position of superiority to *McTeague*, a novel which, after all, admits many dimensions to its panoramic portrait of the mining industry. Nor is there much cause to make claims about any political commitment on Bierce's part to bring mining culture to the surface of nineteenth-century American culture, though clearly he was responsive to that scene in all its dimensions. However, "The Night-Doings" shows the possibilities made available to the writer of mining by the encounter, actual and imaginative, direct and mediated, with mining and its cultures.

Bierce and Norris, although they explore human agency in mining, were apparently also interested in ideas of the agency lying underground in the earth. Over the last thirty years, all kinds of writers have, of course, become absorbed by the idea of a dynamic interrelation between earth, humankind, and what Elliott West describes in *The Contested Plains* (1998) as "the energy that moves continuously around us" (xxi). The limitations of human understanding of such interactions and energies are critical to mining. Humans cannot, after all, make a mine; nor can they sustain whatever precious substances held in the earth once they are depleted. Yet it is quite rare to find the acknowledgment of ideas of earthly agency in the context of recent discussions of mining. Fifty years ago, drawing on "rich mining lore still alive in Europe; on mysterious beings ... phantoms and subterranean spirits," Mircea Eliade, in *The Forge and the Crucible* (1962), described ore as "alive, it moves at will, hides, shows sympathy or antipathy to human beings" (53–54). But the imaginary evoked by Eliade in which miners collaborate in "the work of Nature and assist it to give birth more rapidly" sits uneasily with the contemporary emphasis on mining's extractive and damaging qualities (8).

In the late nineteenth century, though, these ideas of interaction were more familiar. To listen to Henrik Ibsen's miner's son turned banker and speculator speaking at the beginning of the second act of *John Gabriel Borkman* (1896) is to find what is perhaps, for readers now, a surprising form of attention to the responses of the earth itself to mining:

> My father used sometimes to take me with him down the mines with him sometimes. The metal sings down there ... when it's loosened. The hammer strokes that loosen it are the midnight bell clanging to set it free. And that's why the metal sings—in its own way, for gladness.... It wants to come up into the light of day and serve mankind. (64–65)

Something similar appears in Helen Hunt Jackson's descriptions of the Colorado mining landscape. Jackson argues that "You come to feel that you yourself are, as it were, one of the mountain race; the sky is the family roof, and you and they are at home together under it" (302). A literal familiarity with mountains characterized some of the fairy tales of the era. George MacDonald's *The Princess and Curdie* (1883), for example, shows a mountain interacting with humankind to produce mines: "When the heart of the earth has ... come rushing up among her children ... then straightaway into it rush her children to see what they can find there."[28]

It may be argued that such arguments were self-serving, but, for the late nineteenth century, only one generation after the great geological debates about the earth's formation in cataclysmic change, it seems that earth and humankind could easily be imagined occupying separate, differently paced but comparable experiences of reaction and change. Clarence King's *Mountaineering in the Sierra Nevada* (1872) is an obvious illustration of this. His narrative is full of passages that explore natural processes in elaborate metaphors of human movement:

> The whole Sierra crest was one pile of snow, from whose base crawled out the ice-rivers, wearing their bodies into the rock, sculpturing as they went the forms of the valleys and brightening the surface of

their tracks by the friction of stones and sand which were bedded, armor-like, in their nether surface. (4)

At the same time, King draws on mythic texts—in this case the rites of passage suffered and survived in Mozart's *Magic Flute*—to imagine geological formations that have taken millennia to develop, but in which readers can imaginatively engage:

> As the characters of the Zauberflöte passed safely through the trial of fire and the desperate ordeal of water, so, through the terror of volcanic fires and the chilling empire of ice, has the great Sierra come into the present age of tranquil grandeur. (5)

Coming back to John Law's term, then, it seems to me that mining, and certainly the mining under discussion here, is not "singularly tellable." We cannot blithely celebrate mining's acquisition of wealth or the development of technology and ignore its human and environmental costs. It is probably not very useful to think of the movement of people during mining rushes as streams or swarms of insects. Equally, mining may frequently cause wars, and miners may, as David Killick (1998) argues, act as the "shock troops of imperialism," but neither mining nor mines is summarized by those outcomes (286). Miners are not always slaves. This is not to argue that we should romanticize mining, but rather to acknowledge the human and imaginative energies it releases. In the late nineteenth century, these energies formed multiple places and situations, as well as worlds of speculation and fantasy. In the following chapters, I examine some of those places, situations, and imaginaries. First, though, I want to turn back to the problem of mining's relationship to writing that I raised in the introduction. In chapter two I consider how the Gold Rush writers conceived of their task and what we have made of their efforts.

CHAPTER TWO

Mining and Writing

∞

⁕ MINING AND WRITING HAVE A SPECIAL RELATIONSHIP. AS DAVID Goodman (2004) has pointed out, mining strikes were, in an important sense, "literary events" (15). Descriptions of mines and their prospects, accurate or otherwise, were always critically important to players in every dimension of the industry, for they drew in prospectors and miners, and financiers and investors, as well as those whose task it was to represent and regulate the mines. Writing could literally create a mine, as it did in the case of James Townsend's resurrection, in 1888, of the *Homer Mining Index* on the behalf of the owners of a moribund mine, solely in order to reassure investors that profitable work was happening. All the time that Townsend claimed "there [was] nothing new to report," and work on the failed mine was "progressing about the same as usual," his words translated into investment (108).[1] To this extent at least, then, writing about mining operated both as a critically important stimulus to the industry and as an anticipated by-product; a mass of writing and visual representation was produced by the mines alongside the silver and gold.

Interestingly, historians often suggest that mining is not merely dependent on writing, and consequently productive of it, but that mining is particularly writable and even that it is like writing. Malcolm J. Rohrbough (1997), for example, is not unusual in arguing that the Gold Rush events "seem to call for a Homer, a Cervantes, or a Tolstoy to chronicle the ambitions, experiences, successes, and failures of the hundreds and thousands of Argonauts" (295). Michael Kowalewski (2000) suggests the Gold Rush had the "composite intricacy and scope and the multiple cross-hatching plotlines of a Dickens novel" (207). He asks us to imagine that a rush was generically plotted with its strike, its conflict over access to land, speculative activity, and so on. And, in European culture, if mining is perceived to be like writing, then writing is understood to be like mining. Writers mine subjects, they mine for meaning, they follow veins, and they penetrate the depths in their search for narrative and meaning. Francis Bacon's (1623) words, "The truth of nature lies hidden deep in mines," are often quoted because depth and precious metals, even treasure, have become so utterly familiar as ways of thinking about the quest for understanding as to seem scarcely to merit comment (343). Surface and the exhaustion of an imaginative "mine" encode failure and the dearth of artistic power and intellectual fulfillment.

My discussion in this chapter considers some of the tensions in these relationships between mining and writing and depth and surface, with an analysis that examines the published work of people who joined the California Gold Rush. Initially, I want to look briefly and more broadly at the work of two writers of rushes who focus in different ways on mining's relationship with language: Prentice Mulford, who followed the Gold Rush to California in 1856, and J. Ross Browne, who reported on the rush to Washoe in 1859. It is the writing of the great literary star of Gold Rush writing, Bret Harte, however, that forms the central reference point for this chapter's discussion, for several reasons. Firstly, this is a writer whose oeuvre and reputation have always raised questions about the representation of the Gold Rush and its aftermath. Indeed, Harte has become something of a focus in the field for the discussion of how mining should *not* be written. Secondly, Harte is a useful figure through whom to consider those metaphors that use mining to give depth and profundity to the work of writing, because his writing of the Californian mining camps has been identified as without depth. Finally, in Harte's "shallow" work, we can find a fictional mode that pulls away from narrating mining within broader formations and roams the scarred, disintegrating surfaces of Californian mining culture in the era after the Gold Rush.

Mining needed and demanded to be written, as I have suggested, in order to encourage speculative as well as imaginative investment in mining, and to bring capital as well as miners to the mines. The exploration of the ways in which mines were floated on words was, unsurprisingly, rarely attempted in explicit terms, but Prentice Mulford is a striking example of a writer who set the play of language at the heart of his commentary on the experience of the California diggings. Mulford stayed in California for sixteen years. Like many other writers of the Gold Rush, he worked at the diggings, drifted through a series of occupations, and then moved into writing for the new weeklies and monthlies in San Francisco. He enjoys, in consequence, the rare distinction of a writer seeming to know what he was talking about as far as mining is concerned, at least in the view of Franklin Walker (1935), who gives Mulford his highest (and probably Mulford's only) accolade as a writer of mining.[2] In his autobiography (1889), however, Mulford summarizes his experience not as an encounter with mining or as a move into journalism, but as the reading and then the abandonment of a scrap of newsprint:

> Five years was the longest anyone expected to stay. Five years at most was to be given to rifling California of her treasures, and then that country was to be thrown aside like a used-up newspaper. (7)

Mulford's strategy in his Gold Rush writing was to denigrate the excitements and boosterism of the newspapers and to shut speculation down. At his most distinctive, he produced writing that was the opposite of the breathless prose in which the prospects for would-be miners were regularly reported, starving his reader, as it were, of imaginative oxygen, and stripping the rush of significance in terms of action and experience. So, for example, his faux-autobiographical account of a Californian miner, "Peleg Cowcopper" (1867), consists of a narrative of seven pages or so chopped into five brief chapters. Each chapter offers a collection of simple statements:

> I heard, however, of big diggings at Oak Flat, and went there, but there was no water. Bigger diggings were reported in Mariposa. I went there. There was no water. (12)

This mining experience is best conveyed, Mulford suggests, in a form that evokes the most limited grasp of, or access to, information. Accordingly, there are no details of a locality or a landscape here, nor does any reaction achieve sufficient elaboration to give form to random experiences:

> It is hard work to mine when one gets no pay. I had rather tend hogs. So I did tend hogs for a person at Rat Flat. (13)

His only means of stringing these statements together is through running jokes and especially puns, and, in "Peleg Cowcopper" at least, it is with these linguistic tricks that Mulford leaves us:

> Life at sea is very monotonous, except in a storm, or when one is seasick or drunk. We saw flying fish and some albatross. We also saw a school for whales. Whales go to schools in order to furnish scholars with the midnight oil. (9).

Elsewhere, Mulford (1873) suggests that Californian fantasies, as they appeared in writing, were not only wholly unconnected either to the place or to his experience, but also performed a strange, even perverse, psychological work for all concerned. Asked to wrap himself in the glory of his trials and tribulations as a pioneer in California, through telling tales, he responds:

> When a man finds, ready made for him, such a robe of dark and tragic hue, should he not wear it—especially when the public insist on admiring him wrapped, stern, bloody, vindictive and sanguinary therein? I like it. I never harmed man, woman, or child; yet, now, I feel permeated by the reckless, life-scorning, murder-loving spirit of my countrymen. I count my victims by the score; I see them lying weltering in the usual gore; I travel through my own private necropolis; I visit my own private dead-house, full of my slain, as yet unclaimed, unrecognized. (42)

Mulford argues that he is willing to take up the "robe" of his audience's expectations, and to offer the fictional mining adventures that they insist on projecting onto him. At the same time, though, he leaves the reader to reflect on the purposes to which he is putting this performance, its psychological impact on him, and indeed what actual experiences this "robe" conceals. Here and elsewhere, then, Mulford's eccentric writing refuses his reader the materials with which to construct an adventurous or profitable Gold Rush, insisting instead on bringing our attention to its formation in language alone.

An approach comparable to Mulford's was taken by the government officer, traveler, and journalist J. Ross Browne, writing about the first rush to "Washoe," one of the names used for the silver mines of the Comstock Lode in what quickly became Nevada. He also insists on the relationship between mining's origins in wild speculation, and he distorts the narrative to do so, describing events almost too chaotic for continuous prose. So, for example, in *A Peep at Washoe* (1860), he writes of the rush as a pandemonium of disjointed experiences, some real, some dreamed:

> [W]ho could slumber in such bedlam, where scores and hundreds of crack-brained people kept rushing up and down the passage all night in and out of every room, banging the doors after them, calling for boots, carpet sacks, cards, cocktails, and toddies; while amid the ceaseless din arose ever and anon that potent cry of Washoe. . . . I turned over and over for the fiftieth time, and at length fell into an uneasy doze. A mountain seemed to rise before me. Millions of rats with human faces were climbing up its sides. . . . Soon the mountain began to shake its sides with suppressed laughter, and out of a volcano on the top burst sheets of flame, through which ten thousand grotesque figures in the shape of dollars with spider legs.[3] (19)

One of Browne's tactics is to scatter references in such a way as to make his reader scurry mentally in different directions in the mode of his subjects. In likening the serving of supper at an inn to a battlefield, Browne produces gold seekers, uncontrolled and violent, in a series of unrelated and unconnected battles:

> At the first tinkle of the bell the door was burst open with a tremendous crash, and for a moment no battlefield in Waterloo, no charge at Resaca de La Palma or the heights of Chapultepec, no Crimean avalanche of troops dealing death and destruction around them, could have equaled the terrific onslaught of the gallant troops of Strawberry. (36)

The hectic, garbled discourse of newspaper reports is ever present, too, in Browne's prose: in the cartoonery of the dreams, in the constant reference to war news (at what was, of course, the outset of the Civil War), and in the truncated slogans of headlines:

> As I live, it is a cry of Silver. Silver in WASHOE! Not gold now, you silly men of Gold Bluff; you Kern Riverites; you daring explorers of British Columbia! But SILVER—solid, pure SILVER! Beds of it ten thousand feet deep! Acres of it! Miles of it! Hundreds and millions of dollars poking their backs up out of the earth ready to be pocketed! (11)

In Browne's work, the narrator's personality organizes the narrative in a convention that Mulford does not want to adopt. It is always easy to grasp his position as the horrified rationalist. But Browne's grotesque effects, jumbled lists, and huge numbers take an aggressively satirical position toward the reporting of rushes and strikes.

The examples of Mulford and Browne suggest that, for at least some writers, the representation of the Gold Rush demanded, first and foremost, an analysis of how the rush was formed, and indeed distorted, in language. In turning now to Bret Harte, the first writer of mining during this period to make, and indeed to maintain, a national and international reputation, we find a figure whose writing has been understood to use language, specifically literary language, to *mis*represent mining; to do, in some sense, what confidence tricksters did in writing cheating reports on mines. Of course, much writing did misrepresent mining, but in linking Harte in particular to deliberate distortions of fact, his critics have thought of him as mirroring everything that was most repellent about the industry, or even becoming implicated in its abuse of people, its corruption, and its lack of scruple, as well as its dramatic, overheated claims. Harte is judged to have exploited his brief encounter with mining, selling his audience a worthless portrait of the mines.[4]

In looking at these arguments about Harte, my interest is partly in defending a writer who could be discerning in his analysis of the world of the diggings in ways that I shall come to later in this chapter. At the same time, though, I want to suggest that Harte's poor reputation derives from broader assumptions about mining and writing, and indeed, from beliefs about how mining should be narrated.

Harte is, in the view of the majority of his late twentieth-century and twenty-first-century critics, a literary miner—"a casual clever literary miner" in Stanley T. Williams's (1955) fine phrase (211)—that is, someone who, like the mining camp storekeeper or the launderer or the owner of a saloon, mined the miners. In Harte's case, he mined miners by selling writing about them or even, as Gary Scharnhorst (1992) suggests, using "nuggets" of topical comment and local color to "salt" his fiction, thus sprinkling with glittering signs of value a worthless piece of rock in order to lure buyers (19). James D. Houston (1987) rehearses a common, and perhaps more serious, complaint about Harte's career: that this was a man who was not prepared to do the "real" work of mining but who resorted instead to the easier work of exploiting the experience of others for profit, careless of any responsibility for representing his mining subjects' difficult circumstances. Harte did well financially (at least initially), and, as Houston puts it, proved "that there was more gold to be found in writing about the locals than in panning streams with them," but Harte's earnings heighten his critics' sense that Harte's impulse was to exploit rather than to work earnestly (340). Within the substantial body of criticism of Harte's "lack of literary conscience" in exploiting and prettifying real work in his fiction, and what Joseph H. Gardner (1971) calls his "desire for pecuniary gain" (9), we find Harte even accused, by Patrick Morrow (1979), of "strip mining" his subject, that is of permanently damaging the field of writing about the Gold Rush and its aftermath, and perhaps even spoiling it for subsequent writers (8).[5]

Clearly, Harte's work, which was almost exclusively concerned with post–Gold Rush California, might well be expected to attract mining metaphors. His extraordinary popularity and literary success were as sudden as a strike, coming at a point when he had only published the poem "Plain Language from Truthful James" (1870) (popularly known as "The Heathen Chinee"), along with a few sketches, short fictions, and "condensed novels." To be paid as much as Harte was in advances—$10,000 for exclusive rights to publish his work in the *Atlantic Monthly* for a year, a record at the time—inevitably raised issues of literary as well as market value. But it is the rapid collapse of his good fortunes after the early 1870s that completes the metaphor of the promising vein struck and quickly exhausted. Wallace Stegner (1969), writing of Harte, is moved to refer first to his "lucky strike in subject matter" (223), and then to the "boom-and-bust freakishness of public favor" (230).

But these boom and bust circumstances, although characteristic of all kinds of contemporary settings, do not satisfactorily explain Harte's reputation as an exploitative miner, a man who preferred to write second-rate material rather than do justice to his subject, or indeed the antipathy toward the man and his work. After all, his career followed a trajectory much like other writers of the period who wrote about the Californian rushes. Born in Albany, New York, Harte spent seventeen years in California between the ages of eighteen and thirty-five. At the beginning of that period he lived in some of the small mining camps, worked in a variety of jobs, and, for a few days, tried out gold mining. However, after having built a career as a journalist and editor and made his reputation as a writer of Gold Rush fictions, Harte left California for the East and never returned. Although one can easily see how this might be interpreted as plundering the West for subject matter and then pocketing the proceeds, it is important, I think, to remember that other writers made the same career moves (as Mulford's comments about discarding California, already quoted, suggest). As Kevin Starr (1973) puts it, Harte was one of a number of "outsiders with other places and other commitments on their minds" (134).[6] Twain used the lore of the mining camps as a springboard for his entrance into eastern publishing and subsequently promoted himself as a bohemian frontiersman. Yet, having arrived in Nevada in 1861, Twain left the West permanently in 1866: a mere five years to Harte's seventeen. Twain, however, has emerged untouched by accusations of exploitation.[7]

If the view that Harte *in particular* got to California, got rich by exploiting the miners, and then got out is difficult to justify, then we are left with a question about the precise nature of his misrepresentation of mining in writing. This misrepresentation is variously described, but Nicolas S. Witschi's (2002) argument gives a good indication of the form of the charge against Harte: he turns away from depicting the grim truth about mining, especially in terms of human suffering, and he aestheticizes the mining camps in forms, specifically the forms of sentimental writing and melodrama, that were inappropriate to his subject, simply because such forms appealed to his national audience. For Witschi, there is a "fundamental crisis of the mining life" that lies in the physical damage suffered by human bodies in the mines (24). Thus to form mining cultures into sentimental or melodramatic "tale-telling" traduces the suffering and dislocation of Gold Rush reality (39).

It is certainly true to say that Harte has little to say about the impact of mining on the body of the miner. On the other hand, as I suggested in my introduction, mining cannot be defined exclusively by the danger it presents to the human body, nor need the representation of mining take that danger as its sole focus. One might argue, after all, that other aspects of the Gold Rush—aspects that Harte does address—might equally be judged fundamental to the validity of a portrait. Environmental ruin, for example, is clearly a critical point for commentary on the problems caused by the Gold Rush, and Harte's first mining camp story, "Mliss" (1860),[8] begins with this very issue: with "Smith's Pocket" and the "weird aspect of that vicinity," its "huge fissures in the hillside, and the displacements of the soil," the ugly flume and the "sallow depths" of polluted ditches (82). The camp itself is grim, with its "out of the way places, low groggeries, restaurants and saloons . . . gambling houses and dance houses," and its "reeking smoke and blasphemous cries" (87). In a later story, "Mrs. Skaggs's Husbands" (1873), we find Harte depicting California in the late 1850s and 1860s in descriptions of a landscape strewn with "oyster-cans, yeast-powder tins, and empty bottles that had been apparently stranded by the 'first low wave' of pioneer waves" (170). This is a pretty accurate picture, as we know, of the prevalence of trash in the diggings. It places the "pioneer waves" in a distinctly unflattering light and evokes the threadbare justifications adopted by a society that routinely blames another "wave" for the mess, literally and in more general terms, that they are in. Here is a portrait, then, with which historians of our own day might concur.

In these stories, too, Harte makes much of the social and emotional consequences of the rushes: for example, in the portrait in "Mrs. Skaggs's Husbands" of the hopeless drunk Johnson, the adolescent son whom he refuses to acknowledge, and their relentless movement between the saloon and their half-abandoned claim, drinking and gambling compulsively as they go. The same scene of psychic damage appears in "Mliss," too. Mliss's father, Smith, has constructed his life around a gamble on wealth that winds up with him committing suicide. Mliss herself, apparently the winsome poppet of Victorian taste, displays disturbing psychological quirks. Harte's vignette, for example, in which Mliss hammers the head of her blond, blue-eyed doll against a rock in a rage because it reminds her of a rival for the schoolmaster's affections, is grotesque.

Certainly, the corrosive social world of the camps was dealt with in more broad terms by other writers. John Rollin Ridge, for example, in *The Life and Adventures of Joaquin Murieta* (1854) did more to evoke, and perhaps to critique, the imperial aggression and vicious ethnic rivalry of the camps. Ridge's Murieta and his band are victims of racist hatred, and they create new victims:

"Well," said Jack, "I can't help it, but somehow or other I love to smell the blood of a Chinaman. Besides it's such easy work to kill them. It's a kind of luxury to cut their throats." (63)

This is the "almost unending round of ethnic hostilities" that historians find so central to the life of the camps.[9] Although Harte has been praised for his support for native nations and his interest in Spanish culture, he tends to people his mining camps with American, Irish, and British miners, apparently fulfilling the fantasy of American miners that all rival populations in the region might be expunged from the rush for gold.[10] One cannot imagine him putting the "xenophobic violence" that James J. Rawls (1999) finds in Californian mining culture during this period into the mouths of his own characters, as Ridge gives them to "Jack" (9). Nonetheless, Harte's is a portrait of Californian mining that addresses the endemic strains of a migrant experience bent, to the exclusion of all else, on the extraction of wealth.

Harte's critics are, of course, quite right that other writers stay closer to the day-to-day experience of the miners. Alonzo Delano, writing as "Old Block," is an obvious example of a writer who not only stays close to the labor of the miner but who also deals subtly with the experience and the attitudes of incoming hopefuls. Michael J. Gonzalez (2002), for example, has commented upon how the brutalizing work required of Gold Rush miners was especially troubling to those who had assumed hitherto that such toilsome work was for men of a lower caste (125). Delano, in *Pen-Knife Sketches* (1853), describes just such attitudes when he links the miner to men of color. "The miner," he writes, "notwithstanding his toil, has his fun and frolic, as well as a *white* man" (13):

> At home he had seen men at work carrying the hood, digging canals and lifting heavy packages, and though it was beyond his strength there and beneath his dignity, here in California he recollects that he must encounter toil. But he mentally exclaims "I didn't think it was so hard." (10)

Without doubt, Delano is a canny, thoughtful observer of mining experience. But the difference between his analysis and Harte's portrait of the psychological, social, and environmental fallout of the Gold Rush is not one of relative accuracy. Harte is quite as attuned to the experience of the camps. The difference here, rather, is one of authorial tactics.

CHAPTER TWO

Delano's strategy is to close the gap between mining and writing by claiming that his writing is always close to manual work. His works are not, as he wittily puts it, the "inklings of leisure" but rather the whittlings of a homely penknife: chips from "Old Block" (29). In making this claim, he styles his activity in authorship as practical (in working with a penknife rather than a pen), and quotidian (like mining). He adopts a marked aggression in his engagement with his subject, not the reflective or ironic pose characteristic of the professional writer:

> My Pen-Knife—Don't touch it, for I have been grinding it a little, and it may cut your fingers. Although the *stuff* is not bad, the spring is a little wayward, and, if it occasionally wounds, it will not cut deep unless pressed hard. (9)

Delano strives, then, to come as close as he can to suggesting a vision of the author as a man of the camps amongst other miners.

Harte does the opposite, drawing on the tactics of melodrama—popular, vivid, hyperbolic, full of coincidence, and providential plots—and it is striking how frequently reference to this mode of writing is used to condemn him. Starr's judgment that he converted the mining camps to "quaint comedy and sentimental melodrama," "an uproarious Dickensian saga"—both of which epithets are, for Starr, deeply critical—is often quoted (49). Melodrama is not always unacceptable in the writing of the Gold Rush. In Ridge's *Joaquin Murieta*, for example, it is judged wholly appropriate. Berkove and Kowalewski (1998), for example, find the "daring and bloodthirsty exploits" of Ridge's text well-judged given that the writer is depicting the guerrilla tactics of a displaced subject, and that Ridge was the victim of violence against the Cherokee nation (101). In the portraiture of the camps by a writer who is no longer mining, however, it is judged unacceptable.

I shall return to the question of melodrama and sentiment's roles in mining writing, but I want to pause here to consider the forms in which the best-favored portraits of the Gold Rush appear. Which writers are judged to produce the most finely observed picture, and the most attentive to the difficult life of the diggings? Delano and Ridge, though praised, remain quite obscure. The key figure, a writer found singularly true to Gold Rush circumstances, and to whom Harte's casual clever literary mining is most often compared—to Harte's detriment—is Louise Clappe, "Dame Shirley." Indeed, some have suggested that Harte actually mined her record for material and converted it to crowd-pleasing melodrama.[11] I want to argue here that the difference between them takes a quite other form to the divide between truth and its cynical distortion: a difference in literary tactics exists, certainly, but there is also a difference in their judgment of the qualities of Gold Rush society and their broader significance. Certainly their subject matter overlaps: they are both concerned with re-creating the world of the camps. But these two writers have very different perspectives on what they have seen. That difference has been characterized as one of closeness and accuracy on the one hand and distance and cynicism on the other. I would suggest that we are dealing, instead, with contrasting political outlooks.

Clappe's series of twenty-three letters from the Californian mines were written to her sister, though probably with publication in mind, because she had previously published short pieces and poems in the *Marysville Herald* in Sacramento. The letters were printed in *The Pioneer* or *California Literature Monthly* in 1854 and 1855 under the pseudonym "Shirley."[12] Like Harte, Clappe was an eastern migrant to the West, and, like him, she had limited experience of the mines, staying in two camps for around a year. She was well educated yet not from a literary family, nor a prosperous one. For Clappe, too, the sojourn at the mines formed a decisive phase of her life: married at around thirty, she migrated with her new husband to San Francisco in 1850 and visited the camps with him as he tried to make a living as a physician. Returning to the city, separating from her husband and then divorcing him in 1857, she taught in schools until retirement, at which point she returned to the East for a period of close to three decades.

The sense of veracity that is frequently attributed to Clappe's work derives, in no small part, from her skillful use of the truth-telling rhetoric of travel narrative. In writing this kind of text she engages, in a way that Harte, as a writer of fiction, does not, in offering empirical observations that are both fresh and consistent with her readers' expectations about the quality of life in the camps.

> Now you may rest assured that I shall assert nothing upon the subject [of mining] which is not perfectly correct.... Did I not martyrize myself into a human mule by descending to the bottom of a dreadful pit ... actuated by a virtuous desire to see with my own two eyes the process of underground mining, thus enabling myself to be stupidly correct in all my statements thereupon. (129–30)

Literary travelers must always demonstrate their readiness to penetrate new spaces in order to gather knowledge for readers at home. Thus Clappe weaves her "stupidly correct" knowledge into the enjoyable literary material that "a shivering, frail, home-loving little thistle" floating to a "far away spot" might be judged qualified to deliver (3):

> If I could coax some good-natured fairy, or some mischievous Puck, to borrow for me the pen of Grace Greenwood, Fanny Forester, or Nathaniel Willis, I might be able to weave my stupid nothings into one of those airy fabrics, the value of which depends entirely upon the skilful work—or rather penmanship—which distinguishes it. (175)

At the same time, travelogue must contain the recognizable along with the surprising. Clappe embraces the language of travelogues and guides that described new homes in the West: Frenchman's Bar is "a most sunny little spot covered with the freshest greensward, and nestling lovingly, like a petted darling, in the embracing curve of a crescent-shaped hill opposite" (78). An imperial eye is at work here, too: Clappe observes native women with all the condescension of the winning side. They are "poor creatures," gathering flower seeds with baskets "woven with a neatness which is absolutely marvelous, when one considers that they are the handiwork of such degraded wretches" (8). At this moment, she carefully maintains the colonial traveler's distance between herself and the working body:

> It was, to me, very interesting to watch their regular motion, they seemed so exactly to keep time with each other; and with their dark shining skins, beautiful limbs and lithe forms they were by no means the least picturesque feature of the landscape. (9)

Clappe is a sophisticated observer, attentive to the desires of her readers and skilled in her delivery of a combination of the strange and the predictable.

Returning, then, to the comparison between Clappe and Harte, it seems that we are not dealing with a difference between accuracy and misrepresentation, close observation and dilettantish distance, integrity and crowd pleasing, but between travelogue and melodrama. If we turn to what has become a standard contrast between Clappe's eleventh letter and Harte's short story,

"The Outcasts of Poker Flat" (1869), a more pointed set of contrasts emerges. In Clappe's "Letter Eleven" we find an account of the "harmless" William Brown, who steals some gold dust and is entrapped and lynched by the "more reckless part" of the mining community. This example of the violence of law enforcement produced by unregulated societies is followed by the description of "a catastrophe in many respects more sad" than Brown's hanging (98). This second episode involves the fate of "a hardworking, industrious laborer" returning to the States with his gold, whose two companions rob him and leave him to freeze to death in the snow (100). These men escape unpunished. Thus vigilantism on the "frontier" results in the execution of the harmless and the failure to restrain the vicious. Clappe is addressing a well-trodden subject: the operation of the legal systems of the center on the colonial periphery. The letter is, in effect, an argument for the expansion into California of standard legal machinery, and of systems for the delivery of punishment for criminals.

"The Outcasts of Poker Flat" shares this interest in how punishment is disposed in circumstances where no legal machinery exists, as well as a general sense of the harshness of the fate meted out to ordinary and insignificant people in California, but Harte arrives at very different conclusions. The story describes the ejection, by the morally outraged Poker Flat, of the suave gentleman poker player John Oakhurst, along with two female saloon workers and Uncle Billy, "a suspected sluice-robber and confirmed drunkard" (19). Harte's position with respect to this "criminal" element is quite different than Clappe's. Firstly, the criminality of the four outcasts is doubtful: no gambler in a place called "Poker Flat" could be called a criminal; to be a "suspected" robber is not grounds for extradition; nor did saloon workers trade illegally. Secondly, the position of those who dispose rough justice here is rendered not as "barbarous," as in Clappe, but as hypocritical. The story begins with Harte's ironic commentary on a community pretending to be in "virtuous reaction" against criminal activity: Poker Flat "had lately suffered the loss of several thousand dollars, two valuable horses, and a prominent citizen" (18). The town's judicial response to this loss is the indulgence of the inhabitants' "local prejudice" in the expulsion of the overly successful Oakhurst and a few other random souls who can be ejected without consequence to the residents (19). The little band camps out on the way to safety in the next town, along with a couple of passing young lovers, Tom Simson and Piney Woods. With the exception of Uncle Billy (who steals the mules and runs off, proving he is a scoundrel) and Tom, who goes to fetch help, they all die there. Only Oakhurst chooses not to freeze to death and, leaving his own provisions for others, withdraws and shoots himself. What has happened here is that these people have been ejected without fairness or redress, discarded as annoying and, in any case, superfluous. The reader is not asked to imagine that Poker Flat will be a better place in consequence, or that gambling and sex will cease.

What Harte adds to his tale of the rather abject victims of hypocrisy, to the distaste of his more recent critics, is a portrait of the common cause found amongst the group in these circumstances, as they save their food for young Piney. It is passages such as the following that seem cloying to some readers:

> Toward morning they found themselves unable to feed the fire, which gradually died away. As the embers slowly blackened, the Duchess crept closer to Piney, and broke the silence of many hours: "Piney, can you pray?" "No, dear," said Piney, simply. The Duchess, without knowing exactly why, felt relieved, and, putting her head upon Piney's shoulder, spoke no more. And so reclining, the younger and purer pillowing the head of her soiled sister upon her virgin breast, they fell asleep. (27)

The "pure" and the "fallen" sisters sleeping in one another's arms, the appeal to the reader's sympathy for their suffering, the move beyond the historical situation into generalized religious feeling, the iconography of white snow, the embrace of the tactics of sentimental writing: these are effects that allowed those who were socially secure to empathize—however one constructs that process of identification politically—with those whose security was compromised.

Harte clearly expects his reader to "feel sorry" for the Duchess as well as for Piney. However, this passage is not as conventional in its sentimental effects as it seems, at first, to be the case. The western innocent, Piney Woods, has none of the homely prayers we might expect of her. Her "soiled sister" feels "relieved" because she is *not* going to be reminded prayerfully either of her shortcomings or her hopes of a spiritual rebirth in the afterlife. In a conventional sentimental fiction, one would surely expect the women to pray together, perhaps for the "soiled sister" to experience a religious awakening before she expires. But no one, in Harte's story, engages with the possibilities of redemption, not even Oakhurst, whose suicide, gracefully as it is performed, merely enables the others to last a few hours longer before they freeze to death.

Actually, the story is indebted as much to melodrama as to sentiment: the complexities of the world of the camps are rendered through the farfetched interactions of a small group of "characters," criminal and innocent; forces beyond the characters' understanding drive the plot; that plot is organized around a gathering crisis involving physical danger. As Elaine Hadley (1995) has argued, melodrama during this period was a mode that offered its audiences a position of dissent from new and ever more forceful social structures that practiced regulation and differentiated on grounds of class. Its plots dismissed new social conventions, erased class difference, and celebrated crises in which characters helped one another.[13] "The Outcasts" is typical of melodrama in all these ways, exploring as it does the corrupt classifications of crime and punishment in Poker Flat, the position of society's least welcome, and the collaborative efforts of the abject in hopeless circumstances.

In Harte's stories, traces of his fondness for the French as well as the English literature of social outcasts—Dumas and Hugo as well as Dickens—are ever present. These are writers who give vernacular voice to the mundane routines of ordinary people and to the wretchedness of the bereft and bereaved, combining both of these strands with exotic and bizarre events and figures. For some American critics of the era, Hugo's "plea for the outcast, the criminal, the spurned, the scorned, the revolting," was judged politically or morally dangerous, especially given his sympathy for working people's resort to transgressive behavior, and his contempt for the hypocrisy of institutions. In 1862, the *Atlantic Monthly* review of *Les Misérables* actually proclaimed the reviewer's preference for the "bigotries of virtue" over the "charities of vice"; that is, the writer stated a preference for hypocrisy over open-mindedness if the latter was going to involve such explicit treatment of the circumstances of "the revolting."[14]

Harte shows a preoccupying interest in ordinary people and their treatment at the hands of an eastern value system, in "Miggles" (1869), for example, where the reader is faced with the circumstances of Miggles's acquaintance with a stroke-ridden ex-customer whom she cares for, a situation involving sex work and perhaps the ex-customer's sexually transmitted disease. The central concern of the story, however, is not her predicament but the response of the eastern travelers who chance upon her: the women think her contaminating, whereas the men are fascinated by the vision of the sacrifice of this beautiful young woman to a speechless male invalid. At the close of the story, restored to an inn, one of the male visitors, a judge, proposes a toast to Miggles: "Well, then, here's to *Miggles*, GOD BLESS HER" (39). But numerous problems are left unresolved: What are we to make of Miggles, and how are we to judge the platitudes of the judge?

The comparison between Clappe and Harte, then, has dimensions perhaps more diverse than has usually been argued. Clappe is charmed and, at times, horrified by the wildness of the "frontier" and engaged by the complexity of the questions raised by the thorny problem of freedom from control. She is clearly aware of the limitations of administering any system of punishment. In the end, though, in "Letter Eleven," her preference is for a standardized, centralized system. Harte's post–Gold Rush California is also a margin. His readers in the nineteenth century found it vividly sensuous.[15] But it was clearly corrupt as well. Where Clappe, as a travel writer, and perhaps by inclination, situates herself as a cultured easterner and judges California from that perspective, Harte is more interested in, and highly critical of, the all-powerful incursion of eastern American values into the diggings, and the impact on the largely poor population that live there.

Alongside the argument that Harte exploits and distorts mining and its culture stands a related argument about the shallowness of his literary mining. Harte has been characterized as a placer miner, an "old literary placer" in Stegner (1969), a "pocket miner" (that is, one who seeks out a visible accumulation of alluvial gold) in Fred Lewis Pattee (1923), and a writer aiming to "expose" rather than to penetrate in David Wyatt (1995).[16] The placer mining of the Gold Rush involved the panning and sluicing of alluvial deposits on or near the surface. This was the form of mining characteristically undertaken in the opening phase of the Gold Rush by the Americans, Hawaiians, Mexicans, native peoples, Australians, and Chinese who dominated the first wave of the mining population.[17] The parallel made between Harte's writing and placer mining, then, sets his writing of mining alongside the work of those panning for gold either without prior knowledge or with the ten minutes' instruction apparently necessary to enable a would-be miner to work in this way.[18] Placer mining is a routinized search, a scrutiny of the surface for traces of gold.[19] Characterized as a literary placer, Harte is transformed into a writer without skill, merely picking up or sifting materials. I have found only one reference to Harte as a placer miner that flatters him:

> Among the miners there was a phrase which indicated the superlative for a claim. In such diggings, there was no need to labor for days to strip the worthless surface-gravel; one had only to pull up the sod and shake "gold from the grass-roots." So it was with Harte's California stories.[20]

Even this confirms his lack of skill.

To be a literary miner of the surface is a problematic position altogether, then. It speaks decisively of superficiality. But metaphors of deep mining—of elusive and productive veins—and of mining for meaning are also problematic, depending as they do upon imagining that what is profound must lie far beneath the surface. Of course, creativity has been linked with journeys to the underworld in many myths, most familiarly, in Western mythology, in the hazardous voyage to Hades of Orpheus, the poet and singer. There is the sublimity, too, of deep time: the earth changes through processes of corrosion and decomposition scarcely accessible to human imagination. Mines are subject to these processes, and human penetration is insignificant in comparison with them.

Metaphors of mining distinctively require us to imagine movement within an absolute density of matter where rich veins are traced by the patient, skillful, and reflective "miner." This is conceived of as solitary, invisible work without the climaxes and losses of journeys to the underworld or treasure hunts. Rather mining is used to suggest a careful process of seeking out the precious and inexhaustible matter that is hidden deep in unyielding rock. A fine attention to these mysterious and otherworldly surroundings—surroundings invisible to others who do not venture below ground—is demanded. This is the mining of Hawthorne's (1850) "dark miner," Roger Chillingworth, as he penetrates the "poor heart" of Dimmesdale "like a miner searching for gold; or rather like a sexton delving into a grave" (146–47). The excavation and penetration of the self is integral to the process: one thinks of Melville's reference in *Moby-Dick* (1854) to "the subterranean miner that works in us all," and to "our attempts to hear his shaft by the ever shifting, muddled sound of his pick" (233).

This tradition of thinking of mining as a metaphor for creative thought, intellectual quest, and the search for self-knowledge is what supports the familiar association between mining and writing. This is what underpins ideas of writing as mining rich seams, or as following a vein with skill and concentration. This is the metaphor, too, that awards deep mining the profound respect without direct acknowledgment of its dire threat to the human body. It is a trope that insists that deep mining is intimidating and demands courage, and that it is a profoundly serious calling appropriately surrounded by thought and ritual, but it appropriates deep mining to elevate a very different activity.

The relationship between deep mining and writing mystifies both activities. Mining is usually dangerous, for example. It is work that many refuse and dread in ways that are not easily or necessarily comparable to writing. The threat of death, a slow death from poisonous substances and suffocation, or sudden death from terrible injury is seminal to the experience of mining. By contrast, writing may certainly be politically dangerous, but it is not always, inescapably so. Hard rock miners have continually warred with mine owners whose interest is in the success of the mine. Writers are rarely involved in labor wars. Deep mining involves careful teamwork and the development of trust. Writing, conventionally, does not. Mining metaphors, then, are mobilized to surround intellectual activity, including writing, with the dignity of difficult work and the weight of danger, but the connection is evasive about what is at stake for the human subject in either activity. By contrast, writing that sifts the surface runs the risk of being judged superficial in its engagement.

Placer miners who picked up gold from the ground or out of the rivers ran none of the risks faced by hard rock miners, and, if we pursue the comparison between miners of the surface and Harte's placer mining, we come back to that sense of Harte's writing as casual and without skill. Yet we extend no such contempt to placer miners. On the contrary, we think generally of the forty-niners (and later the Klondikers) as brave, dynamic, and doughty; vulnerable in the face of alienating conditions. If the camps are socially corrosive, we do not attribute this to the migrants' fault, but to the circumstances of the rush. Nor do we disapprove of those who turned their hands and skills to other projects in order to survive economically.

Perhaps, in fact, it is in this very gap between what we find worthy of praise in the forty-niners' placer mining and worthless in Harte's work that the source of the disapproval directed at Harte can be found. Harte gives a devoted attention to the "shallowness" of social behavior in the camp, especially as it is "civilized": its hypocrisy, its thoughtless ejection of those it does not want, its sentimental and aggressive fantasies, its tawdry attempts to ward off loneliness. There is no hopeful future, no likely progression available to the inhabitants of his camps. As Stephen Fender (1981) writes, "California was all so insubstantial, really; founded on illusory hopes" (127); Starr, in the same vein, argues that life in California by the late 1860s had failed to "[transcend] the search for wealth that had filled it in the first place" (129). This is the predicament with which Harte's ordinary people are forced to deal. The interactions between Johnson and Tom in "Mrs. Skaggs's Husbands" make the point:

"Wot do you say" said Johnson slowly, without looking at his companion, but abstractedly addressing himself to the landscape beyond: "wot do you say to two straight games for one thousand dollars?"

"Make it five thousand," replied Tommy reflectively, also to the landscape, "and I'm in."

"Wot do I owe you now?" said Johnson, after a lengthened silence.

"One hundred and seventy-five thousand two hundred and fifty dollars," replied Tommy with business-like gravity.

"Well," said Johnson with a deliberation commensurate with the magnitude of the transaction, "ef you win, call it a hundred and eight thousand, round. War's the keerds?" (170–71)

These men are struggling to maintain the gamble that is at the heart of the project of gold seeking, and to sustain the brittle social world in which they have found themselves. Their tactic, like Oakhurst's, is to maintain the thinnest possible surface of social intercourse. This is the shallow world that is Harte's fictional subject.

Within very few years of finding fame, Harte began to be accused of lacking depth, of failing to find new veins, and so on.[21] He was criticized for his "absence of depth" and for "not dealing with complex situations."[22] Some of the writers of the next generation produced parodies that attributed an utter triviality to his work. Frank Norris's "The Hero of Tomato Can" (1897), for example, reads "The Outcasts of Poker Flat" as no more than a series of characters and verbal effects:[23]

> Mr. Jack Oak-hearse calmly rose from the table and shot the bartender of Tomato Can, because of the objectionable color of his hair.... Mr. Oak-hearse's face was pale and impassive, and stamped with that indefinable hauteur that marks the professional gambler. Tomato Can knew him to be a desperate man. The famous Colonel Blue-Bottle was reported to have made the remark to Miss Honorine-Sainte-Claire, when that leader of society opened the Pink Assembly at Toad-in-the-Hole, on the other side of the Divide. (174)

Norris was writing in the heyday of realist writing, of course, and, as Leo Bersani (1984) has argued, the realist writer was devoted to forming experience into "a continuously meaningful chain of events" (55), while "sparing his society the pain of confronting the shallowness of its order and the destructiveness of its appetites" (60–61). Harte, like Mulford and Browne, eschewed realist effects and preferred to explore just that lack of substance in California in the years following the Gold Rush and its expression in the language of the Gold Rush. Again, like Mulford and Browne, Harte apparently took the view that no intervention by the eastern mainstream could civilize or cure the "shallowness" of California's order or the "destructiveness of its appetites." As "Miggles" and many of Harte's other stories showed, that mainstream was, after all, quite as shallow and destructive.

Mining and writing, to sum up, interacted in a number of ways during the late nineteenth century. Writing invented and sold mines, it imitated mining episodes, and it certainly mined mining with a will. Some writers managed their involvement with mining with aplomb: Delano combined writing in various modes with a successful Californian career in, among other things, trading and banking; Ridge and Mulford developed diverse journalistic and activist careers; Louise Clappe moved gracefully (and probably regretfully) on from her appearance on the literary stage. Only Harte, unwilling to abandon the diggings as a subject, became embroiled in expectations of how the whole Gold Rush episode should have been represented, and either could not or would not leave the Gold Rush and its aftermath behind.

All of these writers claimed experience of mining at some level and justifiably so, but none were industry insiders. In my next chapter, I want to look at a cluster of writers, the journalists of Nevadan silver mining, who could claim insider status to the industry in a way that none of the writers

I have discussed this chapter, with their generally transient experiences of the diggings, were able to do. The writing of these journalists, the so-called Sagebrush writers, is generally argued to engage very directly with the industry. In chapter three I want to review those aspects of the industry in Virginia City to which they responded, and those to which they did not.

CHAPTER THREE

Knowing the Mines "Interiorly"

༈ THIS CHAPTER TAKES AS ITS FOCUS THE PRINT CULTURE OF NEVADA in the "silver age" and the journalism of writers such as Dan De Quille, James Gally, Fred H. Hart, Joe Goodman, James Townsend, and, most famously, Mark Twain.[1] This is a body of work, usually gathered together under the name of Sagebrush writing, which responded with an easily recognized and consistent cynicism to the life of the silver mining region of Nevada, a space known variously as Washoe, the Comstock, or by reference to its biggest center, Virginia City.[2] During the 1860s and 1870s, the silver mines in Nevada were, as Bernard DeVoto (1932) writes, "a spectacle" (133): extraordinary and paradigm-shifting in industrial terms, in terms of the wealth they produced, and in the raucous, violent social worlds they generated.[3] The newspapers that the Sagebrush writers filled with their reports, stories, squibs, and hoaxes were, in consequence, read locally, nationally, and internationally for news of prospects and their progress.

What I am interested in addressing here is these writers' approach to writing mining, given their direct involvement in the industry. Twain claimed that he knew the mines "interiorly": "I know the mines and the miners interiorly as well as Bret Harte knows them exteriorly."[4] The thrust of Twain's point here was, as so often, the denigration of Harte, but his comment frames my discussion here. Insofar as the Sagebrush journalists were "insiders" to the industry, as I shall argue they were, how is that position and knowledge made manifest in their writing? I want to argue that their difficult position was shaped by censorship (including self-censorship), and as a result, their work displays a peculiar evasiveness with respect to the conflictual industrial setting of Nevada. Their insider status, in short, precluded the writing of material that did justice, broadly or in specific terms, to the mining industry or the experience of those who worked in it.

Mark Twain's involvement in this scene can loom very large, with Dan De Quille usually in attendance as his first mentor and Virginia City crony. Indeed, much of what we know about the print culture of the region has been gleaned by scholars of Twain. His fellow Sagebrush writers, meanwhile, have become obscure, to the point that, without the research of Lawrence I. Berkove, Richard A. Dwyer, and Richard E. Lingenfelter, most of the Sagebrushers would do no more than fill the lists of writers associated with Virginia City in its boom years, or provide a supporting cast in the opening act of Twain's brilliant career.[5] In this chapter, however, Twain's writing takes its place alongside his fellow journalists', not only because his work, over the few months when he was first publishing in Virginia City, was very similar to his colleagues', but also because my interest here is in the shared situation of a group of writers deeply engaged in the mining cultures of Nevada: in the mines, in the leisure industries surrounding the mines, and in the vernacular culture of incoming migrants.

Scholarship has given us a clear answer to the question about where these journalists stand with respect to Nevada and its silver industry: they occupy it as a remote frontier, a zone of freedom and undomesticated homosociality.[6] The anthology of their work prepared by Duncan Emrich in 1950, Comstock Bonanza, celebrates their involvement as an "intricate fraternity" of young journalists in a highly democratic experience. For Emrich and others interested in the lore of the American West, their work formed part of local and regional culture: "something for the whole camp to laugh over" (xiv). Much more recently, Lawrence I. Berkove (2006) has also drawn on the language of frontier comradeship, though he positions the "fun" against a much grimmer, more problematic space in which "almost anything could be done without regard to long term consequences to the environment or to population centers, because the land seemed empty and communities were disposable" (3).

These journalists are, for Berkove, "literally frontiersmen," living by their wits in an environment of laisser-faire, and developing their writing in the "virile," collaborative world of the newspaper office, rather than the introspective spaces of reading and study.[7] These, then, are the circumstances, along with the magnificent but challenging landscape, that are argued to form the sources of an edgy and "pungent" body of satirical writing that attacks both the gullibility and complacency of their fellow Anglo-Americans in Nevada and elsewhere, and puts up a "frontier" resistance to the polite culture of the eastern mainstream.[8]

These scholars focus especially and vividly on the exhilarating life of the group, the rebellious writing they generated together, and their involvement with the mining society of the saloons and streets of the Nevadan towns. By contrast, I want to begin by rethinking these scholars' sense of place and their circumstances in relation to the mining industry. The first point concerns the idea of the frontier. The conception of a frontier "outside" the cultural mainstream assumes, of course, a center "inside," and one with the power and prerogative to define spaces outside itself. Neither the power nor the right of the U.S. government or mining companies to dominate this space was in doubt among Anglo-American Nevadans during this period; the area was controlled by various armed forces accordingly.[9] Insofar as these writers felt they were on a remote frontier, they clearly shared the assumption that their interests in the region were of paramount importance. Stephen Fender (1981) describes how, to Twain, "the geographical West was pre-eminently a place without history, with no integral culture, no roots, an absurd physical and social landscape" (157). My guess is that much the same might have been said of the attitudes of others of the group. It was on these attitudes, then, that the relaxed homosocial vagabondage of these writers rested, along with their pleasurable sense of rebelling against the eastern mainstream. It was precisely their adoption of such a position that made their work appealing to audiences in that mainstream. As William Dean Howells (1901) remarked on the audience for Twain's writing: "people like things that have at least the appearance of not having been drilled into line" (339). The Sagebrush writers reveled in the appearance of not being drilled in this wild frontier, and they repeatedly represented it for the pleasure of national, as well as local and regional, audiences. Of course, one could only celebrate a frontier as a space in which people might practice unmannered freedom if one ignored or justified the predicament of those displaced and toiling subjects whose freedoms the government and the mining companies felt able, more or less drastically, to curtail.[10]

The second general point that I want to emphasize with respect to these writers has to do with their relationship to the industrial mining complex of Nevada. Generally these men were working at an especially sensitive intersection of mining and writing: the mining newspapers. Many were young, escaping, in some cases, from fighting in the Civil War, or from the working and private lives mapped out for them elsewhere. They came to Nevada, sometimes via California, to make their fortunes. Some had experience as printers before arriving (and thus might be expected to have some experience tinkering with writing copy), and a particular group migrated from working on the San Francisco *Golden Era*. However, others did not have experience as journalists or writers before their arrival in the region.[11] Their primary aim was not literary or journalistic fame, then, but rather to develop prospects in mining. Fred H. Hart, for example, arrived in Austin, Nevada, in 1863, as the town was booming, and began work as a miner, moved east to "Treasure Hill," Hamilton, and then began to support his fortune-hunting efforts through editing (that is, writing, editing, and printing, with the minimum of assistance) a range of more or less securely established papers in the region: the *Gold River Daily News*, the *Hamilton Evening Telegram*, the *Reese River Reveille*, and then the Virginia City *Territorial Enterprise*.[12] The newspapers where these writers found, or developed, work were organs owned or sponsored by mining companies and supported by communities of migrants whose working lives were directed toward prospecting and mining silver. In short, the Sagebrush writers made their living by writing for, running, and, in the case of those who were better off, investing in a range of newspapers. At the same time, these writers were speculating on prospects and mines.

The newspapers for which they worked acted, above all else, as a critically important source of information for insiders and onlookers, speculators and investors, about the prospects and mines of the area. This makes them sound like rather imposing institutions. On the contrary, the *Antioch Ledger*, edited by James Townsend, for example, consisted of a "cramped shed... with no furniture other than the printing equipment and a large dry-goods box... which served as a last rest for all unpaid bills." Even the Virginia City *Territorial Enterprise*, famous, highly profitable, and read internationally, occupied until 1876 a one-story frame building with a shed on one side where the entire workforce, proprietor included, ate and slept in bunk beds.[13] But, imposing or ramshackle, these newspapers required their writers to know mining "interiorly." Richard Lillard (1944), describing Dan De Quille, drives this point home, portraying him not as a writer who covered mines, but as a "miner writing news and feature material for miners":

He held the conviction that first place belonged to accurate mining news—prospects, locations, mills, shafts, ore developments, slopes, essays, bullion outputs. He reported regularly and accurately on Comstock mining developments and also he visited promising districts elsewhere in Nevada and California and sent correspondence to the *Enterprise*. (253)

Writing and mining, as I argued in chapter two, were always interdependent: there could be no mining—no news of strikes, no investment, no migrant workforce—without writing. However, for these writers, the connection between the two was more intimate still. These young journalists, in working for newspapers owned, sponsored by, or working closely with mining companies, were in a position to accept shares in mines as rewards for favorably reporting on, or indeed withholding information about, a particular property. In this context, newspaper men might be leaned on by powerful mine owners to omit unflattering reports, and rewarded with tips or shares in a promising prospect. Dwyer and Lingenfelter (1990) note that De Quille, for example, who wrote for the *Territorial Enterprise* when it was independent and when it was owned by mining companies, "took gifts of stock for favorable publicity and wrote not a word about the frauds, mismanagement, and manipulation of the major mining stocks" (4). As Oscar Lewis (1947) argues, he held throughout his life a "consuming interest" in making money from the mines (ix). James Townsend was more frank than many about the involvement of these newspapers in dealing with prospects, joking that when "funds got low," "a Washoite . . . would slip into the *Enterprise* office and get Sam Martin to print a lot of Kenosha, Pewterinctum or Daly stock and sell it on the 'Washoe Board'" (14).[14]

However, if writing for the Sagebrushers might have insider benefits on numerous levels, their position was, by the same token, far from uncomplicated. Whether or not journalists took payments or gifts, it cannot have been easy to strike a balance between speaking credibly as a knowledgeable reporter and keeping one's mouth judiciously shut for the benefit of the newspaper's owners, or in support of powerful local interests, or on behalf of connections within the industry. No one in a mining town wanted investors frightened away by negative reports, accurate or not. Nor did anyone expect to be deceived by journalists' lies. Joe Goodman's wry account of the struggles of an editor in a small town, "The TRUMPET comes to Pickeye" (n.d.), ends with the following rather rueful "commandments" for a mining newspaper to obey:

Don't try to be funny
Say only pleasant things of Pickeye
Say nothing pleasant of any other camp
Don't speak of a live man except to praise him
Don't speak of a dead man till you know if he left any friends . . .
Eschew politics, further than declaring that the interests of Pickeye are above party and that the *Trumpet* stands for them. (105–6)[15]

Goodman did not "eschew politics," though he ran the *Territorial Enterprise* independently of the mining companies. He and his colleagues relished "trying to be funny," but here he evokes the delicate web of relations between owners, speculators, investors, and prospectors—the population, that is, of all of the silver mining communities of Nevada during this period—within which the Sagebrush writers printed their work.[16]

The work of writing that faced these journalists, then, was not what Lee Clark Mitchell (1989) calls "discursive unbuttoning" on the frontier (70). Certainly, they were in a remote spot and living with evident enjoyment in a relatively informal society and ramshackle conditions.[17] But their work involved keeping silent as well as writing and publishing. Dan De Quille's "Torture Unutterable" (1877) outlines the problems that arise when one is paid to remain silent. A husband promises his wife an extra fifty dollars if she remains silent for an hour. The provocations to speak are great: friends and family seek reassurance from the wife that all is well, and her explicatory gesticulations prove to arouse, and then multiply, their fears. All the wife wants to do is to make extra cash, and her husband is willing to give it to her, but, infuriatingly, she loses the cash when she has to give in and speak to those who are close to her.[18] This story is an engaging one, elaborating as it does on the strains of deciding to stay silent, and the conflicting loyalties that arise. One wonders if it also suggests that communication, for a writer such as De Quille, must be undertaken in the distorted form of signs and gesticulations.

These are the general contexts that we need to consider as we read the journalistic writing of the Sagebrush writers: firstly, their position as young Anglo-American migrants in a space undergoing violent processes of colonization; and secondly, the kind of journalism that they were engaged to do, their status as insiders, and the highly sensitive nature of mining news. If these considerations bring us to a position where their writing appears both likely to be acceptable to the national culture of which they were part and also close to quiescent with respect to the interests of mining companies, then how do we understand their characteristic predilection, as writers, for violent raillery? Are the squibs, satires, hoaxes, tall tales, and humorous anecdotes "insider" jokes the signs and gesticulations of writers making their quiescence clear?

A useful place to begin answering this question is the acknowledgment of where these squibs, satires, hoaxes, and so on were placed. In the first instance, they were usually written as "fillers" to appear on the edges of the fast-changing news of a highly unpredictable industry. Further, much of these writers' time might be spent researching and making reports on the mining prospects and mines. The following is an example of such a piece of reporting written by Twain for the *Cedar Falls Gazette*:

> BULLION—We saw a dozen massive bars at the office of Wells, Fargo and Co, last evening, awaiting shipment. Six of them were for the Gould and Curry Mill, the result of a single day's crushing. We are informed that the average daily shipment of bullion overt the mountains will reach two tons.
> DECIDEDLY RICH—The Maraposa *Gazette* says the quartz vein at New Years, some distance below Coulterville, and formerly known as "Scott's Vein," is said to be paying handsomely, and that $75,000 have been taken out within the space of a week. One of the proprietors says that 3 buckets of dirt taken from the vein yielded 600 ounces, nearly $10,000.[19]

Looked at as a filler for a report like this, a piece like "Torture Unutterable" might appear in a number of lights. Its content might be argued as more or less irrelevant to the important news of the day; a piece of ephemera appearing in the most quickly obsolete of printed forms, the newspaper; trivial fun for light comment. Alternatively, such pieces might either constitute gesticulations from the sidelines, signaling the particular conditions under which the newspaper's content was being produced. Or they might provide a humorous, even anarchic, border to the news. As Lynne Pykett (1990) argues, newspapers may use "oppositional voices and oppositional discourses" precisely in order to give stability to a view that the newspaper wishes to establish (13).

The Sagebrush writers' predilection for directing hostility toward genteel culture might be understood within any of these frames. The relish for transgressing all bounds of bourgeois "taste," especially in the depiction of unrestrained bodies with hilariously disgusting ailments, might easily be positioned within a continuum between adolescent joking and oppositional discourse; or indeed as simultaneously engaging and recognizing the discourses of readers within different social classes. We can see all of these possibilities illustrated in "High Fever" (1878), Fred Hart's anecdote of the "cussedest boy as ever I seed," that eats "a hull lot of eggs" and "a power of milk," before developing a fever. A doctor is summoned:

> The doctor talked to the folks, and felt his pulse, and axed what he'd bin eatin' for breakfast, and the folks said they didn't know, cause he always was eatin' of somethin' as didn't agree with him, and laid heavy on his stummick. Then the doctor looked at his tongue and said the fever was mostly inside, and he guessed he better give him an emetic. So he went down in his saddlebags and got out some truck, and, while three or four of 'em held him, he rammed the stuff down the boy's throat. 'Twarn't mor'n a few minnits till the boy began to git pretty sick, and afore long he commenced throwin' up, and for about half an hour he threw up nothin' but the nicest lookin' custard you ever seed in all your borned days. (89)

This is the kind of filler that might have provoked a chuckle amongst Nevadans, and that the middle-class reader might have found mildly transgressive. In its vernacular humor of the erupting body, it marks material that stands apart from the more important duty of the press to inform readers of "news." Conversely, it is "real" in its address to ordinary lives, rather than wrapped in the complications of speculation. At the same time, it addresses "fever," a condition associated with frenzied speculation, and sets it beside the reports that were supposed to inform investors. This kind of material, then, could perform multiple tasks.

Some stories are open to various readings. In James W. Gally's story "Spirits," a preacher turns up in a mining camp saloon and asks to give a service. He gently draws his audience into listening to him and recalling hymns. The reader is drawn into a sentimental evocation of rough miners softened and elevated by religious feeling. The minister accepts donations toward his work at the behest of the spiritually relieved men. It is only as he leaves and the saloon returns to normal that the reader—or this reader at any rate—is suddenly struck by the way in which a complete stranger has arrived and extracted a substantial sum from his audience. The miners' heart-warming experience may have been wholly bogus or it may not. We have no way of knowing. Perhaps he was a spirit or perhaps spirits imbibed by his congregation clouded their judgment of a trickster. Perhaps it scarcely matters whether congregations can tell a trickster from the "real thing," if their feelings are real. Conversely, perhaps there is no difference between an imposter and a real man of the spirit, and all religious feeling is to be mocked.

Here, I want to pause to consider a comparable example of mining journalism. If we turn to the Witwatersrand and to the Johannesburg of the late 1880s and early 1890s, we are presented with a scene with strong similarities to the Nevada and Virginia City of the 1860s and 1870s: indeed the gold mines in southern Africa have been described as Nevada's doppelgänger.[20] As with Nevada in 1859, the 1886 rush to Witwatersrand began with picks, shovels, and small mining companies, and then was taken over by big corporations with the capital to import technologies that could produce a profitable rate of extraction. Just as the Comstock Lode could not be mined without new drills, new explosives, new pumping devices, or new chemistries of extraction, so the Witwatersrand could not be exploited until appropriate technologies were available—the "blasting gelatine invented in 1874, the MacArthur Forrest cyanide process patented in 1887; and steel alloys, essential for dies and shoes in the mortar boxes of mills' stamps, produced in quantity only after about 1880."[21]

As with Nevada and North America, the Witwatersrand area developed into the most industrialized place on the continent. It also made as much mess. Charles Van Onselon (1982) describes a region "pocked marked with all the signs of an industrial revolution" including "mining gear, ore dumps, battery stamps, reduction works, slimes dams, and the frayed ends of railway lines" (2). Johannesburg, at least as remote as Virginia City, was also "born as a dusty, dirty, mining camp set on a south-facing slope at an altitude of 1740 meters (nominally a mile high)."[22] It was as socially segregated between mansions and shantytowns as Virginia City, and its reputation was as raffish; a "Sodom and Gomorrah reputation" as Saunders and Smith (1999) put it (610).

In my research, no anthologies exist of the print culture of the Witwatersrand, and, apparently, no Mark Twain appeared to reflect glory on the journalists and part-time writers of Johannesburg. But, looking through the Witwatersrand newspapers of the late 1880s, the similarities in the journalism of the mining press are easy to see. The fillers that take digs at polite culture are the same. In response to what was clearly a fatuous report in the London papers that the Prince of Wales was the first heir apparent to wear a beard for many generations, the *Standard and Diggers' News* retorted: "It is a popular belief that the Duke of Edinburgh is the only member of Her Majesty's family who cuts his corns on a Monday" (7); and so on in a long list lampooning the effete and servile interests of a far-off mainstream. The relish for complicated descriptions of physical misfortune is the same, as here in an item in the *Standard and Diggers' News* describing the doomed attempts of a man to kill himself with a lethal saw:

> [He] placed his head where the saw would strike it, and in an instant the scalp and skull had been cut through on the right side of his head, the steel penetrating to the brain ... he instantly raised up and presented the other side of his head to the steel. (1)

Stories of trickery leap out, too. In the *Mining Argus*, a tale appears of a man without funds in search of supper and a drink. Having installed himself in a hotel room, he comes upon a piece of quartz painted to look like gold. He makes his way downstairs to the bar:

> He entered into conversation with some men who were hanging around the bar, and presently he drew out his handkerchief for the purpose of blowing his nose, and in doing so was clumsy enough to pull out the quartz which fell with a clatter on to the ground. He fell on all fours and made a frantic grab at the specimen and hid it, with every sign of annoyance, in his breeches' pocket.

His companions at the bar are hastening to buy him drinks in no time. Alongside such tales of confidence tricks stand comments not about cheating but about gullibility: "Numerous swindlers appear to do a good trade, and always will as long as the public will be so foolishly liberal without troubling to make due enquiries" (8).

For the Witwatersrand writers, too, the mockery of bourgeois values, the gruesome delight in damaged and sickening bodies, and confidence tricks provide the material for fillers. Again, such peripheral material in these newspapers seems both studiedly trivial and also marks the boundaries of the reliable information that it is the business of the paper to provide. It also enjoys representing Witwatersrand culture as rebellious. Not much is offered, however, in terms of satire on the matter at hand: the industry itself.

What, then, do the Sagebrush writers have to say about the "interior" of the Nevadan mining scene? The answer to this question is sometimes couched in arguments about these writers' predilection for pointing out lies, evasions, misrepresentation, and indeed gullibility. It is arguable that this emphasis on lies, tall tales, and hoaxes challenged the industry by mimicking the trickery that was so rife within it. Readers, wary of deception or previously gulled, may have appreciated the cynicism in which the Sagebrush writers' lies and hoaxes were wrapped. Nor was truth a subject that they could have approached disinterestedly. Partiality and susceptibility to corruption aside, these journalists faced a predicament themselves with respect to establishing fact, whatever they printed. Not much information about the Nevada mines could be incontrovertible: mining was dangerous, prospects were speculative, deposits of silver uncertain, the market for silver difficult to manipulate. Placing "lies" at the margins of "the news" simply called attention to the situation.

This is what is happening, I think, with Fred Hart's lies in the Austin *Reese River Reveille*, which he collected in the *Sazerac Lying Club* (1878), a book that was the source of "High Fever," and which went into several editions in the West on the strength of his reputation as a humorist. Hart's lying rests on the conceit of the lying club. The reader is asked to imagine a group of men meeting regularly to hear a "choice selection" of lies. The club's function is to monitor the submitted selection of expected lies for any "insertion of a truth." Those who bring lies to the club may be lying in offering a true story (rather than bringing lies in good faith), but Hart assures us that he will make us aware if any of the lies he is publishing are true. He also confirms that he will guard against "the pit-fall of interspersing the best stories of the club with some of my own" (37). These additions, of course, may be true lies or trick truths.

Hart explains in his preface how we should consider his book of lies. It has been "compiled and prepared in the intervals of daily editorial labor and no claim of literary merit is made for it"; indeed he points out that particular stories have been copied elsewhere already (8). This, then, is not the stuff of copyright, but of a shared joke. A Pickwickian silliness prevails in this lying club, and, for all their fussing, the lies are completely insignificant. Nonetheless, there is evidently a point being made here about the conduct of mining in Nevada. Hart is giving us a setting that has elevated lying beyond the realms of everyday practice to a hobby, and where truth telling has been banned (and in any case is branded as cheating).

Yet what kind of response is this smiling cynicism to the Nevada silver industry? To argue that these writers are repeatedly calling their readers' attention to the lack of veracity in Nevadan silver mining culture begs questions about which "truths" we might hope for them to tell. We cannot expect these newspapermen to write the unvarnished truth about particular prospects and companies: they might have been able to do so in some cases, but they could not have done so in others and kept their jobs. The mining industry in Virginia City and the surrounding areas was truly groundbreaking as well as corrupt. It formed the epicenter of an industrial explosion of tremendous proportions that had profound implications for local populations as well as for the whole region. New technologies as well as frantic activity produced a massive operation: Eugene P. Moehring (1997) lists "more than forty mine, mill, flume, toll, provisioning, salt and railroad towns" developed by 1875 "to supply the core communities of Virginia City and Gold Hill" (334). This was an awesome and dramatic industrial scene lasting as long as there was ore to be profitably ripped out. Nevadan mining culture was also exceptionally cosmopolitan, though work underground was hierarchized according to "racial" difference and Anglo-European preference. It was notoriously dangerous, too. Gunther Peck (2001) lists "fire, poisonous gas, explosions, cave-ins, and other hazards" as having killed more than nine hundred miners between 1863 and 1880. The Comstock had "one of the worst industrial accident rates in the world during these decades" (77).

Nicolas S. Witschi (2008), reviewing Berkove's anthology of the Sagebrush writers, is unique, I think, and certainly well justified, in identifying this writing as a collection of literature emanating from "the new industrial blast furnace," rather than from a wild western margin (88). But what is the nature of the journalistic engagement with this "blast furnace" of activity?

One would hardly expect journalists reporting on mining prospects to draw attention to the carnage in the mines, but Dan De Quille provides an instructive example of the ways in which the Sagebrushers addressed conditions experienced by a large section of their local readership. In three pieces published between 1876 and 1877—two fillers from the *Territorial Enterprise* and a passage in *The Big Bonanza* (1876)—De Quille refers to an infamous phenomenon in the mines of the area: temperatures of up to 130 to 150 degrees Fahrenheit below 1,000 feet, the presence of very hot water underground, and their impact on the workforce. This is how Eliot Lord (1883), in his study of the Comstock, describes the problem:

> View their work! Descending from the surface in shaft-cages, they enter narrow galleries where the air is scarcely respirable. By the dim light of their lanterns a dingy rock surface, braced by rotting props is visible. The stenches of decaying vegetable matter, hot foul water, and human excretions intensify the effects of the heat . . . though naked, they can only work at some stopes for minutes at a time, dipping their heads repeatedly under water-showers from conduit pipes, and frequently filling their lungs with fresh air at the open ends of the blower tubes.

To Lord's description, Richard E. Lingenfelter (1974) adds:

> Tons of ice were sent down daily into the mines where the half fainting men chewed fragments greedily to cool their parched throats, and carried lumps in their clenched hands through the drifts . . . Three gallons of water and ninety-five pounds of ice was the average daily consumption of miners employed in the hottest workings of the Comstock . . . In some of the mines the men had to contend not just with the heat, but with scalding water as well. An incline in the Savage mine tapped a hot stream that chocked the air with steam. Men could only stand for a few minutes at a time near this hot fountain. (13–14)

Lingenfelter lists cramps, dizziness, mental impairment, stomach problems, heat exhaustion, and, inevitably, death, as consequences of these conditions, as well as the pneumonia and blood spitting caused by repeatedly coming up into cold air at the end of a day spent in literally boiling conditions.

It comes as no surprise to find that De Quille, in his magnum opus *The Big Bonanza*, had nothing to say about these conditions. No muckraker in any case, he ruefully admitted giving in to pressure to tell the corporate story in this volume.[23] Here, then, working conditions receive little attention, appearing only as a spectacle. The heat of the mines is rendered in a portrait of the scantily clad miners pictured in superb physical shape:

> All are naked to the waist, and many from the middle of their thighs to their feet. Superb muscular forms are seen on all sides and in all attitudes, gleaming white as marble in the light of the many candles. We see everywhere men who would delight the eye of the sculptor ... Before us we have the Troglodytes—the cave-dwellers.... All are drenched with perspiration, and their bodies glisten in the light of the candles as though they had just come up through the waters of some subterranean lake. In places, in some of the mines, the heat is so great that the men do not even wear overalls, but are seen in the breech clout of the primitive races. (248)

These miners are the eroticized, racialized objects of the onlookers' gaze: men from the distant past, from the underground, from the sites of savagery.

When we turn to a story of a visit down the mines that De Quille wrote during the same period for *The Territorial Enterprise*, we find him still imagining the gaze of a visitor encountering the overheated miners, but complicating that gaze. In "Old Johnny Ranchero" (1877), the conditions in which the miners work are rendered in the delusions of an old man:

> It was summer down thar, and the weather was devilish hot. The doors all stood open, and the folks had nearly all ther clothes off—the men I mean; the women and children I didn't see—all kept inside, I guess ... Everybody was a-drinkin ice water.—blamedest people for iced water I ever seed. Plenty barrels and kegs around too, but nobody offered to treat, but all swollered ice water for dear life.... Sez I to one of the fellers ... "Temperance celebration, sir?" (67)

The story deals with the ultramodern complex of the mine by defamiliarizing it. It is rendered here as a kind of grotesque pastoral, in a description of a summer afternoon's holiday, while a laugh is generated by the naiveté of a foolish old man who finds a ridiculous explanation for what he sees. The effect, again, is to distance the reader, involve her or him in deciphering the interpretation of Old Johnny and not the conditions in the mines, while dissipating the horrors of the miners' desperate thirst in laughter at Temperance workers ceaselessly drinking water.

In the hoax "Eyeless Fish That Live in Hot Water" (1876), De Quille comes back to the scalding heat of the mines in a more opaque form still. Here he adopts the rhetoric of the science paper with its evidence and careful qualifications, and its earnest air of discovery, in order to describe the eyeless fish discovered when two mines, the Hale and the Norcross, are flooded with scalding water:

> In appearance these subterranean members of the finny tribe somewhat resemble gold fish. They seem lively and sportive enough while in their native hot water, notwithstanding the fact they have no eyes or even the rudiments of eyes.

In view of the damage done to human bodies by scalding water in mines, the invention of eyeless fish as the flood's victims prompts a rather hollow laugh, certainly for the reader now. Yet the additional comment that "when the fish were taken out of the hot water in which they were found, and placed in a bucket of cold water for the purpose of being brought to the surface, they died almost instantly," does recall, horribly, the effect that speedy emergence into a cold atmosphere had on miners' health (48). Accordingly, at the time of its publication, local mining interests were annoyed by this hoax because *any* news, real or imagined, of mine flooding was hostile to investment. At least one newspaper, the San Francisco *Stock Report*, argued that De Quille's hoax was calculated to injure the mines he named.

Whatever his attitudes and whatever squibs on conditions underground he had to offer, De Quille clearly needed to keep himself and his readers at a point of distance from which he and they might retreat, always to dissolve shared knowledge with humorous tricks. This is not really satire in the sense of offering a critique, angry or disengaged, of current conditions. This is a kind of feinting maneuver, dodging the anger of the mining companies for the amusement of readers familiar with the conditions in the mines.

I want to turn, finally, to a blunt aggression in these journalists' work: aggression toward the genteel, the pious, the feminine, but especially toward the gullible. Scholars have cast this aggression in different ways: DeVoto sees it as "a violent humor, appropriate to a violent life" (152), Edgar Marquess Branch (1950) calls it "slapstick and nose-thumbing" (84), and Richard S. Lowry (1996) refers to the rhetoric of "vengeful manhood" (11). Critics have had different ways of characterizing this aggression, but they often agree that it makes a dynamic and justified attack on the hypocrisy, sententiousness, and sentiment of mainstream culture (and its preferred forms of literature), especially what DeVoto (writing about Twain) called "the pale negations and paler affirmations of the genteel tradition" (11).[24] I have already argued that the Sagebrush writers' relationship toward the cultural mainstream is one of complicity, and that they tend to use bourgeois culture as a soft target in their journalism. Here I want to consider their satiric aggression in another light.

Satire, the preferred mode of the Sagebrush writers, is often violent in its responses and its jibes. It is generally withering in its portrait of the modern mainstream. It is also a distancing literary tactic. Michael Seidel (1979) argues that the satirist strives to "distance himself from the debasing, deforming, encroaching and contaminating nature of his subject" (14). This is a strategy that one finds across the work of the Sagebrush writers, but that I want to illustrate in a piece written by James Townsend where he describes the work of the journalist:

> A reporter is not ubiquitous, nor has he eyes all over him like a potatoe. He has a sort of negative right to ask folks if they "know anything going on," and when he gets a surly answer he jots it down in the blackbook of his memory against the illbred swine who snubs him, for he knows that a day of retribution will surely come, when he can pile coals of fire upon the heads of those who decline to give a civil answer to a gentlemanly question. It is singular that these same reticent hogs think more of a local item than any other men do. If one of them becomes the father of a scrawny baby with a mouth big enough to feed with a fire shovel, he wants the reporter to say it is a beautiful ten-pounder, with flowing hair and a full set of teeth.[25]

The pressure on the reporter to be like a rotting "potatoe," the aggravation of the silence and snubs of "illbred swine," the imagination of a "blackbook" listing future victims, the plotting of violent revenge, and then the hateful image of the "scrawny" baby with a mouth into which food might be shoveled: this is a small explosion of uncontrollably hostile feeling against subjects who are wholly intolerable. As Seidel remarks, "[O]ne of the more plaguing paradoxes about the satiric mode is that the satirist, having taken on a kind of monstrosity as his subject, makes something of a monster of himself" (3).

What was it, though, that produced this excess of aggression? Certainly, these writers' situation could, as I have suggested, provoke the "unutterable torture" of self-censorship that De Quille describes. Clearly, too, these young writers reveled in the opportunity offered by their circumstances to express unrestrained antagonism toward the social world that they had, for the most part, temporarily abandoned. Yet their belligerence, the sense they give of spoiling for a fight, may have been prompted by living in a setting literally given over to fighting on multiple fronts. The world of the silver industry in Nevada—a state with the motto "battle born"—was, after all, both divided and united by different violent conflicts. These were the Civil War years, of course, and, far away though Nevada was from the theater of war, feelings ran high. Although some historians have argued that the arguments and fights about the war in Nevada were theoretical, Paul Fatout (1964) describes "a nervous climate of opinion" in Virginia City, and describes how the "Western press continually circulated stories of thousands of Californian secessionists migrating to Nevada to take over the government when the territory became a state" and "did their best to create a reign of terror by publishing sinister tales of guerillas armed to the teeth, even with batteries of artillery, mobilizing at secret points from which they would descend upon cities, seize power and set up a Pacific republic" (69). Ronald M. James (1998) describes "vigilantes search[ing] for anyone who would speak ill of the Union or Lincoln" after Appomattox, and finding and giving the lash to a pro-Confederacy supporter (72). Ronald C. Brown (1979), meanwhile, makes the interesting point that, during the industry's heyday, Nevada was hosting a population of "social and psychological casualties of the Civil War," not to mention those finding in mining "a psychological surrogate for the thrill and camaraderie of the campaign" (7).

At the same time, in the period after the Pyramid Lake War of 1860 (a conflict sparked by the killing of five Americans at Williams Street, a stage stop east of Virginia City, in revenge for the capture and abuse of two native women), attacks from dispossessed Paiutes on incomers continued and threatened transportation lines between the Comstock Lode and outside; this became a dangerous zone. Alvin M. Josephy (1991) reminds us that "during the four years of the Civil War . . . more Indian tribes were destroyed by the whites and more land seized from them than in almost any other comparable period in American history" (xiii). Moehring (1997) suggests that newspapers, including the *Territorial Enterprise*, "routinely magnified the danger and rallied public opinion" in favor of hostilities, if not the extermination of native nations (319). At the same time, conflict over mining claims was rife. James W. Hulse (1991) describes the "flood proportions" of "quarrels and litigation" that developed in 1859, and James the "armed conflict," between "eerie subterranean battlegroups" that took place between 1863 and 1864 (61). The Nevada of the Sagebrush writers was something close to a war zone.

Twain's "A Bloody Massacre" (1863), perhaps the most famous Sagebrush hoax, is usefully considered in this context. It concerns a well-known local man, Philip Hopkins, who reads in the *San Francisco Bulletin* that the value of his shares in the Gould and Curry Mine have been inflated by the company. Armed with this information, he sells his shares and, on the *Bulletin*'s recommendation, buys new shares in the Spring Valley Water Company of San Francisco. However, he has been duped. He soon discovers that the Gould and Curry Mine is solid after all, and that the Spring Valley Water Company is not. Furthermore, he learns that the editor of the *Bulletin* has talked up the water company because he has a personal interest in it. This drives Hopkins to a frenzy of violence against his family, and to suicide:

> The scalpless corpse of Mrs Hopkins lay across the threshold, with her head split open and her right hand almost severed from the wrist. Near her lay an ax with which the murderous deed had been committed. In one of the bedrooms six of the children were found, one in bed and the others scattered about the floor.... The oldest girl, Mary, must have taken refuge, in her terror, in the garret, as her body was found there, frightfully mutilated, and the knife with which her wounds had been inflicted still sticking in her side.

Hopkins then rides to Carson "on horseback, with his throat cut from ear to ear, and bearing in his hand a reeking scalp from which the warm smoking blood was still dripping" (21).

Famously, many readers began to panic when they read the piece, though careful reading, as various scholars have pointed out, should have made it obvious that these events were impossible, certainly for locals who knew Hopkins, an unmarried man.[26] Here, they argue, is Twain proving the gullibility and propensity to hysteria of the mass of the population. Equally, it is pointed out that there is a moral here about reading with care and consideration, especially at a time of war. These arguments about Twain's motives may be disingenuous, though. If George D. Lyman's (1934) account is to be credited, Twain wrote the hoax as a result of being approached by the Gould and Curry mining company, who were irked at the *Bulletin*'s attack on their company's integrity and annoyed by their praise for a another company that had, or that they believed had, cooked their books to deceive investors (246). However carefully Twain's readers examined "A Bloody Massacre," they could not have gleaned this agenda without prior knowledge. At the same time, the actual violence that surrounded the Comstock Lode and its various and far-flung mining settlements was very real. Most of Twain's readers, apparently, did not anticipate that there might be an approach to the story of a massacre that would render it as simply amusing, and surely not surprisingly so.

It is possible to think of the aggression of this piece and the violence it visits on its subjects as a means of teaching readers a lesson, though the lesson seems a rather punishing one. It may be that the writer is striving to separate himself from the gullible, somehow to prove his own resistance to being fooled by hoaxing others. Equally, this may be satire as a defensive tactic, a series of threatening and exaggerated behaviors performed to drive danger away. This is how Alvin B. Kernan (1973), drawing on the behavior of frightened and endangered animals, describes a strain of satire in which "the aggression is too direct, so violent, and so sustained as to make us distinctly uneasy" (117). Hoaxes like "The Bloody Massacre" or "The Eyeless Fish," or indeed the stories of boiling vomit or mechanical saws out of control, make the reader uneasy. In the dangerous mining cultures of Nevada, frightening readers may have proved the best salve for these writers' own fears.

In this chapter I have examined the writing of a group of mining insiders who claimed to understand the Nevadan silver industry "interiorly," and who seemed to embrace the vernacular culture of the mining towns. They were, like many immigrants to Nevada, "luck hunters" rather than hunters after truths about the industry and its position in the region.[27] But the Sagebrushers seem to have had no more fellow-feeling for their readers than for the "genteel" objects of their contempt. Perhaps they saw themselves as subjects emancipated from social networks and obligations. Where they do clearly seem to have placed faith, however, was in the power of words to control and manipulate their multileveled situations, and their facility for doing so "interiorly." For all their lying jokes, the Sagebrushers took no liberties whatsoever with their own position as insiders.

In this chapter and the previous one, I have looked at writers using language and genre to re-create different forms of response to mining and mining societies. In all cases, their impulse has been to address the fragile surfaces and assumptions shaping mining worlds of the period, and to give a sense of styles of engagement appropriate to these circumstances. I want to turn now to another series of writers, many of them with less direct experience in the industry, who nevertheless strove to find ways of truthfully representing mining societies using broad canvases. The strategy that links them is their use of romance.

CHAPTER FOUR

The Romance of Mining

☙

✢ IN THIS CHAPTER, I AM RETURNING TO SOME OF THE POSSIBILITIES of representation raised in chapter one, and to the sweeping portraits that late nineteenth-century writers developed to try to understand the mining industry and to plot its position in time and space. I am not revisiting the paeans to human progress or the gloomy projections that I quoted there, but rather the work some journalists and writers undertook to understand the effects of the industry on contemporary experiences and understandings of time and space. For the writers I discuss here, those effects were profound, and they turned to forms of legend and romance to deal with them. Such an artistic turn has done them few favors in terms of their current critical status: legend may seem an evasive form with which to represent mining, and nineteenth-century romance is tainted by its hospitality to imperialism. Yet these writers were ambitious in their approach to the demanding task of representation, and it is with their attempts to do justice to the industry that I am concerned here.

The gold and silver mining industries of the decades after the Californian Gold Rush were not easily plotted.[1] Certainly, by the 1870s, mining was modernizing, in the sense of becoming a more complex and institutionalized industry, in terms of the operation of finance, the professionalization of every phase of the operation, and the fast-moving shifts in mining technology, not to mention the energies produced by the transnational reach of gold and silver mining. There was a trajectory of progress to be followed here. Yet this was a scene of modernization full of contradictions: mines were urbanized and yet remote from the center, manifest in their impact on people and landscape and yet dependent on impersonal systems of speculation, the focus of technological ingenuity and yet essentially primitive in their extractory activity, highly localized and yet evidently operating in a transnational setting. Furthermore the industry was characterized, in the final decades of the nineteenth century, by erratic movement: the constant, unanticipated movement of prospectors, miners, and speculators, as well as those supplying and supporting them; and the ceaseless displacement experienced by native nations in the face of these transient activities and populations. One strike was succeeded by another and another, driving people to new places tens, hundreds, and thousands of miles away. Contradictory and volatile movement was scarcely exclusive to the mining industry, of course, but the continuation of strikes and rushes that might prove to be of world significance, short-lived, or utterly misguided made mining's contradictions and volatility especially evident. It was not easy, then, to generate plots to organize mining imaginatively, nor to conceive a single context for mining plots.

Even to describe *where* mining was proved challenging. No single geography was evidently appropriate for the task. The boom in precious metal mining and its escalating industrialism generated multiple geographies. Of course, the mining industry and camps of the American West could be mapped by participants and onlookers as colonial hinterlands, but to what centers were these peripheries tied: to San Francisco or Denver, to the corporate interests of the East, or to the financial houses of European investors?[2] Alternatively, mining sites in the American West could appear central to a transnational mining scene during this period, as William G. Robbins (1989) has argued, sharing patterns of intensive industrial and social development with other mining centers in Australia or southern Africa;[3] or they might suddenly seem a poorer prospect by comparison to such other sites;

or become past episodes in a narrative that had moved on to new dramas. On a localized scale, single mining towns, as Donald L. Hardesty (1988) has explained, operated as focal points of local, native, regional, national, and transnational industrial activity: creating and exporting wealth, generating instant cities, and causing profound changes to people and landscapes.[4] Some centers of mining activity were current or recent war zones.

Setting mining in time was difficult, too. The late nineteenth-century predilection for thinking about the search for gold as an essential human impulse stretching back through history into myth produced descriptions of miners as Argonauts. Wayland D. Hand (1942) describes how western miners liked to tell tales of gold growing on trees, much like the legendary golden apples of the Hesperides (153). Instead of reaching backward into mythic time, it was, of course, possible to think in terms of national and imperial expansion buttressed by technological progress, or the spread of the Anglo-Saxon race. However, these temporalities were disrupted by the appearance, in mining sites, of the disorienting, filthy, and chaotic "instant cities."[5] Instant cities were not a late nineteenth-century phenomenon, of course, but a form of urban space produced, from ancient times, by the discovery of precious metals. As Gunther Barth (1975) explains, these places were always isolated, always "transplants" from imperial and national centers, "pieced together from a mosaic of practices," insecure at all levels (xxii–xxiii). Late nineteenth-century observers, however, tended to see a place such as Leadville, Colorado, at its moment of boom in 1879, as a setting so full of contradictions as to be difficult (though important) to describe or theorize.[6] This "city" was not where one would expect an industrial powerhouse. It was a "cloud city"—a place defined by its airy inaccessibility—and yet apparently a site into which all too familiar processes of urbanization could somehow be pumped in a matter of months. It was plainly comparable to the burgeoning industrial cities of the day, but how could that comparison be formulated? For example, did somewhere like Leadville intensify the development of the vices of city life, or produce them in a distorted form? How could the speeded-up twenty-four-hour social life in such places be understood? It was evident that organizations normally dominant in urban centers were turned upside down in favor of a leisure industry catering to miners around the clock. There were, at the height of Leadville's fame, "five banks, three newspapers, department stores, seven churches and schools," but "120 saloons, 110 beer gardens, 118 gambling dens."[7]

The journalistic interest in finding geographies and temporalities with which to explain these places to national readers was, not surprisingly, intense. The simplest solution was to make recourse to literary conventions of describing Gold Rush camps, and, accordingly, many writers of the period deftly positioned the mines by reference to the coordinates provided by Bret Harte. Richard Harding Davis provides a wonderful example of this in *The West from a Car Window* (1892), where he describes the "dim and commonplace" Coloradan silver-mining town of Creede as lacking "the sharp, clear-cut personality of Bret Harte's men and scenes": it is "like a negative of a photograph which has been under-exposed, and which no amount of touching up will make clear" (60). Equally, writers could evoke the carnival produced by "vice," concluding simply that instant cities were places that were subverting mainstream culture for some period of time. Oscar Wilde, for example, described his visit to Leadville in April 1882 in "Impressions of America," focusing on an anarchic, alcohol-fueled violence. As he told it, he had been warned that "if I went there they would be sure to shoot me or my traveling manager," and he describes a lynching having taken place on the theater stage before his talk began. He goes on to describe the Leadville miners' interest in the whereabouts of the subject of his talk, the Renaissance sculptor Benevenuto Cellini. When his audience learns of Cellini's death, claims Wilde, they ask "Who shot him?" effectively eliminating other times and places (31). Nothing of this actually happened, but such details performed the task of summarizing Leadville mining culture with the use of an enjoyably familiar trope.[8]

The journalists who ventured to place somewhere like Leadville and its mining in the broader but more detailed narrative of national development clearly found the task arduous. A year into Leadville's boom, A. A. Hayes (1880), in his piece in *Harper's New Monthly Magazine*, began by drawing confidently on national history—America is a nation "continually attracted to new discoveries"—before sweeping into a continental history stretching back to Spanish occupation of part of the continent (381). But faced with positioning Leadville within that trajectory, Hayes quickly loses the thrust of his argument. When he suggests that this is a "new country" for "busted" men who "were just *dead broke* at home" and are "ready for a new country," we seem to be getting close to a statement of the safety valve theory of the "frontier" that we associate with Frederick Jackson Turner (380): the traditional fantasy of returning to a backwoods economy in order to make a fresh move forward to a socially and politically healthy future.

But, as Duane A. Smith (1992) wryly puts it, "Only by stretching the imagination could one call the mining camp a safety valve" (247). Hayes is forced to conclude that Leadville is a new place, but not one that can develop from frontier "new country" to American community:

> Mining camps, in the nature of things, grow to towns and cities, as boys grow to men; but as there are those humans whom we declare not to be men, but overgrown boys, so is Leadville not a city, but an overgrown mining camp. (394)

By the end of his piece, Hayes has turned from this argument about the arrested life of the town to illustrating the decay festering at the heart of the boom. He describes the streams' "banks rent and torn into distressing wastefulness by the gulch miners of the old days," the trees "mostly burned into leafless, sometimes branchless, stems," surroundings "positively weird in their desolation" (394), the "reeking garbage of the town," the "sulphurous fumes from a smelter" (396).

On a number of grounds, then, single themes and rationalistic explanations failed satisfactorily to summarize the industry or its manifestation in instant cities. Writers were much more successful when they abandoned the tropes of vice and topsy-turveydom, and the relations of cause and effect. In Hamlin Garland's *Hesper* (1903), for example, we have a rare and wonderful embrace of different geographies in his description of Cripple Creek in 1894:

> Just west of Le Beau's Camp ... stood a symmetrical peak which some missionary to the red people had called Mount Horeb. About the year 1870 some persons not missionaries planted gold in the soil in convenient places and raised a mighty shout over the discovery of a new El Dorado. A rush took place and to the outside world the region became known as the Mount Horeb Mining District, and was alluded to with deep resentment ... But there were miners whom neither the dogmatic opinions of geologists nor the tricks of schemers could turn aside from a faith that somewhere on the mighty slopes of Mogalyon lay veined of gold and these continued to chip and to dig, and to hammer. (122)

Garland captures the projection of meaning onto space on the part of groups both unconnected and in conflict. He assembles the different temporalities of native activity, biblical events, missionary pursuits, and geological assessments. He creates a sense of Cripple Creek as a focus for diverse and competing projects of occupation.[9] *Hesper* goes on to deal with the Cripple Creek mining war horizontally in the form of a "tale of two cities," in which the mining camps of Cripple Creek and the nearby town inhabited by its wealthy investors, Colorado Springs, are locked in conflict.[10] Garland manages to create all kinds of other relationships across space: between the ranching and mining industries, for example, and between local capitalists and upper-class easterners coming for a cure. His well-researched novel is both striking and unusual in its desire to acknowledge this range.[11]

Garland clearly sensed that he needed to be inventive if he was to represent mining in temporal terms, following tradition in his choice of a title. Hesper, the evening star, is associated with the Hesperides, the three nymphs who, in Greek myth, tended a blissful garden with golden apples in a far western corner of the world. But he seems also to want to give greater complexity to the mine's position in deep time in *Hesper*, setting aside the sweep of transhistorical generality, and using instead a tactic of dissolving past and present in the eyes of his protagonists. Theirs is not a commanding gaze so much as one that is aware of landscapes and social forms merging in the experiences of migration:

> As the big barge drew out into mid-stream, the wharfs, the four story tenements, and the business blocks rose in dim terraces, one behind the other, till the highest of them all loomed like the crest of a mist-lit mesa, and the lights in the dusk of the lower levels allured like camp fires in the deeps of wooded vales, while between the little group on the stern of the boat and this smoke-hid range of mysterious peaks the cold gray water rolled, ever widening, menacing, inexorable as death. (1)

However, with all that he achieves in evoking a setting for Cripple Creek—and indeed with all that he knew about it—Garland finds it difficult to develop a *plot* in the setting he has created: the references are too diverse, the populations are operating either on different planes or moving awkwardly between them.

This sense of deep time is used more successfully by Robert Louis Stevenson in his meditation on a ghost town in *The Silverado Squatters* (1884). The book derives from a series of articles giving an account of his honeymoon, during 1880, in the ruins of a deserted Californian mine in Silverado.[12] Stevenson had camped in a ruined boarding house that had served the miners of the Calistoga Mining Company in Silverado, California. It was, in Richard Aldington's (1957) words, "a smashed and littered-up miners' doss house" (122). The Company had opened a mine on this spot in 1872 and, in an elaborate ceremony in October 1874, inaugurated a town to service the business of the mine. By October 1875 the miners had left, taking all the buildings except for the hotel.[13] This was, of course, a familiar circumstance in mining. Stevenson stayed in Silverado for a few months and afterward published his account of the trip in *Scribner's Monthly* in 1883, before revising it in *The Silverado Squatters*.[14]

Stevenson re-creates Silverado in layers of speculative prospects: as a relic of the past, as a remote space in the imagination, as a perch in the wilderness. It is a ruined ancient city, a remote fairyland fastness, a castle in the air, and "the temple of some forgotten religion" (252). It is a world that may be layered with imaginative significance both in the way that the earth is geologically layered and as the mine is successively "discovered" by different groups or generations of miners. As the reader settles to this sense of a space imagined in multiple dimensions of the past, and indeed to the notion of the cosmopolitan writer perching on a mine, lost in his own speculations on Silverado, Stevenson completes the logic of his argument: the mine's owner reappears, all set to start gathering capital in order to work the mine again. In defiance of the behavior expected of ruined objects of poetic contemplation, this place is about to find a new history.

In the end, however, Stevenson's landscape, like Garland's, offers nothing in the way of a mining plot. For plots centered on gold and silver mines that do justice to these multiple temporalities and geographies, we need to turn to the narrative patterns of romance.[15] Romance revels in places that are different, undetermined, unfamiliar, and, above all, remote. It embraces the transhistorical, not only in its habit of using the plots of myth and legend, but also in charging those contexts with political and psychological meaning for the reader in the present. As Gillian Beer (1970) writes, romance universalizes experience: legendary kings and knights "are our representatives," there are "primary sources of experience," and "we have all in our time been princes and giants and royal pretenders" (3, 72). The continuities of social systems do not register in a world defined, above all, by what Richard Chase (1957) describes as defined by "radical even irreconcilable, contradictions" (7). At the point when the argument between romance and realism was at its height during the 1880s, romance was dismissed by some as offering stories that were no more than "poor silly toys that many grown people would still like to play with," and even apologists referred to romance's capacity to "lighten the burdens of life by taking us for a time out of our humdrum and perhaps sordid conditions."[16] What I want to argue here, though, is that this form, "overstepping" as it does "the limit by which life is normally bounded," is peculiarly attuned to mining, and on a number of levels.[17]

Mining lore has always generated legend, romance's key source, and, in the late nineteenth century, the legendary was embraced in tales told by miners.[18] The following passage comes from a tribute given to a pioneer prospector in Virginia City in 1871. There is certainly nothing here of the progress of the industry or the development of Virginia City. Instead, the speech evokes the world of the Harz miners' stories, with their magical transformations and bright sensuous detail, their acknowledgment of the vitality of the earth, and drama of the underground. Here the speaker describes the prospector:

> He climbs like a huge fly upon the bald skull of some lofty mountain, and the primeval hills welcome his daring footsteps. He taps with the prospector's pick at the adamantine doors of the earth's treasure chambers, and at his demand they reveal their shining secrets. His glittering ax lays low the green plumed forest monarchs, and on the surface of emerald prairies he marks the site of cities yet to be.[19]

In a different example, a coal miner's tale, free of the florid quality of the public speech, we find a narrative that moves through different dimensions, real and magical, natural and supernatural, in succession of unrelated, unexpected events, rather than in the relations of cause and effect. The tale has romance's quality of linking the transhistorical and the abstract with the specificity of local detail set in real time:

> I worked in the Enterprise mine when it was only a drift many years ago. The vein didn't have much surface on it, and when I threw a fall, the damn toppin' caved in on me—sand, slate, coal 'n' all.

I shook it off all right, but when I cleared me eyes I found meself face to face with a buck which had pretty two-pointed antlers. "I guess we're into it, butty," says I to meself, "and so let's make the best of things." Well, sir, the buck he gave a snort and started to run off. I caught him by the tail and lifted meself onto his back. Then I took hold of his antlers. Bucky ran from one breast to another and then into the gangway, and from the gangway he hopped out of the mine to the surface, and with one leap he bounded up to the top of the mountain.[20]

I am arguing here that both the protean shapes of the mining industry and the lore of miners during the late nineteenth century brought mining into conversation with romance. Yet the writing of mining as romance has seemed, to many critics, deeply distasteful. It is argued that mining romances produce self-serving imperial fantasies of extraction and removal of precious metals by Anglo-Saxon heroes, erasing the toil of miners and the conditions of the industry altogether. More broadly, romances are argued to reproduce an imperial geography, in which Anglo-European culture appears "as a zone of relative order, security and secularity," whereas other spaces are fictionalized as places "of magic, mystery and disorder."[21] H. Rider Haggard's *King Solomon's Mines* (1881) seems almost to have been written to illustrate these arguments, with its Anglo-Saxon drive into South Africa, its flimsily justified quest, its horribly breezy conversion of native nations to children and witches, and its chilling fantasy of endless wealth stacked up a few yards beneath the surface. Mining romance could certainly flatter the scramble for precious metals, by Anglo-European and American corporations and governments, erasing the human costs paid by miners and local populations. However, not all mining romances were as crude as this.

The romance that inspired Haggard to write *King Solomon's Mines*, Stevenson's *Treasure Island* (1883), demonstrates disillusionment with British culture, beginning on a rather frayed edge of England, apparently suffering from economic depression and depopulation. In Stevenson's romance, the forces of social order—the headstrong country squire and the doctor—rush to Treasure Island, entranced as much by the opportunity to leave their allotted roles as by the idea of getting their hands on "free" gold; there is certainly no breath of "Protestant piety" here. Also, contrary to his apparent function as a beacon of upper-class Anglo-Saxon capability, Squire Trelawney is quickly revealed to be a fool. Our flawed heroes find the opposite of escape, and are drawn into a fight in which success depends on the risky manipulation of shifting collectivities rather than the assertion of Anglo-Saxon muscle. The character that achieves the greatest realignment as a result of the book's events, and manages to make that change stick, is Long John Silver, the story's ostensible villain.

Stevenson's romance operates between two peripheries. In Joseph Conrad's mining romance, *Nostromo* (1904), the distinction between center and periphery and between rational and irrational realms is lost altogether. Terry Eagleton (1970) has argued that Conrad projects a "sense of... the impossibility of grasping at the heart of a fragmentary universe," and this is certainly true of the Sulaco silver mine (22). This mine becomes the focus of the obsessive attention of a diverse collection of stakeholders locally, nationally, and worldwide: governments and factions within Costaguana and their representatives in Sulaco, investors in San Francisco, international transportation firms, engineers from Britain, Italian workers, French radical opinion, and Charles Gould, the mine's superintendent, for whom the necessity for protecting the mined silver trumps all other relationships. At first it seems apparent that the Sulaco Mine is the creature of an American investor's fancy and Gould's filial loyalty. But this mine does more than simply possess the imagination of these and other men, as happens, for example, in *King Solomon's Mines*, or disrupt social collectivities, as in *Treasure Island*. It wholly colonizes the efforts of everyone concerned with it. It may be incorporated into proliferating political, economic, and individual projects, but, from the start of Conrad's retrospectively organized text, these projects have already been thwarted, interrupted, and dissipated.

Neither of these examples of imperial romance deals in a direct way with the mines themselves, or with the work of mining. They hold fast to the obsessive, compromising process of ransacking spaces in which precious metals have been dumped, stored, or hidden. In turning now to a discussion of Mary Hallock Foote's mining romances, I want to consider the attempt of a writer to use romance not only to plot the power of mines, but to examine the industry itself.

Foote wrote three novels set in Leadville: *The Led-Horse Claim* (1883), *John Bodewin's testimony* (1886), and *The Last Assembly Ball* (1889). In the case of the first two, she used disputes over mines to structure her plots.

The Led-Horse Claim deals with a violent conflict between the superintendents of two mining companies over access to a particular lode. *John Bodewin's testimony* focuses on the legal battle between a local industry insider and a Kansas investor over the alteration of a boundary set between two claims. Foote's focus on legal argument was no accident. Her husband, an engineer and mine manager, was involved in cases on which Foote could draw.[22] The absence of any federal law about how to deal with mining rights before the mid-1860s, and the difficulties produced by the Apex Law when it was passed in 1872, made legal disputes endemic to the industry.[23] Indeed, according to Malcolm J. Rohrbough (1986), the law to which judges made reference in making decisions "lay abandoned" in Leadville, when "juries refused to bring verdicts supporting the owner of the apex," and "local hostility overrode the clear intent of the law" (96). In focusing on legal dispute, then, Foote was moving to the heart of the industry as it was experienced locally and within every dimension of the mine's work. It was for this reason, I imagine, that her writing was considered very accurate by industry insiders.[24]

A century or so later, however, Foote's analysis of the mining industry has been dismissed.[25] The knowledge and understanding gleaned over many years of marriage to a man struggling unsuccessfully to make his way as a mining engineer, living in mining communities at New Almaden, Leadville, and Grass Valley, are, it seems, neutralized by her gender and class. As a young artist from a Hudson Valley Quaker farming family who came to California, Colorado, and Idaho via a successful career as an illustrator, she has not appeared, to the majority of her critics, to be equipped to grasp the nature and workings of an industry operated by men. I want to argue otherwise, for it seems to me that Foote brought to her portrait of the industry a distinctive and fruitful cluster of preoccupations. Trained as an illustrator by an artist with close connections to the Pre-Raphaelites, Foote kept, for a long time, something of the Pre-Raphaelite interest in using the broad vividly realized landscapes of Arthurian and medieval legend to engage with contemporary psychological states. At the same time, she shared the interest of that group in the fine description of nature, particularly rocky ground. And, like the Pre-Raphaelites, Foote was deeply engaged by the concept of a "frontier" that offered respite from the encroaching wasteland of industrialism.[26] It is this complex aesthetic position that allowed Foote to find a geography of mining, and explore its psychic fallout, while also addressing the position of places like Leadville within the national geography.

From her early short story "In Exile" (1881), set in New Almaden, California, we can see Foote drawing these elements together. She writes a portrait of a natural landscape in the process of being destroyed by mining, but the plot moves forward in a series of tableaux soaked in medieval reference: the encounter at a bright fountain in a deserted space, the vision of the entrapped woman at her needlework. The sensuous impact of bright fabric brings the story to a close. The two protagonists, engineer and schoolmistress, knight and lady, occupy a space defined both by their shared late-nineteenth sense of themselves as in exile on the frontier, but also by the emblematic landscape of legend.[27]

Foote's love of Tennyson, a poet revered, of course, by the Pre-Raphaelites, gave her further tools for imagining how this space was being occupied (as well as several plots).[28] Foote described migrants to the mining camps as exiles ancient and modern: as "lotos eaters."[29] These are the heroic adventurers of *The Odyssey* who, having arrived in the land of the lotus eaters, quickly become addicted to the narcotic plant, and also convinced that they are in a wonderful place. All thoughts of home are erased along with any other sense of purpose. They have been away from home for decades and, in any case, this new land has become their central point of reference. The parallel that Foote was making between the mining industry and the pursuit of an addictive substance in a place far from home scarcely needs glossing. Of particular interest in relation to Foote's location of mining, though, is her sense of the way in which a place first imagined as a focus of discovery is transformed by the longing for material satisfaction into a desert in which the mines form the only reliable reference point. In Tennyson's "Lotos Eaters" (1832), the fate of the adventurers is given another twist: these are men whose imagined and expected escape to a land of effortless fulfillment has produced, in Isobel Armstrong's (1993) words, "a condition without sequence, of repetition without progression and disjunction without change" (88). Foote's lotus-eating becomes a dreary obsession with consuming the landscape of California and Colorado.

The Led-Horse Claim brings these Pre-Raphaelite and Tennysonian strands together to produce another remote, dusty land with mining work at its center. The plot is a simple one. Virtuous Hilgard and corrupt Conrath are the eastern superintendents of the Led-Horse and Shoshone mines. They come into conflict when Conrath begins to mine a vein of silver which is legally part of the neighboring Led-Horse claim. The argument between the two companies escalates into armed warfare during which Hilgard shoots Conrath by mistake. The situation is complicated by the developing love affair between Hilgard and Conrath's sister, Cecil. This element of the plot, couched in the terms and the symbolism of chivalric love plots, is written in a series of set pieces: in summer and winter scenes, at the place where surveyors have marked out the boundaries of the claims, underground in the mines. The effect is not, as in Garland, Stevenson, and Conrad, of mines in the West as a place of innumerable projections on the part of outsiders. Rather, *The Led-Horse Claim* rests on the proposition that sites such as these produce a terrible new geography. This is no bright frontier of possibility but a permanent exile in a new industrialism, and there is certainly no homeland to which to return. The East of the novel consists of a bleakly impersonal hotel and the emotionally arid home of Cecil's aunt. Hilgard and Cecil's future, like the prospects of the mining towns, will consist of "drifting about unsteadily" (1), a point that Cecil's dour aunt confirms after the protagonists' dreary eastern wedding: "Journeys, journeys, nothing but journeys . . . rushing back and forth, thousands of miles at a stretch" (271). The lure of the mines and the intensity of mining interests have eliminated the home place.

At the same time, the battle over the mining claims of the Led-Horse and Shoshone Mines rests on the much more precise demarcations of law and warfare. As an underground battle over mining rights begins, Cecil looks at the destruction of the landscape and the placing of a flag amongst the rocks, and assumes that a battle has taken place above as well as below ground. Hilgard's explanation that this is the work of a mining survey party does nothing to dispel the sense that the mining and fighting are inextricably linked. Although Hilgard and Conrath are too young to have fought, direct and oblique references to the Civil War dot the text. Foote seems to want to recall full-scale war in her imagery of flags, barricades, rifles, and Conrath's large-scale funeral, even to prompt the reader to think of the mining war as an extension of the national war, and of the West as the focus of continual war. As the references to the mine as a battleground accumulate, one even wonders if the reader is being asked to remember the conflict between native nations and "mining interests" that characterized the establishment of new mines. Conrath's mine, the Shoshone, after all, is named for a native nation.[30]

Foote's interest in imagining a national landscape centered in the West and epitomized by mining is taken further in *John Bodewin's testimony*. Here, Foote evokes a landscape defined by some of the qualities of

Victorian Camelot. Tennyson's Camelot is, as Inga Bryden (2005) argues, "like Arthur himself... simultaneously substantial and insubstantial... a constructed illusion caught in the process of being built" (143). It is set in a forlorn world of hostile peoples, giving Arthur and his knights a ceaseless task of subjugating malign enemies. Their hopes for success lie in the idealism of Arthur's virtuous knights, but, of course, in Tennyson especially, those bright expectations have already been compromised by sexual betrayal. Foote uses this idea of the compromised Arthurian ideal in a hostile landscape from the start of *John Bodewin's testimony*, as a group of representative Americans watch the dignified Bodewin on horseback picking his way across a plain. The scene is the opening trope of traditional romance, but here the landscape is horribly burned, and the inhabitants of the camp are subdued. The plot rests on the difficult and destructive situation created when Bodewin, a mining engineer, adhering to codes of chivalry rather than of law, decides to favor the claims of the man who has saved his sister from a compromising situation over the claims of the rightful owner of a mining claim. When Bodewin is kidnapped, however, he forgets chivalry, and favors the claims of instinct and feeling first. By the end of the novel, Foote is identifying him as an Arthurian figure especially associated with a compromised and adulterous Camelot, John *Tristram* Bodewin.[31]

The fact of the matter is that the West organized by mining has become a setting where no code has much hope of prevailing or even allowing actors on a sense of occupying the moral high ground. Finding a new setting and making a new start offers no solution either. At the end of the novel, as Bodewin and his new wife Josephine arrive in a fresh and apparently empty western space to begin their lives afresh, Josephine makes to embrace the familiar, expansive future promised by this new, as yet uncorrupted, space. There is a brief sense that Bodewin may even be able to regenerate Camelot. In a moment, though, all the couple can hear above the wind is the railway and the sound of the telegraph machine, ceaselessly conveying information between here (which seems hardly to be a place) and there (which might be anywhere in the world).[32] There are no points of security here.

I began this chapter with an emphasis on the instability of the mining industry of the last decades of the late nineteenth century, and with all that was unpredictable and difficult for onlookers to locate the mining industry. I have also argued that some writers made use of romance to trace the geographies of mining, to open up its temporal complexity, and to explore the problems of living in the worlds that mines create. Now I want to return to the problem with romance that I mentioned earlier: in reaching across space and time these texts render the vertically organized spaces of mining and the life of underground workers far less visible. The most popular romances of the era tend to convert the underground—and the mine—to the cavern, and to spaces that can be accessed horizontally, rather than by journeying down into the depths of the earth. Equally, tales of treasure of the period are wont to imagine riches already converted into coins and jewelry, erasing the processes of production involved in mining.

We can take a number of approaches to this apparent absence. It may be explained by reference to a lack of knowledge, class background, or personal qualities of the writers concerned. It may be argued that writers like Foote or Stevenson share a sense that their very literary writing should refer to the human condition, penetrating the darker aspects of human experience rather than the working life, above or below ground. Or perhaps the nineteenth-century novel was just inhospitable to downward movement. David L. Pike (2007) makes the point that nineteenth-century novels are organized around upward movement and mobility, and that downward movement is what happens to the scoundrel and the failure, the unworthy poor (43). Even Garland, the great proselytizer for heroic toil, refers, in *Hesper*, to mining as an "unholy business" for slaves (149).

Equally, as Pike (1997) describes the underground generally as "a site of crisis," he reminds us of the dread of the underground and work that is undertaken far beneath the earth's surface. This is not just the dread experienced by onlookers. Hand (1942) describes how "the mingled feeling of awe and fear that grips anyone descending into a mine as a visitor for the first time is a feeling shared in some degree by miners themselves, even those of many years' experience" (127). He says, "Lore centering about accidents and deaths in mines is common; in fact there is little folklore underground that is not in some way connected with the fears and apprehensions of miners for their welfare and safety while in the bosom of the earth" (140).

Foote provides an example of this profound sense of crisis in her description of Cecil Conrath, in *The Led-Horse Claim*, sitting alone and in the dark of the mine:

> What a mysterious, vast, whispering dome was this! There were sounds which might have been miles away through the deadening rock. There were far-off, indistinct echoes of life, and subanimate

mutterings, the slow respirations of the rocks, drinking air and oozing moisture through their sluggish pores, swelling and pushing against their straitening bonds of timber. Here were the buried Titans, stirring and sighing in their lethargic sleep. (113)

There is a wealth of association here with the Gothic tale with its subterranean settings, and also with the popular renderings during this period of Scandinavian mythology, which is full of mining reference. The underground has an eroticism, too. What we are reading here are the familiar Victorian associations between wetness, the underground, the sluggish and sub-animate and the world, terrifying and preferably invisible, inhabited by working bodies.

A common strategy for enabling the exploration of the problematic, dangerous world of the underground mine is to project it onto the life and death of an amorous relationship that takes place aboveground. Richard Harding Davis's imperial romance, *Soldiers of Fortune* (1897), is a case in point. The novel is notorious for its portrait of American corporations stripping non-industrialized societies of valuable metal deposits and for inspiring the aggressive imperial ventures of the period.[33] Davis's hero, Robert Clay, works on engineering projects—in this case an iron mine—on behalf of stockholders. He describes mining in remarks about how he has "discovered and planned and opened them," and made sure that they are systematically run, but the work of mining, as opposed to its management, is barely acknowledged except to remark on Clay's command of an army of workers (63).

Clay's plan, however, is to abandon all day-to-day contact with mining, to marry a highly sophisticated "society" woman, and to become an independent traveler and advisor to companies and governments. His marriage plan is initially unsuccessful, though, because his intended, Alice, cannot even bear to think of his association with "dirty" mines. Alice encounters the site of the iron mine on a visit arranged by Clay, who has anticipated that his success in this tough masculinized setting will make his intended bride admire his manliness, and that she will agree to marry him. In fact, when Alice encounters the life of the mine, she rules out becoming engaged to anyone involved in such work. She finds the site "noisy, hot" and "grimy" (112); she is shocked by its ugly intrusion on the landscape. Far from admiring Clay's work, Alice is horrified by it. Perhaps Davis intends some of the sexual associations of the "hot" and "grimy" that other writers make more explicit; there is certainly a lot of commentary on black smudges on white dresses. However, the novel ends with Alice rejected in favor of her sister, Hope. Alice is appalled by the mines and their works. Hope, by contrast, is happy to get "dirty" exploring the mines, but also happy to brush off the experience. Accordingly, she is rewarded with the sophisticated pleasures of Clay's new life.

Davis's story shows various degrees of separation between mining work and the social world aboveground, of which he judges complete separation as most appropriate; and he models that separation in the relationships between men and women. Clay cannot marry a woman who is troubled by the human and environmental realities of the mines. He needs, in Davis's view, a woman who can see them and then erase them from her mind. This is a preposterous argument, of course, although it should remind us that mining has long been steeped in matters of gender and sexuality, and that mines are suffused with the tensions of gender politics and charged with eroticism. These issues are the subject of the next chapter. For now, however, Davis's imperial romance serves to exemplify all that romance can achieve in obscuring the life of mines. Foote, Garland, and Stevenson have often been accused of failing to portray the world of mining, or preferring to remain blind to its cruel and destructive works. In this chapter, I have explored some of the challenges facing writers that tried to represent mining's different dimensions during this period, both its transnational power and its local impact. The forms of romance to which they turned offered opportunities for engagement with a complex industrial world and, I would argue, their work deserves greater respect than it has received.

CHAPTER FIVE

Sex Work

✣ MINING IS GENDERED AND SEXUALIZED, MARKEDLY AND OBVIOUSLY so.[1] Its cultures and traditions have been permeated by questions, problems, and arguments about gender and sexuality. This chapter looks at how gender and sexuality figure within the mining cultures of the late nineteenth century, and at the ways in which sexuality, in particular, lent meaning to the work of the camps and towns during this period.[2] This is not a tidy field of enquiry, and not only because camps and towns enabled and contained a range of gendered and eroticized relations, and, by representing them, made them available to interpretation by national and international as well as local audiences.[3] It is unruly because the miners brought to the surface—quite literally—critical questions about gender, sexuality, and power. Indeed Michel Foucault's (1978) much-quoted point that sexuality is "an especially dense transfer point for relations of power" seems very apposite in a setting involving so many "transfer points": conquest, aggressive competition, the displacement and devaluing of various populations by incoming Anglo-Europeans, the extraction of metals, the demographic domination of men over women (103).

In this chapter I examine some of the most familiar and traditional conventions of gendering and sexualizing mining within and beyond Anglo-European culture: conventions of thinking of mining as more or less exclusively male, as polarizing and exaggerating norms of masculinity and femininity, and of mines as sites of violence, actual and symbolic, against women. Perhaps slightly less familiar, though equally traditional, is the association made between the mining cultures of the gold and silver rushes and liberatory sexualities. Before considering these two strands, though, and the nature of their relationship to one another, I want to look first at a gendered and sexualized figure of particular importance in mining cultures, and of special significance in the popular imagination of gold and silver mining. This was the highly visible figure of the female "prostitute." Cyprian, fallen or fancy woman, lady in the trade, red light woman, soiled dove, sporting girl, summer woman: her many names give some indication of the importance as well as the complex cultural position—and intense interest—of a woman who entered (full or part time, or occasionally) the sex industry of the mining camps, or who entered into a range of sexual relationships with men to support herself economically.[4]

This has not been a consensual figure. For Elliott West (1979), for example, writing about the saloon in the Rocky Mountains, these are abject figures: "tired and haggard woman," "a few hardened hussies" (48–49). The figure of the Chinese prostitute also has, until recently, acted as the focus of longstanding arguments about the abjection of sex work and sex slavery within patriarchal systems.[5] At the opposite end of the attitudinal spectrum, in Donald L. Hardesty's (1998) portrait of the world of the more remote camps, prostitutes form an integral part of a rebellious sexual and emotional economy.[6] Still other scholars draw our attention to the range of economic relationships involving sex between men and women, a range poorly summarized by the term "prostitution." Alexy Simmons (1998), for example, foregrounds the flexibility of prostitution as a form of work and its availability as a temporary means for women to earn a living. And, as James Ferguson (1999) helpfully points out, there is no virtue in imagining relationships between miners and women selling sex as non-normative when normative relationships would be "preposterously . . . out of place" in transient mining communities (167).

These conflicting viewpoints reflect, to some degree, the range of cultural attitudes to prostitution in Western society now. However, the arguments around the interpretation of the prostitute's work of selling non-reproductive sex are secondary here, I think. Prostitution was more than present or prevalent in mining communities; it was, as Julia Ann Laite (2009) argues, a "defining" feature at the heart of the work culture of the mines (743). This begs a question about exactly *what* the presence and prevalence of prostitution "defines" about mining and its cultures. It is sometimes argued that prostitution is a kind of variant on the exploitative nature of the work cultures of mining. Firstly, it proliferates in mining camps and towns precisely because women are seeking their fortunes alongside men, but are excluded from mining (a point to which I shall presently return). The two businesses were thus bound within a single communal project of extraction around which everyone's life was organized. Secondly, as Paula Petrik (1987) and Simmons (1998) have pointed out, miners and prostitutes shared many of the same work experiences. They were usually migrants looking to make money quickly; many worked seasonally or according to need and they moved from place to place across networks of fellow workers. Both forms of work, though stigmatized, were easy to enter. Both were hierarchized according to the ethnic background of workers. The trajectory of the two businesses was also shared, as workers moved from independent and small group activity into a form of managed, routinized, and waged work capitalized by others. It is no wonder that capital "secretly flowed between the two sectors."[7]

But, above all, both mining and prostitution demanded heightened performances of conventional norms of gender. Both demanded that workers made their bodies wholly available to the task, frequently to the point of destruction. Both worked in exceptionally dangerous conditions, facing diminishing prospects as they aged. It is this particular set of shared experiences that is critical here, I think, because where these destructive conditions and grim experiences are regularly admitted of mining work and mining bodies, they are regularly obscured, or complicated, in what quickly became a popular pleasure in recalling prostitutes, in various guises, in mining camps and towns. Conversely, although the bodies of miners of this period are rarely pictured, those of prostitutes are frequently presented without the mainstream displeasure directed toward these workers in other contexts.

What seems to be happening here is that the still highly visible figure of the prostitute is acting as a kind of surrogate for the miner: she may be the object of ambivalent feelings, but, in this context, she is apparently a much less troubling figure than the miner. Her rebelliousness, for example, is perceived to be of trivial economic or political significance by comparison with the threat of the miner's strike or war. The prostitute's demise or death is accepted as the inevitable consequence of her dance with danger, and therefore less shocking than the miner's accident, the outcome of hazardous work, mistakes, and corruption. David Belasco's highly successful melodrama *The Girl of the Golden West* (1905) seems to bring about this surrogacy. Belasco places the indistinctly formulated figure of "The Girl," a character that has many associations and attributes of the mining-camp prostitute, as his central figure. She runs a saloon and she lives alone with "only" a "lax voluptuous squaw"—a figure who effectively acts as a prostitute's maid—for company (10). All the miners that The Girl serves pursue her, and their desire for a "girl's" company and attention is made evident. Her conversation with the new arrival, Johnson, about her status as a saloon worker—someone that a visitor might expect to be a full- or part-time prostitute, or a woman who might be prepared to have sex with a stranger—acknowledges the likelihood that The Girl has been "corrupted" by these circumstances:

JOHNSON: I'd like to ask you a question.
GIRL: I know what it is—every stranger asks it—It's this: Am I decent?

Though Johnson's response is to insist that she is "worth" "something better than this" (50), The Girl pleads, in the mode of the sexually or morally compromised woman of Victorian fictions, that Johnson will not "expect too much" and "bring out the best" in her, even redeem her from her life (56). Yet, at the play's climax, The Girl invites Johnson (a man that we know is a Mexican bandit in disguise) up to her cabin, where they enjoy a passionate embrace, before, with the arrival of the sheriff, Johnson is forced to hide in The Girl's bedroom.

This is comprehensively disgraceful behavior for a woman according to conventions of the time, though Belasco's New York audiences presumably excused it as typical of the Wild West. What is interesting here, though, is that Belasco keeps insisting that The Girl is not a prostitute at all. From the start, he insists that she is not the "soiled dove" that we assume her to be, but a subject operating independently from all that we know of her life: "The Girl ... is rather complex. Her utter frankness takes away all suggestion of vice—showing her to be unsmirched ... untouched by the life around her" (8).

It is possible for her to live as a saloon worker, and yet not be physically and psychologically vulnerable, or "smirched."

It might be argued that what we have here is a character typical of the contemporary taste for sexually compromised women with redeeming moral urges: another Mrs. Tanqueray or Mrs. Warren.[8] But here a different parallel is traced in the way the surprising figure of The Girl and the disquieting figure of the miner, both of whom seem able to do their work without being "really" dirtied or damaged. When, at one o'clock in the morning, alone in her cabin, The Girl kisses Johnson without restraint, Belasco treats the audience to a range of extraordinary effects:

> GIRL: 'Taint no use. I lay down my hand to you. (*She runs into his arms.*)
> JOHNSON: (*Embracing and kissing her*) I love you! (*All EFFECTS. BREAKAWAY.*) SNOW *bags: FANS* R *and* L. SNOW effect over door; canvas and silk machines R and L. A loud SHRIEK on the air tank is the direct cue to set everything in motion for the Breakaway. When this is heard windows R.C. and L.C. open and close; now appliances over windows work; inside and outside doors c. open and close as though blown by the wind; curtains on canopy over bed are first blown in . . . and then blown out by fan in rear; small basket on wardrobe up L is knocked off; pot with flower is knocked from stand R.C.; blankets in loft shake, but not too violently. Several pieces of white tissue are blown from under bed by means of the fan in rear. All these effects must come simultaneously. (76)

Before our eyes, the effects dissolve the walls of the cabin, and set The Girl right at the heart of the turbulent mining camp. The industrialism of the setting is recalled in the banging and shrieking of the effects; the sounds of shaking, the loss of light, seem even to suggest some mining disaster. All this occurs as The Girl kisses the stranger: her brave performance of independence and self-determination collapses at the moment that the world worked by the miners receives is finally acknowledged in the play. The Girl has previously remarked that the miners' position is one of complete subjection—"they eat dirt, an' they sleep dirt, an' they breathe dirt till their backs are bent, their heads twisted, their souls warped"—and that subjection is mirrored in the surrender of her own body (54).

At the core of most discussions of mining and gender, however, lies a very different set of interests. The view that mining is an activity usually, perhaps appropriately, even naturally, performed by men has long prevailed.[9] This argument is of special relevance here because the late nineteenth century did indeed see a masculinization of mining.[10] Of course, this was not a process that was quickly and evenly achieved. Indeed, looked at transhistorically, this late nineteenth-century masculinization seems to have been a rather exceptional episode in mining's history. In the rush to the Gold Coast in West Africa in the late 1870s and 1880s, for example, male-dominated European enterprises run by men coexisted with longstanding practices of placer mining dominated by women. Raymond E. Dumett (1998) describes how Akan women's skill in panning for gold was the object of admiration on the part of incoming Anglo-European miners (53). Meanwhile, women in Latin American mines and in the Far East mined on into the twentieth century; and now women have returned to underground mining all over the world.[11] Nonetheless, during the period under discussion here, women were excluded, if unevenly so, from most American and Anglo-European enterprises. Native and Mexican women, and some migrant Anglo-American and Anglo-European families, worked in placer mining during the Gold Rush in California, and some women were successful in prospecting and managing mines throughout the period of the rushes; but generally, as particular mines required larger workforces, more expensive technologies, and more capital, men were employed exclusively, and women were, as much as possible, relegated to unpaid work in the home, or forms of ancillary work.[12] The Klondike rush, at the turn of the century, was a last gasp of the placer mining that involved family parties and single women.[13]

This process of masculinization has been understood in a number of ways by scholars of the mining scene. As Anne McClintock (1995) and others have explained, this was an historical moment at which Western bourgeois cultures in general found the idea of men and women working side by side in any setting unattractive, but responded with extreme antipathy to the spectacle of white women working in the mines. The well-founded association of mining with brutal toil and visions of the exposure of the body to "dirt" (as well as, perhaps, the traditional link made between mining and the penetrative sexual domination of the female, to which I shall return presently), made the presence of women in the mines disturbing to the dominant mainstream in Europe and the United States. Middle- and ruling-class cultures were united in wishing to link women, especially white Anglo-European women, with work that could at least be imagined as light and clean, and in insisting that the absolute biological and mental differences between men and women be mirrored in the undertaking of different work.

Alongside this argument lies another longstanding contention that the rushes generated unfettered heterosexual freedom, as young men managed to escape from the repressive sexual economy of the Victorian mainstream of Anglo-America. To some scholars, rejection of the female or relief at women's absence has seemed the joyful consequence of the whole adventure, the implication being that it was women especially that enforced repressive sexual and social practices.[14] But this is a complex issue on two counts at least. Firstly, although Anglo-European women may not have joined some rushes in large numbers, it did not follow that women were absent from the diggings. Some native women, and Mexican women who lived locally, were already at the mines when immigrants appeared.[15] Secondly, this argument is muddied, I think, by the assumption that the migrants were trying to extricate themselves from a home life shaped by a nineteenth-century cult of domesticity. If male migrants were escaping, they were escaping from multiple formations of home, according to class and place, and were doing so in different ways: sometimes temporarily, sometimes for protracted periods, sometimes forever. Surely countless variables were in play as far as possible attitudes and practices on migrants' parts were concerned.[16]

The masculinization of mining in the late nineteenth century, wherever it occurred, coincided with a broader miners' tradition that held that the mine was not simply a masculine workplace, but a space in which beliefs about an absolute and essential difference between men and women could be explored, and, in certain situations, acted upon. It has often been reported that the exclusion of women is believed by miners to be necessary in order to avoid bad luck or danger in the mines.[17] As Wayland D. Hand (1942) found in researching the lore of western miners: "One of the most universal of miners' superstitions" had to do with the "fear of accidents, cave-ins, and other untoward happenings" if women entered a mine and the suspicion that women's presence might cause the ore to "pinch out" (134). Gier and Mercier (2006) suggest that such ideas are "superstitions" that have been mobilized cynically in order to exclude women from some of the better-paid work within the mining community (4). But this may be a simplification.

Such work lore may derive from, or be linked with, ancient ideas about the femininity of a productive earth. So, for example, in *The Forge and the Crucible* (1962), Mircea Eliade reaches back into ancient thought about mining to explore the conception of earth as a woman growing ores in her womb. He describes the way in which mining is envisaged as a process in which the miner may "intervene in the unfolding of a subtle embryology: they accelerate the rhythm of the growth of ores, they collaborate in the work of Nature and assist it to give birth more rapidly" (8). One can certainly find traces of such ideas in miners' writing of the period in question here, for example in an early volume of poetry from the Australian Gold Rush, *The New Rush and Other Poems and Songs* by J. Rogers (1864):

> To Earth's aurifrous centre
> We'll wedge our weary way,
> She beckons us to enter,
> And let us not delay:
> There gold, man's envied treasure,
> In our degen'rate day,
> The source of Love and Pleasure
> Will all our pains repay. (55)[18]

This is a poem about seduction and desire, as well as about the fecundity of the earth, and indeed mines have long been eroticized by miners as sexually powerful and possessive. Pascale Absi (2006) writes of how, in Potosi's Pachamama, the miners speak of the mountain they are mining as appropriating to herself the miners' "desire, and the eroticism of their bodies" (61). One can also find discussions of a more aggressively sexualized vision of mining. Thomas M. Klubock (1996), for example, quotes Chilean miners describing the "threatening, consuming and vengeful female presence" of the mountain, which they cannot abandon "no matter how hard [they] work" (443). T. Dunbar Moodie (1994), writing about mining cultures in the Witwatersrand mines, describes the pervasive use of "sexual expletives and crude accounts of sexual activity" (18). Janet L. Finn (1998), comparing the mining cultures of Butte and Chuquicamata, notes the use of women's names for mines as a "warning of 'insecurity, capriciousness, betrayal, hopes and fears, habitual characteristics of the relationships'" between men and women (127).[19]

It is no simple matter to position this accumulation of research about miners' gendering and sexualizing of their work within the particular historical setting of the late nineteenth-century mining rushes, or alongside the late nineteenth-century masculinization of mining in the West, or against scenes of demographic imbalance. We can only struggle to imagine the attitudinal specificities of local mining cultures made up of more and less experienced miners or complete novices of all different and hybridized ethnic and cultural backgrounds. It is difficult to make confident assertions about how the lore and cultural practices surrounding mining might have been disseminated or assimilated within the myriad and often transient settings of camps and towns.[20] However, some research has shown how male workers, faced with extremes of toil in an industrial setting, turn to heightened performances of masculinity in order to express a sense of vulnerability. In this context, as Moodie argues, references to dominating women, for example, may form part of a tactic for "keep[ing] at bay incapacitating fears," as well as the threat to "personal stability" posed by facing danger day after day (18).[21] A highly industrialized mining setting is being referred to here, but surely the fear of humiliating failure haunted the experience of the placer miners of, say, the Californian or Klondike rushes, as well as migrants to the dangerous silver mines in Nevada, Colorado, and elsewhere. Insofar, then, as miners may have practiced and performed aggressive masculinities in order to maintain a sense of the agency in these circumstances—and in circumstances in which migrants struggled to eliminate the claims of rivals—they certainly had a wealth of mining lore and tradition on which to draw.[22]

These aggressions may have fused with a "conquest mentality" on the part of Anglo-American immigrants, so that relations between men and women were further distorted by hierarchies produced in the service of a colonial project.[23] Such a conjecture is easily illustrated. Mrs. Lee Whipple-Haslam, in *Early Days in California* (1925), describes the Cherokee Wilse Walkingstaff murdering James Ham over a "young squaw" (15). Albert L. Hurtado (1997) gives the particularly troubling example in his account of an incident when:

> a young one-eyed Indian woman had intercourse with a miner for food, [and] her husband appeared and threatened her. The next day another Indian came to the camp and begged the whites to leave the woman alone. He added that among his people the penalty for adultery was the loss of an eye. (135)

Hostility on the part of men as a response to relations with women pervades scenes of married life. In Anne Ellis's *The Life of an Ordinary Woman* (1929), the author gives a disturbing sense of a threatening gender hierarchy in the domestic sphere:

> All this first winter, George is trying to train me. I find men who have led a wild life are more exacting of their womenfolk.... After, when we had moved to Cripple Creek, things are running smoother. I say "We seem to be getting along better"; his answer was, "Yes you are getting some sense." (182)

In the journalism coming out of mining towns, not only masculine hostility toward women, but an insistent impulse to eradicate attitudes attributed to them too, seem to be rehearsed relentlessly. So, for example, the squibs of the male writers publishing in San Francisco and Virginia City during the 1860s celebrate the irrelevance or separation of women—family members and wives—from the male subject.[24] Here is Mark Twain (1867) heaping contempt on the advice to be expected from a female relative. "Aunt Nancy" is the object of derision:

> DEAR MARK: We spent the evening very pleasantly at home yesterday. The Rev. Dr Macklin and wife, from Peoria, were here. He is a humble laborer in the vineyard, and takes his coffee strong. He is also subject to neuralgia—neuralgia in the head—and is so unassuming and prayerful. There are few such men. We have soup for dinner likewise. Although I am not fond of it. O Mark! Why *don't* you try to lead a better life? Read II. Kings, from chap 2 to chap 24 inclusive. It would be so gratifying to me if you could experience a change of heart. Poor Mrs Gabrick is dead. You did not know her. She had fits poor soul. (27–28)

Here the joke is on a woman, steeped in the domesticated, religious culture of small town society, whose mind runs between the trivial and the half understood, and who cannot imagine what will be helpful, much less interesting, to her correspondent—a portrait unleavened even by affectionate patronage. Dan De Quille (1862) takes a similar position when he makes fun of the "married lady" in a "Letter" to the *Cedar Falls Gazette*. The piece has to do with a discussion about the worth of having a wife in the Nevada silver mines: whether, and the matter is put bluntly, the sexual and comestible comforts she may provide can compensate for the expense of keeping her. The piece is laced with double entendre around the sexual attractiveness—or lack of it—of the married woman: "There might be but little flour in the barrel, not a joint in the larder, and no sugar in the bowl. Yet her temper never lacked sweetness and she always had a smile in store for her husband!" (83). The reader is asked to conclude that the wife really cannot satisfy her husband's appetites sufficiently to make supporting her worthwhile.

Whatever sources we give for the attitudes toward women in the writing under discussion here, clearly we are looking at a strain of expression preoccupied with situating women as the sexualized objects of justified exclusion and aggression. Mining has often been described as the penetration and rape, by men, of a natural world conceived of as feminine. The terms of rape can describe the damage to the landscape by mining, the careless disruption of place, and its equally careless abandonment. "Rape" speaks powerfully to the indifference of miners and mining companies and corporations to spaces inhabited by others, humans, animals, and plants, as well as to the imperial obsession with searching out and appropriation of "resources," especially gold, is well understood.[25]

Yet, after all this, historians over the last decade have found a dramatically different way of reading what was going on in the camps, and have described a quite different scene in which norms of gender and sexuality, far from being exaggerated, could be contested, and where that contestation resulted in enhanced freedom of sexual expression. Jean Barman (2004), for example, writing about native women during the gold rush in British Columbia, explores the existence of liberatory sexual lives even in the face of the colonizing impulses and imperatives underpinning the development of mining. As Barman says, "indigenous sexuality struck at the heart of the colonial project, as a focus both for arguments about savagery and for codification projects" (213). The imposition of systems of gender and sexuality were, of course, critical to the expansion and establishment of imperial power, but these processes were never complete. Consequently, Barman finds evidence of native women in the region maintaining and extending their independence in respect of sexual behavior: "they scooted around, they dared, they were uppity in ways that were completely at odds with Victorian views of gender, power and race" (215). Nor were such experiments the preserve of those judged beyond the pale of mainstream white middle-class systems of gender and sexuality. It was, as Susan L. Johnson vividly argues, "hard to insist on any true order of things" in the transient, multiethnic settings of the mining industry (133).

Certainly, the unraveling of normative practices was a subject to which those who wished to evoke the essential qualities of mining communities for audiences "outside" made frequent reference. Louise Palmer (1869), for example, writing about Nevadan sexual culture in the *Overland Monthly*, described the practice of abandoning monogamy in favor of successive relationships punctuated by easy means of divorce:

> How charmed is Mrs. D to give her first husband Mr. C, her hand in the dance, while Mr. D leads Mrs. C to the refreshment table.... True Mr. C may have been a little shocked a year ago, when he discovered that his wife's mode of paying her lawyer for obtaining her divorce was a promise to marry him. (460)

Some of the fictions published in the West the 1860s and 1870s explored situations in which isolation might offer greater fluidity than this in relationships between men and women. Journalist and writer Frances Fuller Victor, for example, in *The New Penelope* (1877), produced a collection of stories describing diverse and enigmatic sexual situations: "romancing generally" (103). The title story rests on a bigamous relationship, for example, and another on the desertion of a husband bribed by a wealthier alternative. Pragmatism rather than experiment drives the sexual choices of Fuller Victor's society, where gendered and sexual behaviors are uncoupled from convention.[26]

Joaquin Miller's melodramatic fiction, *First Fam'lies in the Sierras* (1876), became one of the great theatrical hits of the period as *The Danites in the Sierras* (1881). Miller's novel also takes the opportunity to abandon convention, showing a range of sexual possibilities as well as norms of courtship placed under stress. Miller had worked as an odd-job man (or, according to some stories, cook) at the Klamath River diggings in California for around three years; and he gave a lifetime's work to cutting a sexually unconventional dash as the "poet of the Sierras."[27] From the start of *First Fam'lies*, he makes the unconventional masculinity of the camps an object of humor: "the men ... shot and stabbed each other in a rather reckless manner, but then they did it in such a manly sort of way" (9). Into this "spicey little camp" (75) come two Nancies: Nancy Williams on the run from the Mormons, cross-dressing as "Little Billie Piper," "a boyish girl-ish-looking creature" with a "cloud of yellow hair" and "small white hand" (15); and Nancy, a pregnant young woman posing as a widow. Both characters present challenges of definition to a society made up of men and "two or three fallen women" (13): Billie is identified as a poet, "no worse than a case of the small-pox" (20), while the widow is examined as if she were a "sort of pickled oyster or smoked ham" (30).

The love-plot that ensues, in which the widow Nancy is courted by the noble though elderly miner Sandy, is fraught with confusion. In an amusing parody of the extremes of distant desexualized worship valorized in Anglo-European courtship conventions, Sandy is simply too embarrassed to speak to Nancy or any other woman, much less court her. While he is tongue-tied and over-awed, Nancy is burdened with the knowledge that she is already pregnant. Seven months after the ensuing, and scarcely legal marriage between Sandy and Nancy, Nancy gives birth, but the innocent Sandy does not understand, as others soon begin to do, that nine months should have elapsed before a child of their marriage was born.

Meanwhile, Nancy is constantly visiting Billie (or Nancy), giving rise to local gossip about their friendship, and questions in the mind of the reader as to who is disguising which sexual identity or preference. The resolution of all of this is complicated and far from smoothly executed, but Miller's "first fam'lies," who might conventionally be imagined settling the area with children produced within marriage, practice instead a range of ambiguous and non-normative relationships.

The writer most famous for western tales illustrating what Henry Adams called "the power of sex" was Harte himself; indeed Adams insisted that Harte was the writer who broke down mainstream barriers to the writing of erotic feeling.[28] "The Idyl at Red Gulch" (1869), for example, shows Harte writing three quite complex sexual histories: the woman with a young child who has become a sex worker; the schoolteacher who is, except for a brief period, at war with desire; and the miner coming back from alcoholism who has loved the former and now loves the latter. Sandy's blond body in "The Idyl of Red Gulch" causes Mary the schoolmistress to cast aside "the purity of spotless skirts, collar and cuffs." She "forgot all, and ran like a crested quail at the head of her brood ... romping, laughing and panting" (54). Here, the mining West forms a setting for unrestrained sexual pleasure, and the opportunity for readers to enjoy the imagination of the male body.

Recently historians have also begun to consider the particular hospitality of the mining camps, with their transient, largely male societies, to the sexual and emotional expression of same-sex love between men. The homosociality of the camps and mining towns was celebrated on multiple levels from the late nineteenth century: as sociopolitically and nationally powerful; as a sturdy work-practice; and in emotional and sexual, or quasisexual, terms. The collaborative friendship between "partners" was associated first with the Californian Gold Rush, as well as with prospecting parties and small settings where placer mining took place.[29] Charles Howard Shinn's study of *Mining Camps* (1884), for example, contained the following, much-quoted statement:

> The early camps of California did more than merely destroy all fictitious social standards. They began at once to create new bonds of human fellowship. The most interesting of these was the social and spiritual significance given to the partnership idea. It soon became almost as sacred as the marriage-bond. The exigencies of the work of mining-claims required two or three persons to labor together if they would utilize their strength to the best advantage. The legal contract of partnership, common in settled communities, the brother-like tie of *"pard"*-nership, sacred by camp custom, protected by camp law; and its few infringements were treated as crimes against every miner. Two men lived together, slept together, took turns cooking, and washing their clothes, worked side by side in dripping claims, and made equal division of returns, were rightly felt to have entered into relationships other than commercial. (111–12)

Although mining, especially underground mining, has often been argued to give primacy, in the lives of miners, to male partnerships and collaborations amongst groups of coworkers, the relationship that Shinn is describing is one that stands as a critique of the formalities and commercialism of the heterosexual partnerships of the mainstream, and to the blandness of the work performed in such settings.[30] In addition, the apparently all-powerful institution of heterosexual marriage is sidelined by the imagination of a homosexual marriage in which the separations of work and leisure, mind and body, and commercial and emotional work that were being enforced on much of the population, no longer obtained. Shinn's use of the term "sacred" implies not only a desire to ward off associations between an institution that is like marriage and the practice of same-sex love, but perhaps also a desire to indicate a benign essence of human sociality free of legal paraphernalia.

If Shinn avoids sexualizing the relationship between partners, however, the artists of the Gold Rush, of whom most painted from observation and memory of the diggings, embraced the opportunity to depict social and same-sexual bliss in the mining camps. Ernest Narjot, for example, a forty-niner who went on to own and work a silver mine in Mexico before settling back in California, produced a series of genre scenes in which men adopted postures of sensuous contentment.[31] In *Miners: A Moment at Rest* (1882, see figure 2), a miner paterfamilias reads the paper while two miners hang on his words. Inside the little log cabin, men smoke and play cards; outside, an empty tin can and few drying clothes demonstrate domestic simplicity free of commodities, while an axe sits by a plentiful supply of logs and a slain deer hangs ready for consumption. In perhaps the most famous painting of mining of the period, *Sunday Morning in the Mines* (1872, see figure 3), Charles Nahl (another migrant to the Californian mines, though one who turned more quickly than Narjot to working full-time as an artist[32]) shows, at the center of the canvas, a portrait of two groups of men in relaxed communion in the sunshine: three are absorbed in a book, their limbs stretched out, their clothes hanging loosely on their flushed and golden bodies; the other two smile flirtatiously at one another as they do their washing. This is a vision of pleasure far from the rituals of normative social behavior and bodily constraint, and one that extends to its viewer the opportunity to imagine the pleasures of unregulated sexual expression.

Representations of happily affectionate and erotic relationships between men provided something more than a fantasy of men without women for an Anglo-American audience. Relationships between "pardners" seem also to have evoked a more generalized dispensation, a transitional period before incorporation into all of the systems of the center. The partner is a fellow in gambling, drinking, or just lying around. He is also a shield against the loneliness and anomie that might result from living outside conventional structures of work and leisure, dealing with the "impersonality of the gold fields," the "competition over claims," and the "fear that partners who slept in the same bed and shared work and leisure might be gone the next week."[33] Harte's "Tennessee's Partner" (1869) covers many of these dimensions: the partners convene at times of crisis but they are not tied to one another; their actions with respect to one another are pragmatic as much as sentimental, for all that the story ends with the mourning of Tennessee's partner for his dead friend.

A useful comparison can be made here with the "mate" and the relationship of "mateship" generated in the gold fields of Victoria in the 1850s and 1860s.[34] This figure has also been credited with creating the building blocks of a democratic but stable society in difficult circumstances far from the center's regulatory powers, but to have done so through substituting

Figure 2: Ernest Narjot. *Miners: A Moment at Rest (Gold Rush Camp)* (1882). Autry National Center; 97.88.1.

marriage to a woman with a marriage-like, but asexual, dedication and closeness to a mate. T. Inglis Moore (1971) makes the comparison with "a man's sentiment for ... his mother" rather than for a wife (204). This has the same quality of rebellion against the institutionalized relationships of the center, and the same association with a love of social equality. The similarity between partners and mates is unsurprising given the similar circumstances of these rushes: the apparent ease of access to gold lying on the earth's surface that inspired the rush of adventuresome young men, and the same transience of communities.[35] And indeed the presence of Americans in Australia, and the powerful cultural influence of the masculinities developed and represented in California in other mining settings made the development of similar formations likely.[36] Both Moore and David Goodman (1994) attribute the development of the "mate" as a cultural type to the popularity in Australian camps of Harte's "Tennessee's Partner."[37]

Figure 3: Charles Christian Nahl (American, born Germany, 1818–1878), *Sunday Morning in the Mines* (1872). Oil on Canvas, 72 × 108 inches. Crocker Art Museum, E. B. Crocker Collection. 1872.381.

The relationship between partner and mate, although it demonstrates the transnational culture of the rushes, in terms of the movement of people and mining texts, should also remind us of how masculinities always carry the impress of local circumstances and the distinctive qualities of particular rushes. While the figure of the partner becomes imbricated in the prolific mythmaking of "the frontier," with its sanctioning of a temporary wildness, that of the mate seems to be much more strongly shaped by a more direct objection to the restraints enforced by institutions. In the Australian Gold Rush setting, precious findings were deemed the property of the crown, and licenses were required to mine.[38] The love of the man for his mate represents a private independence from all such systems. In Henry Lawson's famous short story "An Old Mate of Your Father's" (1889), old mates are an indestructible "relic of our father's past," a bastion in memory against the inevitable entrapment in the shabby routines of marriage and farming (54).

None of these texts delineating the freedom of non-normative sexualities in mining cultures, however, venture to engage indigenous sexualities, much less sexual lives hybridized through new contacts. They are white, Anglo-European stories of playful spaces in circumstances of conquest. As Hurtado argues, other ideas and practices of gender and sexuality (those of native nations in particular) produced misunderstanding, mistrust, and violent aggression (123). These limits are played out in Alonzo Delano's comic melodrama *A Live Woman at the Mines* (1857). Delano presents his audience with two couples: John and Mary Wilson, the aspiring forty-niners arriving in Sacramento hoping to mend their fortunes, and Pike County Jess and High Betsey Martin, a rather wild pair of working-class migrants from Missouri. Mary soon moves from loving wife to surrogate mother when the pair reaches the mines. The miners have been at a loss without women and Mary hastens to fill the emotional and practical gap. Betsey, by contrast, is the bossy termagant of vernacular comedy: carrying all before her, she defies all danger, inconvenience, and advice to capture the man who has left her to go to the mines.

In the case of both figures Delano imagines how these women, had they black or brown bodies, might be treated quite differently. Betsey seems anxious to fight natives throughout, but she herself is mistaken by the camp for a "digger squaw" (96). The miners rush to exterminate her. The arrival of the "live" Mary also prompts some pointed discussion. Old Swamp, "the sermonizer" of the camp, proclaims:

> It has been handed down to us, by various letters through the post-office, that we war born into the world, and that our mothers were live female women. It is so long since we have seen a woman, that we don't exactly know what they are, but the doctor here says a woman is a female man of the human specie; he says too that you have caught the animal and had her alive on exhibition. Now stranger, we want to take a look at the thing, and I pledge you my honor we won't stampede her. (84)

Old Swamp, in calling the woman "a female man of the human *specie*," links women to cash and also to exchange when no cash is available. More than this, though, we are asked to imagine Mary as the "live" creature to be exhibited to the male gaze. Earlier in the play, John is horrified when a stranger offers him money for Mary, but now, amused by the suggestion that his wife may be thought as a "live" exhibit, John replies to Old Swamp:

Ha! Ha! Ha! Gentlemen—well this is a droll specimen of the mines—
yes I have caught such an animal—rather rabid, but if you will risk
the consequences, I'll show her up. (84)

One is irresistibly reminded here of the exhibition of African women during this period, women imagined as excessive in their sexuality, savage, and, of course, needing to be tamed.[39]

I began this chapter with an observation about the unruliness of gender and sexuality in the mines, and their representation in the mines, and indeed there clearly is an array of reference in play. Without doubt this was a setting in which a range of sexualities and sexual practices appeared as part of a mining camp world that ignored norms of sexuality in the same way that it disturbed other conventions. However, the freedoms imagined here were contingent on the occupation—in every sense—of this space, and they were sanctioned for white subjects alone. From this limited and compromised scene of human experiment, I want to move to the last rush, for this was a "poor man's rush" that seemed to offer a last-ditch possibility of independence and autonomy.

CHAPTER SIX

"Talking Klondike"

∽

✣ I BEGAN THIS STUDY WITH A PHOTOGRAPH DERIVED FROM THE Klondike Gold Rush, and it is to the representation of that episode in writing that I want to return in drawing my discussion to its close. This was the last rush westward in North America, transposed now onto a snowy "Northland" first of the Yukon and Alaska. Even at the time, it seemed to be, as Hamlin Garland put it, "the last march of the kind that could ever come."¹ The 1897 stampede first into the far west of Canada and then into America's northern dominion, and the two years of intense placer mining by migrants that followed, formed the dying fall of a phase in which independent prospecting and itinerant mining played a significant role within the industry. By the 1890s new technologies, new professions, and a population of skilled workers were encouraging corporations to exploit existing sites rather than to follow prospectors' new strikes. Yet, if this last North American rush heralded the end of an era, it was also an extraordinary episode: "the most flamboyant... of them all," in William Cronon's words (2003, 1). The publicity generated, the demanding and complex inward journey required of migrants, and the numbers involved created an event full of cultural interest and significance. The writing that it produced was just as distinctive.

The focus of this chapter is on the way in which this episode was, from the start, written, represented, and understood as a poor man's rush. In Klondike writing, the experience of the working-class gold seeker lies at the very heart of interpretations of the meaning and significance of this event. Sometimes this figure is transformed into an everyman figure, sometimes to an indistinguishable speck in the landscape, and sometimes to a suffering and oppressed subject. Sometimes he appears in the form of the dime-novel tough guy from nowhere, straight-talking and practically minded. The experience of these poor men appeared in the writing of working-class migrants and in popular cultural forms, but it was also taken up by middle-class Klondike writers for whom the subject-position of the working-class gold seeker seemed interesting, usable, and even exotic. In the following discussion, I want to examine these various appearances of poor men before moving to looking at the intervention of the most famous working-class writer of the Klondike, Jack London, in this field of expression.

First though, it is worth exploring this conception of the Klondike as a "poor man's rush," a mass movement of those that had been damaged rather than enriched by industrialism, the rise of big corporations and the play of global markets. This is a rush that has long been represented as powered by a more profound disturbance in the U.S. population than the youthful desire to escape from tiresome routine or convention into a western (or northern) adventure. Instead—and unlike the other rushes—it has been interpreted as an outcome of the very difficult economic conditions experienced by the American working classes during the severe depression of the mid-1890s: a last resort, perhaps, for beset industrial subjects.[2] However, there are problems with these arguments. Firstly, they tend to set Americans at the heart of the rush to the Klondike when, according to a recent assessment, they made up only around 40 percent of the incoming population. Around the same numbers came from Canada and Britain, and 20 percent were from other regions.[3] This was, in fact, a "congeries of strikes," as David Wharton (1972) puts it, and different strikes were dominated by different ethnic populations: the Russians colonized Circle City, for example, the Scandinavians Nome, the Italians Fairbanks.[4] Secondly, the rush was not dominated by those made vulnerable by industrial capitalism. A Klondiker needed to be able to raise funds to make the journey to the Yukon (and subsequently Alaska), and to get equipped to spend a year in the area of the diggings. No speedy fortune could be hoped for, in any case, in a setting where miners dug down over the winter months and searched through the excavated material in the spring thaw. On the other hand, we find plenty of evidence in Klondike writing of the presence of wealthier travelers, young men and professionals on vacation, in search of adventure as much as gold. These were figures, furthermore, who were much involved in setting the meaning of the Klondike. Thirdly, the rush was profoundly significant to others besides the immigrant gold seekers. This was an event with important implications both for the Tagish and Tlingit nations, whose trading practices were interrupted, and in some scholars' view irreparably damaged, by the temporary influx of migrant miners and the industrial dredging that succeeded it.[5] The Klondike rush caused the demise of the ethnically mixed trapping and mining economy which was operating in a space of ambiguous borders, and which was now replaced with systems of intensified colonial control and policing.[6] Thus, though it is as the "poor man's" flight from economic depression that the Klondike has always been understood, this is not a conception that securely summarizes what was happening. And, although Klondike writing tends to represent working-class experience, we need to approach this dominant interpretation of the Klondike with the exclusions of that summarizing conception in mind.

In setting the poor man in the foreground, Klondike discourse has tended to focus on his experience of the rush as one of hardship and vulnerability if not defenselessness, and, more than this, to mobilize him as a sign of universal suffering in human experience. A life in a frozen landscape, the toll taken on human bodies in such a place, and the nature of animals' experience: all achieve great resonance in this context. However, it has been the trip to the diggings that has been the Klondike's most charged and powerful trope. The difficult journey undertaken by poor Klondikers is transformed into a moralized progress. The popular historian of the Klondike, Pierre Berton (1960), describes the most difficult part of the journey to the region as "a rough approximation to life itself," a life in which every man experiences his own Chilkoot Pass, his own encounter with a test that seems insurmountable but that must be faced (434).[7]

The emphasis given to the journey in Klondike writing is understandable. It was this, after all, rather than the experience of mining in which most Klondikers participated. Comparatively few of those that left for the Yukon reached the diggings: the final leg of the journey was too difficult, the preparations too expensive, the prospect too intimidating. Those that actually reached the diggings arrived too late to have any hope of making a profitable claim, or indeed any claim of their own.[8] In a real and important sense, the toilsome and expensive journey, with its various stages and stations to the far-off, indistinctly understood Yukon, did indeed constitute the defining Klondike experience. And within that experience, the trek from Skagway and Dyea on the British Columbian coast over the mountain passes into the mining region formed a climax involving, for most people, repeated three-mile, thirty-degree climbs up the Chilkoot Pass, carrying a year's food, clothing, and equipment totaling at least 1,500 pounds. At the foot of the Pass, Klondikers had to shoulder their supplies (this pass was too steep for horses), make twenty or more trips in a long and packed procession to get their supplies over the summit, and then progress down the other side to the next stages of the journey. There were other routes, and later, when other strikes were made further north in Alaska, other destinations, but the journey over the Chilkoot Pass and down to Dawson and the diggings formed the symbolic heart of the Klondike experience.

Compelling as the idea of universal struggle clearly was, however, there was actually very significant variation in the hardship encountered on the journey. This was not unequivocally a common experience. According to the immigrant gold seeker's means, Tagish could be employed to carry packs, freight tramways could pull bags up, and animals could be bought to drag sleighs.[9] It was possible to avoid the whole episode by going straight to Dawson by steamship. Using the alternative White Pass, which was lengthier but less steep, enabled those who were better off to use horses to carry supplies. Conversely, those without money could get trapped in the Klondike. Some "retreating, destitute prospectors" ended up in relief stations set up by the Canadian government, some wandered the streets of Dawson, some suffered from frostbite and "black rheumatism," and some had limbs amputated.[10] Others turned back but lacked the money to get home. Class shaped the physical experience of the Klondike, and indeed, as we shall see, it inflected the meanings given by different participants to the rush.

Nonetheless, contemporary narratives of the journey insistently drew on the most difficult experiences to imagine paradigms of human endeavor and pain in contemporary as well as in transhistorical dimensions. Hamlin Garland, for example, who traveled to the Klondike to participate in a migration he thought of as an adventure rather than to find a claim, saw the stuff of myth in the experience. His description, in *The Trail of the Goldseekers* (1899), of the "Way of Death" imagines the fallout of human greed in an apocalyptic vision of the rotting and carrion-infested carcasses of horses abandoned at the top of the White Pass. The following passage evokes the scenes of slaughter and abandonment characteristic of the landscape of epic narrative:

> The waters reeked with carrion. The breeze was the breath of carrion, and all nature was made indecent and disgusting by the presence of carcasses. Within the distance of fifteen miles we passed more than two thousand dead horses. It was a cruel land, a land filled with the record of man's merciless greed.... The birds sat on the bleak gray rocks in the gathering dusk with the suggestion of being utterly at the end of the world. Their feathers were blown awry by the merciless wind and they looked weary, disconsolate and bewildered. Their faint, sad gobbling was like the talk of sick people lost in the desert. (208)

Garland's description is suggestive of humankind's deadly lack of scruple in the scramble for gain, but he seems also to be evoking the experience of the modern mass: the helpless, wasted horses and anthropomorphized birds, "disconsolate and bewildered," suggest an uncomprehending crowd, even the carnage of the modern battlefield.

Garland's text was written for a middlebrow and literary audience, but Klondike texts with broader audiences strove for similar effects. For example, the photographs of "the bitter, desperate and almost unendurable struggle" over the passes that were sold to the Klondikers showed images of the migrants reduced to antlike creatures toiling to survive in a featureless landscape.[11] In E. A. Hegg's famous image *Packers ascending summit of Chilkoot Pass* (1898), the uninterrupted blankness of the snow strips human action of promise, emphasizing the miserable shuffle uphill, "inch[ing] up the mountain at the pace of the slowest climber." Again, the allusion to shared human experience was obvious, and yet conditions in which a "man who stepped aside to rest might wait hours for a chance to get back in line" clearly had contemporary relevance.[12] Such a photograph vividly illustrated Social Darwinist assumptions about the inevitable fate of the slow-climbing majority.

Accounts of the journey written by middle-class Klondikers read the journey as a test of individual "character": "My object in writing up a description of this trip is for the purpose of giving my friends an idea of the endurance and hardship one experiences on a jaunt of this kind." Frequent

Figure 4: E. A. Hegg. *Packers ascending summit of Chilkoot Pass* (1898). P124-03, Alaska State Library, Eric A. Hegg Photograph Collection.

reference was made, in letters and accounts, private and published, to the prime importance of responding to this test appropriately. "Quite a number of boys failed to put a sufficient supply of nerve in their outfit."[13] In their many published letters and journals, middle-class Klondikers re-created the journey in terms of a series of structuring, and potentially empowering, moments on the trail: the encounter with natives, especially "squaws," the experience with the wild dogs, as well as the Chilkoot ordeal or its equivalent on another route.

Contemporary Klondike fictions also focused on the psychological implications of the experience, elaborating on the enhanced performance of masculinity under pressure. In G. Manville Fenn's novel *To Win or to Die* (1904), for example, two adventuresome Klondikers, highly strung Abel and sensible Dallas, are subjected to multiple tests of character during "stern winter in its wildest" from the repeated, sadistic attacks of men and beasts to the psychological torture of nightmares and "the horror" of the dreary life of the diggings (255). Dallas chides Abel for his lack of courage—"You don't make the best of things, old chap" (221)—yet even he buckles under the strain of the adventure, burying his face in his hands, and giving "a strangely harsh, hysterical laugh" when the pair finally strikes gold (400). Clearly, the Klondike experience offered writers the opportunity to elaborate modes of masculine behavior favored by the middle classes during this period, and to show the fittest surviving.

If the photographs of the Chilkoot, with their emphasis on generalizing the experience of the Klondike, evoked for some a test of character or grit, their meaning to poor men must surely have been differently as well as similarly nuanced. Images such as Hegg's perhaps indicated different vulnerabilities for working-class purchasers: suffering demanding "grit," certainly, but also the susceptibility of specks of humanity to organized exploitation. Poor and, especially, poor and inexperienced Klondikers were not only subject to the weather conditions and physical strains emphasized by their better-off fellow travelers, but their defenses were weaker with respect to the high prices demanded for the range of supplies needed.[14] This was a major focus of commentary in popular organs with audiences amongst working miners. In September 1899, the *Sunday Gleaner*, a Dawson newspaper published for a working-class readership, made the following point about "good bright fellows":

> Some good bright fellows have been fleecing the people of Seattle. Just think of that statement gentlemen! . . . If any person or persons did step into that city of large grafts and peddle out to them a series of beautifully printed and engraved mining shares, which represented nothing but the printer's art, the Seattle suckers were only handed a slight dose of what some Seattle merchants passed over to many a man and miner now living in the Klondike Country . . . in the shape of mackinaw clothing, "perforated" eggs, "embalmed" meats, exaggerated statements.[15]

Resentment at such exploitation clearly represented a significant part of the experience for working-class Klondikers, a resentment that is most evidently explored in all kinds of references in Klondike writing to the relations between dogs and their "masters." As Rebecca Onion (2009) argues, dogs are given a peculiar agency in Klondike writing, appearing in "parables for the lives of white men on the frontier; and as useful analogues for the actions of men fluctuating between the life of the city and the lost vision of the frontier" (132). More than this, dogs appear as politically charged beings, both as strong and indispensable working creatures who are kept hungry by their "masters," and also as starving beasts that are ever close to rebellion. Anecdotes such as the following (presumably apocryphal) example abound:

> And when the animals don't do as wished, some of their masters beat them savagely.... After seeing the look of furious hatred in the eyes of some huskies, I can believe the incredible stories we hear. Probably some of you have heard about the fierce team—half wolf, half dog—that turned on its tormentor. Nothing but the abandoned sled, torn clothing, and a blood colored watch remained.[16]

In addition to these problems, poor Klondikers needed "grit" to withstand the hostility on the part of the Canadian bureaucracies that flourished in the wake of the rush. A Mounted Police report quoted by Coates and Morrison (1988), for example, which refers to poor incomers as "the sweepings of the slums and the result of a general jail delivery," suggests the kind of treatment that working-class Klondikers could expect (98). The police who were posted to make sure migrants had sufficient resources and supplies to stay at the diggings all winter were equipped with machine guns and 300 rounds for each man's rifle.[17] Worst of all, perhaps, was the corruption around recording claims. Prospectors wishing to register their claims were made to queue for long periods, running the risk of losing claims which had to be registered within three days to be established. Nor were applicants allowed to check with their own eyes that records were being accurately or fully recorded. Looked at in this light, the Chilkoot photographs of an inching mass may have served to represent, to some Klondikers, the need for the continuing exercise of determination in the face of the oppressive and exploitative practices as much as a generalized human quest.

It also seems possible that poorer purchasers of these photographs may have wanted to see people like themselves pictured as part of what was often referred to as a stampede. Immigrant gold seekers landed in the region, as Wharton explains, "on the average of one boatload every eight minutes"; "people were never out of sight of one another for long" (269). Once at the diggings, the horde of people meant that every new prospect was quickly crowded, as Fred Baker found:

> Got wind of a new creek discovered to the upper fork of the Clondike. Shouldered a little grub and a blanket and started at 3 in the morning. Traveled until 8 in the evening and it rained all day. Started at

sun rise the next morning which is about 1/2 past 3 and was there in the middle of the [afternoon] and not a minute too soon. Had just got through staking when the crowd came in and in less than 5 hours she was staked from top to bottom [a distance of about seven miles].

Baker's conclusion was that "in this country ... you have got to get a hustle or you will get left."[18] At the same time, there seems no reason not to interpret the photographs as a shared adventure. Some texts suggest a joking camaraderie as well as sharp competition amongst the crowd. One Klondike memoir describes a notice that a prospector had erected to mark his claim, marked with the words: "I claim all on this side of the river." Those who came after him soon added:

So do I
I claim this swamp for a fever ranch
I claim this tree for a bird roost
I claim from here to the North Pole
I claim this rock for scenic purpose[19]

Nonetheless, where working-class Klondikers' writing has been preserved and published, it too comes back insistently to conceptions of the Klondike experience as the struggle facing every man, even if the nature of that struggle is differently inflected. Volney Rowland, a grocery wagon driver from Visalia, California, left home with some inkling of what was waiting for him in the Klondike, having had some experience in mining.[20] His father had migrated from Kansas in the late 1870s to work in the silver mines, and Volney had worked on his father's claims. He did not, however, anticipate a system in which you worked on a claim, gave half your findings to the owner and 10 percent to the Canadian government; or where your work, through the wintry twilight, involved gathering, hauling, and cutting wood for fires to burn a shaft through the permafrost down to the bedrock, digging and piling up the dirt and gravel until April, then washing the gravel with hot water to find what flakes of gold might be present; or where your wages depended on the success of the claim, and failure might mean no wages and effective entrapment in the region.[21] Rowland did not construct his chances of success or failure by reference to "character." Rather, in writing from "Carribou" in May 1898, he stressed the shared experience of the "hard struggle" that he and his friends were suffering, and the sense of foolishness at having taken himself to such "the frozen north" at all:

> You bet we five will be the same as brothers the rest of our lives I think, if you see any of Jeans or the Jasper boys folks tell them that they are alright and getting along fine and some day these strayed sheep or mutton heads, more planer, will some day wander back for their flocks and be satisfied with shorter grazing on the plains of the San Joaquin Valley, but not until a hard struggle for better in the frozen north is made. (34)

Rowland's letters are unusual in recording a working-class Klondike experience autobiographically. A more common strain in the writing of the "poor man's rush" involved assuming a working-class voice as a means of authenticating stories of disastrous, if exciting, experiences of the Klondike; a strain, too, that adopts a rebellious response to suffering. This is precisely what we find in the work of the popular balladeer of the Klondike, Robert Service. Service, as is well known, did not reach the region of the Klondike until he took a job as a bank teller at Whitehorse some six years after most outsiders had left.[22] The Dawson that he subsequently encountered in 1908 was no longer worked seasonally by struggling stampeders, but day and night by mechanical dredgers. By this time, this former center of Klondike culture was dominated by a middle-class enclave and, according to Carl Klinck (1976), on its way to becoming a ghost town.[23] That enclave was Service's first audience as well as the rather prim social group against whose tastes he defined the working-class experience that he imagined as excitingly wild.[24]

Nonetheless, the opening verses of Service's first published volume, *Songs of a Sourdough* (1907) evoke the full-throated patriotic imperialism of the contemporary white population of Dawson:

> This is the law of the Yukon, and ever she makes it plain:
> "Send not your foolish and feeble; send me your strong and your
>   sane.
> Strong for the red rage of battle; sane for I harry them sore;
> Send me men girt for the combat, men who are grit to the core;
> Swift as the panther in triumph, fierce as the bear in defeat,
> Sired on a bulldog parent, steeled in the furnace heat." (11)

Here is also the familiar statement of the need for manly grit to survive the Yukon setting, extended through a series of similes of fighting and war. Once again, the universalizing impulse proves irresistible. The very verse form calls up a sense of overpowering human drives. Service seems to have thought of mining and war as linked by "primal facts of life": "I don't believe in pretty language and verbal felicities, but in getting as close as I can to the primal facts of life, cutting down to the bedrock of things."[25]

This all sounds rather like the imaginative world of Manville Fenn, Dallas, and Abel. Yet Service, the versifying bank worker and devotee of amateur theatricals and concerts, was also a part-time "vagabond," who liked to wear rough clothes, and to mingle with a working-class audience and imagine himself as one of their number.[26] His verses, full of slang, jokes, and dime-novel reference, imitated Kipling's use of music hall ballads in writing against the grain of middle-class mores and taste.[27] They evoked the scene of the mining saloon of dime-novel fame, and looked to wrest laughter from gruesome tall stories. In "The Cremation of Sam McKee," for example, Service revels in the deadpan tone of his narrator as he describes frying a corpse in the freezing snow:

> The flames just soared, and the furnace roared—such a blaze you seldom see,
> And I burrowed a hole in the glowing coal, and I stuffed in Sam McGee,
> Then I made a hike, for I didn't like to hear him sizzle so;
> And the leaves scowled and the huskies howled, and the wind began to blow. (38–39)

Reading this it comes as no surprise to discover that Service's Dawson audience found his work too crude for their tastes, both in its language and in its reference to rougher lives and impolite stories.[28] It is perhaps more interesting to find Service apparently drawing here on a common strain in the representation of the poor man's predicament in the Klondike, in which the suffering subject showed a salty and contemptuous attitude to friends, fellow miners, bosses, and bureaucrats alike.

The following song, "Just from Dawson," printed in the *Klondike Nugget* in 1898, deals in much the same rebellious and slightly grotesque strain that we see Service using five years later. (By all accounts, it was the "old timers" of the Klondike who provided Service with his material.[29]) The vision of a man freezing into a solid block is treated with a ghoulish humor, and any sentimental response prompted by the scene of a man confiding in his comrade as he fades away is soon dispelled as the dying man produces a nugget for his family that has been pilfered from a fellow miner:

> A Dawson City mining man lay dying on the ice
> He didn't have a woman nurse, he didn't have the price.
> But a comrade knelt beside him as the sun sat in repose
> To listen to his dying words and watch him while he froze.
> The dying man propped up his head above four rods of snow
> And said I never saw it thaw at ninety eight below.
> Send this little pinhead nugget that I swiped from Jason Dills
> To my home, you know, at Deadwood,
> At Deadwood in the Hills.
>
> Tell my friends and enemies, if you ever reach the east
> This Dawson City region is no place for man or beast.
> That the land's too elevated, and the wind too awful cold.
> The hills of South Dakota yield as good a grade of gold
> Tell my sweetheart not to worry with a sorrow too intense
> For it would not thus have panned out had I had a lick of sense . . .
>
> Tell the fellows in the homeland to remain and have a cinch,
> That the price of patent pork-chops here is eighty cents an inch.
> That I speak as one who's been here scratching 'round to find
>   the gold,
> And at 10 per-cent of discount, I could not buy up a cold.
> Now "So long," he faintly whispered, "I have told you what to do."
> And he closed his weary eyelids, and froze solid p.d.q.[30]

What we have here is a text that represents the predicament of the poor man, but no way of knowing its provenance. "Just from Dawson," wherever and however it was performed (if indeed it was recited or sung at all), was printed in the Dawson *Klondike Nugget* in June 1898, as were other similar songs about miners dying and falling on hard times. The *Nugget* was by no means a newspaper for the working-class reader, although Lea Kajati Ehrlich (1983) argues that it was "quite popular with miners" (13). Actually, songs and poems such as this appeared alongside material that focused on economic opportunities and worthwhile investments for business interests. The special souvenir edition of the *Nugget* printed in November 1899 printed an editorial that cast scorn on "the fabrications of returning miners," and argued that "the ups and downs experienced by the average man ... the hopes and disappointments, visions of wealth and hard rubs with poverty" needed to be "stripped away," if readers were to reach the *Nugget*'s measured view that "this district is considered by those best acquainted with it and most capable of judging one of the greatest mining camps of modern times" (6). Yet the ballad printed in this souvenir edition, again a dying miner song, this time written or set down by the assistant editor, contributes some intensely hostile sentiments toward capitalists and "scheming politicians" to the usual lament of the miner dying in the snow:

> Men who never saw a rocker, of our habits make a mocker—turn up their dainty noses at our jeans.
> And who hold their nostrils tight if they happen into sight of a Sour Dough at his meal of pork and beans ...
> O, by royalty they've done us of our ground our grit had won us, they have legislated all our rights away.
> They have forged the chain around us, into serfs they near have ground us, and I fear the leeches all have come to stay.[31]

These sentiments may be styled as material filling the gaps in a popular publication, either to attract as broad a readership as possible, or to shore up, by means of contrast, the upbeat sentiments that dominate the newspaper. By November 1899 the "poor man's rush" was itself in its death throes. Perhaps the Dawson newspapers wanted to announce the ascendancy of a new economic setting over the dying traces of a "poor man's rush." Quite clearly, however, the frequent appearance of these miners dying or lingering, down on their luck, in frozen wastes in these newspaper songs, and their similarity to Service's ballads suggests that published Klondike writing of the "poor man's rush," at least, favored portraits of unsuccessful poor men, cynical but passive in the face of their experience, and conveniently "dying out."

The representation of the Klondike included, alongside a lore of universal human experience, a body of expression that articulated the working-class culture of the "poor man's rush," often on the poor man's behalf. This writing drew on a limited repertoire of tropes, as we have seen, and was sketchy in depicting the region, ignoring the complex history of mining and trading that had been going on since the 1870s.[32] It was preoccupied with a North American white male experience, and it ignored circumstances where Tagish and Tlingit people were not only very visible to immigrants and frequently entering into economic relations with incoming gold seekers, but were also key to the often-told stories around the "discovery" of gold in the region.[33] In turning now to Jack London's work, I want to consider both his debt to the forms of "talking Klondike" that I have been discussing and his address to just such omissions and exclusions.

Jack London's relationship to the experience and representation of the "poor man's rush" is an intriguing one. He was a young working-class man, as Jonathan Auerbach (1997) puts it, "an ambitious working-class Nobody with no cultural capital" (xvi). He responded to the publicity around the Klondike by rushing to the region, seeing the trip as a "breathing space" from his life in California. He gave the work of mining a brief, unsuccessful trial, and, within months, returned home.[34] This is something of a representative experience of the Klondike for all participants, regardless of class. However, London's journey to the Klondike also gave him opportunities that other mining settings had proffered to many of the mining writers with whom this study has been concerned: to live the "vagabond" life available in various forms to young men at the time, and to provide the setting and the material, as well as the audience, for launching a writing career. Where London is unusual is, firstly, in writing fiction about mining settings out of a working-class experience, and, secondly, in encountering a context that, as we have seen, had established a discourse of the "poor man's rush."[35] He also proved unusual in the importance that he continued to give to using his Klondike material. Here, though, I want to focus on London's first fictions of the Klondike, written in the months after his return in August 1898 and published in January and February of the following year.[36]

Turning to his first story, "To the Man on the Trail" (1899), one can immediately see how London has assimilated the terms of "talking Klondike." He has turned to the conventions of saga rather than epic to evoke universalizing registers of human experience, and we are presented here with northern European saga's interplay of feats of quest, courtship, and feasts followed by storytelling. In London's Klondike, as in the sagas, the dramatis personae is restricted to ruggedly brave warriors and meek womenfolk, fierce dogs, and creatures from "outside." Accordingly, the men with whom he presents us at the start of the story are gathered together in a cabin while hostile weather rages outside, wassailing, recalling past exploits and triumphs. London adds the saga's characteristic trope of a supernatural challenge when a huge and mysterious "Frost King" appears:

> Then came the expected knock, sharp and confident, and the stranger entered.... He was a striking personage, and a most picturesque one, in his Arctic dress of wool and fur. Standing six foot two or three, with proportionate breadth of shoulders and depth of chest, his smooth-shaven face nipped by the cold to a gleaming pink, his long lashes and eye-brows white with ice, and the ear and neck flaps of his great wolfskin cap loosely raised, he seemed, of a verity, the Frost King. (45)

In such a setting the performance of masculinity so central to Klondike writing is critical to the achievement of heroic success. The "Frost King's" skill with dogs, his physical hardiness, and indeed his "nerve" sit comfortably with the Klondike valorization of individual "grit."

London's protagonists occupy essentially the same unforgiving and unvarying landscape as we have seen elsewhere in Klondike texts. Dramatic contrasts are made not only between the warm fastness of the cabin and the howling cold outside, but between the "inside" of the Klondike and the "outside" of civilization. London's adoption of the modes of saga allows him to re-create the region as radically separate; more separate certainly than the peripheries, frontiers, or colonies of a metropolitan center. Susan Kollin (2001) describes how Alaska is written, during this period, as "an ineffable landscape," "an infinite space" (29); though she glosses this strain as "generat[ing] images that celebrated the nation's course of empire" (35). London's "white silence" does not empower his characters in such a way. On the contrary, it has a physical and psychological impact that they barely withstand.

London's story also draws on the understandings of working-class experience characteristic of the Klondike. The drinking with which the story begins recalls once again the scene of working-class leisure so detested by the middle classes:

> "Dump it in."
> "But I say, Kid, isn't that going it a little bit strong? Whiskey and alcohol's bad enough; but when it comes to brandy and peppersauce and"—
> "Dump it in. Who's making this punch anyway?" And Malemute Kid smiled benignantly through the clouds of steam. (43)

The drinking is followed by a song which links "the grape" with the enjoyment of other "forbidden fruit":

> There's Henry Ward Beecher
> And Sunday-school teachers,
> All drink of the sassafras root;
> But you bet all the same,
> If it had the right name,
> It's the juice of the forbidden fruit. (44)

Meanwhile, along with these familiar strains of "talking Klondike," London picks up on Klondike class inequalities, and represents them in familiar forms. The plot of "To the Man on the Trail" is organized around the pursuit of the young Frost King by the mounted police, a project that sets the powers of the police in direct opposition to the natural justice that allows a swindled man to recover his money. The Malemute Kid not only supports the fugitive on principle, but he makes it clear to the policeman that he is doing so. In the references to men's management of dogs, too, London covers familiar ground in evoking the quality of boss worker relations, and exploring the preoccupying balance of power between "master" and the rebellious, starving creatures on whose strength and vitality his very existence depends. The inhabitants of the cabin can assess a man by listening to how he deals with his dogs, assess a journey in relation to how the dogs will need to be fed, and, more broadly, assess the extremity of their position as subjects by reference to the frantic aggression of cold and hungry animals: "the snapping jaws and the wolfish snarls and yelps of pain which proclaimed to their practiced ears that the stranger was beating back their dogs while he fed his own" (45).

London does not merely recast, or give greater vitality or mysteriousness to, the tropes of Klondike writing. He gives much greater emphasis to economic vitality and to the dignity of work. This is especially marked in London's second story, "The White Silence," which configures the same characters in ways that bring their respective kinds of work into the foreground. We begin with Mason's skill in chewing ice out of Carmen's foot, the Kid's and Ruth's knack with their "meager meal" (1). This is followed by Mason's competence with dogs that are starved and footsore, the comment that "the toil of the trail" will not "permit" the "extravagance" of talk: "of all the deadening labors, that of the Northland trail is worst" (3). The work is "breaking": "heart-breaking" and body breaking. Carmen falls down exhausted, Mason is fatally injured by a tree, and the team of dogs has to be beaten off the food supplies with axe and rifle. Through it all, though, and in a landscape that reduces them to "maggots," the characters make constant recourse to skills practiced with their hands and experience with their tools (4). This is a poor man's experience of work that is neither a soul-destroying routine reducing the subject to an automaton, nor an idealized display of individual talents and commitment. It is the work of hands and bodies in a working world that no one would knowingly choose, but in which experience and a collective consciousness is respected. The representation of the dignity of work fills "The White Silence."

It may be pointed out that London's writing, set in the social world on which the Klondikers intruded rather than the life that their interventions produced, scarcely gives an account of the toilsome mining work that he witnessed and briefly tried out. In fact, in these stories, gold seeking takes place alongside other economic activities, as it did for most of the populations, native and migrant, in the region. Klondike work is contrasted to past workplaces and forms of labor. It forms different kinds of interlude in a range of life histories. Julie Cruikshank's (1990) insights are useful here. In her account of interviewing native Yukon women, she describes how she expected that her interviewees' recollections would regard the Klondike rush as a pivotal episode their lives. However, "from the beginning, several of the oldest women responded to my questions about secular events by telling traditional stories . . . and elaborating mythological themes"; their emphasis was on "landscape, mythology, everyday events, and continuity between generations" (2). The working lives in "To the Man on the Trail" and "The White Silence," too, have unfolded in very diverse contexts of place, family, tradition, and necessity.

Perhaps even more importantly, London, in turning back to the culture of the Klondike before the rush, creates a setting in which class and ethnicity are only partial predictors of experience. In "The White Silence," we have three human protagonists: Ruth, a native woman, married to Mason, an American immigrant, and the Malamute Kid, as well as, alongside, a team of dogs. Ruth, loyal and subservient, is named for the Biblical figure, the gleaner working in a foreign land, and is pregnant by Mason. The Kid evokes the popular cultural form of the dime novel, yet his nickname, Malamute, is the name for the local dogs. The gender and naming of the failing dog, Carmen, evokes an altogether different Hispanic setting and subjectivity. Mason hails from the American South, a place from which he has escaped and to which he has hoped to return.

It seems possible that London was drawing, in "The White Silence," on the opaque and shifting circumstances that preceded the rush to the Klondike, in which different communities and populations, separate and interlinked, pursued both common and distinct aims.[37] Again, Cruikshank's (1996) research evokes a very modern scene in which native nations' relations with one another, and with incoming groups, produced new and not necessarily welcome formations. Marital and sexual relationships between different populations, in particular, fractured allegiances as well as sealed them, and caused different projects to collide as well as to become productively enmeshed with one another.[38] Cruikshank records the involvements of a single family with different marriages, some informal and some passing relationships, the naming and renaming of family members, and the difficulties of maintaining social systems in such circumstances. London himself was plainly fascinated by the evidence he saw of relationships between native women and Anglo-European men, and baffled as to how to interpret what he observed.[39]

The unfixed identity of London's characters in "The White Silence" may derive from London's observation of the ethnically and occupationally mixed population of the Klondike and the confused and complex processes of change in the region. Or it may be, as Mark D. Steinberg (2002) suggests, that this liminal and unstable setting was particularly attractive to a writer dealing with the unfamiliar position of being a "worker author" (1). Certainly, London does not place the American poor man in a separate category, set him in generalized portraits of every man, or imagine his miserable end as a failed gold seeker. Mason's end, on the contrary, is caused by a terrible accident that crushes his body, and leaves bereavement and a fatherless child in its wake.

Of all the rushes, the Klondike produced a very coherent and easily recognized set of tropes: the Chilkoot Pass, the dying miner, the expression of "grit." It also produced two writers in London and Service who were able to form a writing of working-class mining experience that appealed to a large and diverse audience. "Talking Klondike" seems also, in some important ways, to have represented the experience as it was for many participants. It told of a very modern experience of mass movement and of the difficulty of sustaining an individual project in testing conditions; it described a bitter hostility between stakeholders; it addressed the punishing work involved. By the time much of the material I have been discussing appeared in print, that experience was utterly finished, and readers were able to combine the sense of experience that these texts gave with a realization that the gold and silver rushes were well and truly over.

Afterword

∞

☆ I OPENED THIS STUDY WITH A DISCUSSION ABOUT THE FEAR THAT mining has long aroused and the painful difficulty of representing it. Outsiders to the industry may find it easiest to avert their gaze. Mines are, after all, characteristically remote and invisible to the center. Participants, meanwhile, may be deeply troubled by their mining experiences. The late nineteenth-century response to mining encompassed the same reactions: distaste and evasiveness toward the mining cultures from outside, and deep cynicism and uncertainty from within. The writers of mining romance depicted the exhaustion of people and relationships as well as landscapes and mines. The Klondike writers dwelt not on sparkling northlands but on appalling frozen wastes. Prentice Mulford's response to the deceiving claims of Gold Rush publicity and his experience of their fallout was terse. The aggressive squibs of the Sagebrush journalists, although apparently deflecting engagement with the terrible conditions in Virginia City's silver mines, nonetheless echoed their reverberations.

The diversity of these responses matched the "fabulous complexity" of the industry, as well as reflecting the range of writers' and artists' positions in relation to particular sites, experiences, and aspirations. As I have argued, the mining rushes opened up artistic as well as economic prospects for participants, producing eddies of new and unexpected artistic as well as extractive activity. There were ancient and traditional models of explication available, of course, and apparently plenty of opportunities to think expansively across national boundaries: to adapt, say, the sexualities to which Harte gestured to the colonial context of Australia; or to use transatlantic Arthurianism to recast the American West. Twain was convinced that his success in publishing about Nevada equipped him to work up the Kimberley diamond strikes in South Africa, too. Equally, though, for other writers and artists, the rushes demanded a response nuanced to specific circumstances: to the proximity or distance of investors; to the qualities, physical and affective, of local landscapes; to new relationships with animals; to the absence of Anglo-American and European women; to local surges of hostility towards Chinese populations; to endemic legal impasses; and so on.

For once, this was an industrial situation where those who had worked in and around it moved regularly into writing, painting, and photography. Their stances were not those of the awed visitor or the investigative journalist, but of the ex-miner, the ex-prospector, the ex-manager, and the local mining journalist or photographer. These people were well informed. This is not to say that they necessarily made common cause with miners or sided with them in various types of dispute; in many cases it would have been difficult for them to do so. Nevertheless, this was an industry and an intricately imagined and ritualized work culture in which the writers and artists discussed here had variously been involved. Theirs was an output that made a very different response to industrialism and its effects to those forms of documentary and muckraking, realism and naturalism with which we are usually dealing when looking at the expressive response to the outcomes of industrial capitalism during the late nineteenth century.

As the rushes and strikes came to a decisive end, however, and as mining excluded amateurs and discouraged migrants, and different discourses took over within the industry, this series of gold and silver rushes lost cultural weight. Of course, the Gold Rush has never been invisible to mainstream culture, and places like Leadville and Virginia City have provided the setting for hundreds of Westerns. Nostalgia for the Old or Wild West has enabled some former mining towns to sustain themselves through tourism and has preserved others as ghost towns. Historians of the American West have recovered the rushes and strikes in different forms and have variously reviewed their impact in human, environmental, and political terms.

Still, it comes as something of a surprise to find, at the turn of the twenty-first century, a string of new attempts to revivify the world of the strikes and rushes. These attempts are various in their preoccupations and in the forms they use. When one examines them closely, however, it is not the vitality of their recovery of events in the light of modern preoccupations and subsequent insights that stands out. On the contrary, approaches taken in our own day to narrating and interpreting the rushes draw attention to the energy and insight with which the mining writers of the late nineteenth century represented the new societies and radical responses produced by the rushes and their industrial aftermath.

What seems especially noticeable, when one compares recent portraits of the rushes with late nineteenth-century works, is the continuing contemporary engagement—their investment as well as their rejection—in grand narratives of emigration and frontier. Isabel Allende's *Daughter of Fortune* (1999) and the HBO TV series *Deadwood* (2004–2006) are two obvious examples. Each strives to realize the circumstances of the rushes and the mining societies they generated. Yet both restore the rushes to the conventional frontier narratives of progress and disintegration. Allende's novel takes up the familiar emigrant narrative of a rite of passage from trauma through recovery into assimilation into a new society, giving it a feminist charge. Her half-Indian, half-English heroine, Eliza, finds new possibilities for self-realization through leaving domestic life and Victorian values behind and lighting out for America. She does not merely escape conventional marriage, unplanned parenthood, and the oppression of women in the domestic space, she also embraces desire, sisterhood with prostitutes, and men's clothing, eventually finding a "feminine" expression in the construction of a recipe book. As with several fictions of the same period (Rose Tremain's *The Colour* [2003], for example, as well as Maggie Greenwald's earlier film *The Ballad of Little Jo* [1993]), the radicalism attributed to Eliza's escape is underwritten by the heroine's sexual relationship with a Chinese man. The Chinese, famously the focus of loathing within the dominant culture in the late nineteenth century, have become a popular locus for doubts about the outcomes of the rushes. Here in their fictional form, Chinese men also become figures at odds with Anglo-European patriarchal masculinity. Thus, in Allende's novel, gender and ethnic inequalities summarize various tensions and blockages in mainstream Anglo-European culture, and romantic love in the California of the Gold Rush serves to resolve them. It is difficult to think of a late nineteenth-century mining fiction that offers mining cultures as a context for any such resolution: one thinks of the coupled protagonists of "Mliss" and *John Bodewin's testimony* stranded at the end of the text, or the lengths to which Richard Harding Davis is forced to go in order to get his mining engineer hero happily married. Even in the 1850s, Californian writers had left faith in norms of heterosexual marriage behind.

Deadwood uses the particular circumstances of Deadwood—founded in the wake of Custer's first campaign against the Sioux, but before Sioux land had been annexed by the U.S. government—to revisit and politicize familiar ideas of the frontier. This setting, literally as well as effectively lawless, is used to turn the screw on some familiar preoccupations in western literature, as well as scholarly and popular history: violence, the fragile status of the law in the camps, and the problematic relationship between "frontier" conditions and "civilization." But *Deadwood* is perhaps most concerned with turning the audience's gaze on a place free from big government, and utterly dominated by the pursuit of wealth. The viewer cannot avoid making the obvious, dispiriting parallel to post-Enron America. This use of the rushes to reflect upon a profoundly disappointing present is not unique to *Deadwood*. Elliott West (2001), in his updating of Rodman Paul's classic study of "mining frontiers" of the American West, is irresistibly and regretfully reminded of contemporary American culture:

> A gold or silver camp was primitive and alien; it was strikingly familiar. It was unlike any city or town of its day; it was a fabulous overstatement of every trait and trend pulling an earlier America toward the one we know. Maybe this is why mining frontiers hold so many of us in fascination. We look back and marvel at American history's true Land of the Odd—men grubbing for meal money and then eating like anacondas, towns consuming themselves in the name of progress, families searching for structure in times of dizzying flux—and something nags at the edge of our awareness. Then we see it. This artifact of strangeness was as well as a grand anticipation. Goggling at this distant and exotic past, we realize with a shock that we are looking at ourselves. (283)

Both texts locate the rushes of the late nineteenth century as the origin of a modernity that is difficult to like. They share with some of the writing of the late nineteenth century a sense of the profound significance of the rushes in historical terms. Garland depicted the Klondike as a climactic episode in a process of destruction too painful to summarize; Foote saw the mining of the American West as a new scene of human experience arising from the wreckage of prior ideals. In London's work, contemporary America presses inexorably into the Yukon. What is so striking about a contemporary text such as *Deadwood*, however, is the simplicity of the link it makes between past and present. By contrast, Garland, Foote, and London were peering uncertainly into the future.

Not all portraits of the rushes in our day have chosen to hold to conventions of imagining the West. As some of the nineteenth-century literature of mining struggled to narrate mining's "fabulous complexity," so some of the contemporary treatments of the rushes represent them in the form of compulsive routines, scrambled stories, and confused investigations. Jason Rhoades, for example, in his New York installation, "Sutter's Mill" (2000), showed a makeshift model of the famous mill being constructed from metal tubes, disassembled, and then reassembled into a second model that was simultaneously being disassembled, as soon as it was built, for reconstruction: a compulsive routine of discovery and abandonment, as well as an unnerving portrait of the cultural practice of constantly reiterating narratives such as the story of John Sutter's "discovery" of gold.[1] The models dominated the physical space in which they were erected and dismantled, reaching right to the ceiling, filling the room; but at the same time, video monitors showed film of the same installation in Germany, as well as another film of a wooden Sutter's Mill being built. These competing versions of the same "event" raised questions about what relationship they might have, whether they were the same or different, whether one "event" might have an effect upon another, or cause a perceptual change in the mind of the observer.

In the same year, Michael Winterbottom's movie, *The Claim* (2000), brought a range of fictions to bear on his representation of a late nineteenth-century mining town. Different versions of nineteenth-century experience converge rather than interact in *The Claim*. The plot is reminiscent of Thomas Hardy's *Mayor of Casterbridge* (1886); the setting and dialogue is similar to Robert Altman's *McCabe and Mrs. Miller* (1971); and the central scene, in which a whole house is carried down a mountain, vividly recalls a famous episode in Werner Herzog's *Fitzcarraldo* (1982) in which a steamship is carried over the mountains. Nastassia Kinski, who plays the wife who has been sold and now returns, played in Roman Polanski's film of

Hardy's *Tess of the D'Urbervilles* (1892), *Tess* (1979); and her father, Klaus, starred in *Fitzcarraldo*. Where Rhoades's installation draws attention to a shared and routinized national engagement with the Gold Rush's founding moment, Winterbottom's plethora of different explanatory tools is used to disorient his audience. Even the narrative force provided by the parallel with *The Mayor of Casterbridge*—with its portrait of inevitable technology, uncontrollable forces of Nature, and the works of fate—cannot apparently help us to plot this mining town.

In a comparable vein, Anita Desai's *The Zig Zag Way* (2004) depicts the dispirited, self-lacerating academic, Eric, searching for traces of his grandfather's life in the mines in Mexico in the late nineteenth century. Desai finds numerous ways of disconnecting Eric's investigation from the grand narratives of the past: against the references to imperial histories, the quotations from accounts of Spanish mining; against Eric's encounters with various postcolonial projects that appropriate Indian cultures and strangle indigenous projects; against the planned career trajectory of Eric's girlfriend and the construction of a new life by the aging Vera. Eric and his mining forbears follow a much more "zigzag way," disengaged from the plans their bosses, communities, and partners have fashioned for them.

Rhoades, Winterbottom, and Desai have all chosen the gold and silver strikes and rushes of the late nineteenth century as a setting through which to review the conditions of modernity. The complexities of the mining scenes they describe invigorate texts that are full of claims, and indeed qualms, about whether or how mines and miners might be represented. My own argument in this study has been that we can find similarly ambitious and compelling claims pursued with great energy during the late nineteenth century, and that their authors did justice, in a range of ways, to episodes that were clearly indicative of new conditions, but hard to gauge or describe. Our own contemporaries have tended to emphasize, above all, the problems of depicting these events. The late nineteenth-century subjects of this study certainly experienced difficulties on a number of levels with writing mining. They grappled, in a range of encounters, with the different strands of mining culture. In retrieving some of these engagements, I hope I have both recovered a field of writing, and found traces within it of the extraordinary and profoundly significant scenes and experiences of late nineteenth-century gold and silver mining.

Notes

INTRODUCTION

1. All such generalizations have to be qualified. Martin Lynch argues in *Mining in World History* that the first modern gold rush was sparked by a strike in Siberia in 1832 (London: Reaktion Books, 2004), 119; nor was the California Gold Rush the first rush in U.S. history. Nonetheless, the cultural response that forms the subject of this study begins with the 1849 California Rush. William P. Morrell, *The Gold Rushes*, chapters 1 and 2, gives a broader colonial context to the gold rushes on the continent (London: Adam and Charles Black, 1940).
2. Events were not, of course, as neatly bracketed as this summarizing statement suggests. The new technologies of mining that brought this phase of rushes to an end were first available in the 1880s, and indeed, 1880 is the date at which the standard study in the field, Rodman W. Paul's *Mining Frontiers of the Far West, 1848–1880*, rev. ed. (1963; repr. Albuquerque: University of New Mexico Press, 2001), finishes and the point at which Keith L. Bryant, writing "Entering the Global Economy" in *The Oxford History of the American West*, ed. Clark A. Milner II, Carol A. O'Connor, and Martha A. Sandweiss, argues that "the days of people racing from one place to another, having little or no hard information and enduring hunger, danger, and frequent death, had almost disappeared" (New York: Oxford University Press, 1994), 205. The Klondike Rush, which seemed at the time to form the end of an era, the last gasp of an opportunity for ordinary people to light out and get rich, seems now to have been something of an anachronism.

3. The details of the injury are described in captions placed next to the photographs of the Klondike Rush collected by William E. Meed between 1898 and 1953 and housed at the University of Washington Library. These captions are derived from Meed's journal.
4. *Hard Places* is the title of Richard V. Francaviglia's study of the archaeology of mining camps. He reflects on the description in his conclusion (Iowa City: University of Iowa Press, 1991), 214–15.
5. Langston Hughes, "In the Johannesburg Mines" (1928), in *Collected Poems*, ed. Arnold Rampersand (New York: Vintage, 1994), 43.
6. The work of the Kinsey brothers has been searched out and published by Norman Bolotin in *Klondike Lost: A Decade of Photographs by Kinsey and Kinsey* (Norman: University of Oklahoma Press, 1980) and *A Klondike Scrapbook: Ordinary People, Extraordinary Times* (San Francisco: Chronicle Books, 1987).
7. The photograph was part of a series of indicative scenes of Klondike mining. The series comprises three images: "Going down the shaft"; "Overcome by gas, the rescue"; and the photograph under discussion here. I have no information about whether they were intended for sale as a set or were taken for the pleasure of the participants.
8. See Bolotin, *A Klondike Scrapbook*, 33, for a rare image of Hayden's work.
9. Eugenia V. Herbert offers a detailed description of the two modes of mining in her writing "Mining as a Microcosm in Pre-Colonial Sub-Saharan Africa," in *Social Approaches to an Industrial Past: The Archaeology and Anthropology of Mining*, ed. A. Bernard Knapp, Vincent C. Pigott, and Eugenia W. Herbert (New York and London: Routledge, 1998), 141–49. See also Ronald H. Limbaugh, "Making Old Tools Work Better: Pragmatic Adaptation and Innovation in Gold-Rush Technology," in *A Golden State: Mining and Economic Development in Gold-Rush California*, ed. James J. Rawls and Richard J. Orsi (Berkeley: University of California Press, 1999), 27–46.
10. In *Roaring Camp: The Social World of the Californian Gold Rush*, Susan Lee Johnson describes how hard rock miners kept placer tools ready for use, should any news reach them of hopeful prospects (New York: W. W. Norton & Company, 2001), 274.
11. For some examples of historians approving use of literary writers as sources for knowledge on the ground, see Johnson, *Roaring Camp*, 334–42 (on Harte); Patricia Nelson Limerick, *The Legacy of Conquest* (New York: W. W. Norton & Company, 1987), 56–58, 187 (on Twain); and Richard E. Lingenfelter, *The Hardrock Miners: A History of the Mining Labor Movement in the American West, 1863–1893* (Berkeley: University of California Press, 1974), 20, 23–24, 26 (on De Quille).
12. Limerick, for example, finds the miner and the prospector lacking in glamour, despite "the floods and tides of nostalgia poured forth by veterans of Western mining rushes." Her tentative (and tongue-in-cheek) suggestion is that the miner lacks the dash of a cowboy mounted on a horse (*Something in the Soil:*

Legacies and Reckonings in the New West [New York: W. W. Norton & Company, 2001], 217). In a similar vein, the mining historian Duane A. Smith notes in *Rocky Mountain Mining Camps* that "the mining frontier has failed to capture the pens of authors" or even the producers of films and TV series (Niwot: University Press of Colorado, 1992), 255.

13. Surveys and anthologies such as Lawrence I. Berkove and Michael Kowalewski's "The Literature of the Mining Camps" in *Updating the Literary West*, Western Literature Association (Fort Worth: Texas Christian University Press, 1997); Michael Kowalewski's *Gold Rush: A Literary Exploration* (Berkeley: Heyday, 1997) and "Romancing the Gold Rush: The Literature of the California Frontier," *California History* 79, no. 2 (Summer 2000): 204–25; and Lawrence I. Berkove, *The Sagebrush Anthology: Literature from the Silver Age of the Old West* (Columbia: University of Missouri Press, 2006), as well as his essays in various essay collections on Twain and western writing, have been indispensable to this study, as have the studies of various Sagebrush writers by Richard A. Dwyer and Richard E. Lingenfelter. The more recent work of Nicolas S. Witschi, especially *Traces of Gold: California's Natural Resources and the Claim to Realism in Western American Literature* (Tuscaloosa: University of Alabama Press, 2002), is also bringing the nineteenth-century writing of mining back into focus.

14. See, for example, C. Grant Loomis, "Bret Harte's Folklore," *Western Folklore* 15, no. 1 (Winter 1956): 19–22; Don L. Griswold and Jean Harvey Griswold, *History of Leadville and Lake County, Colorado*, vol. 1 (Denver: Colorado Historical Society and University Press of Colorado, 1996), 54 (on Mary Hallock Foote); and Marvin Lewis, "Humor of the Western Mining Regions," *Western Folklore* 14, no. 2 (April 1955): 92–97 (on De Quille and the Sagebrush writers). These and other sources assume either that these writers' published work constitutes folklore in a lightly mediated form or that the writer practices a simple conversion from folklore to literary writing.

15. Two commentaries on mining and its cultural significance in the late nineteenth century that have proved of particular importance and influence in thinking about the link between mining and documentary are Alan Trachtenberg's essay "Naming the View" in *Reading American Photographs: Images as History, Mathew Brady to Walker Evans* (New York: Hill and Wang, 1989); and Allan Sekula's "Photography between Labor and Capital," in *Mining Photographs and Other Pictures, 1948–1968*, ed. Benjamin H. D. Buchloh and Robert Wilkie (Halifax: The Press of Nova Scotia College, 1983), 193–268.

16. The anonymous review published on March 6, 1872, 7, is reprinted in Frederick Anderson, ed., *Mark Twain: The Critical Heritage* (London: Routledge and Kegan Paul, 1971), 46–47.

17. For a range of discussions of the relationship between literary writing and folklore, see, for example, Daniel R. Barnes, "Towards the Establishment of Principles for the Study of Folklore and Literature," *Southern Folklore Quarterly* 43 (1979):

5–16; Frank De Caro and Rosan Augusta Jordan, "On Literary and Artistic Uses of Folklore," in *Re-Situating Folklore: Folk Contexts and Twentieth Century Literature and Art* (Knoxville: University of Tennessee Press, 2004), 1–22; Richard M. Dorson, *American Folklore and the Historian* (Chicago: University of Chicago Press, 1985), 204–9; Cathy Lynn Preston, *Folklore, Literature and Cultural Theory* (New York: Garland, 1995); and Bruce A. Rosenberg, *Folklore and Literature: Rival Siblings* (Knoxville: University of Tennessee Press, 1991).

18. The sources that I have found most helpful in exploring the ways in which mining has charged intellectual activity have been: Mircea Eliade, *The Forge and the Crucible* (Chicago: University of Chicago Press, 1978); Carolyn Merchant, *The Death of Nature* (San Francisco: HarperCollins, 1980); and Wolfgang Paul's eccentric compendium, *Mining Lore: An Illustrated Composition and Documentary Compilation with Emphasis on the Spirit and History of Mining* (Portland, OR: Morris Print Co., 1970). Although they say little about mining, Rosalind Williams's *Notes on the Underground* (Cambridge, MA: MIT Press, 2008); and David L. Pike's *Metropolis on the Styx: The Underworlds of Modern Urban Culture, 1880–2001* (Ithaca, NY: Cornell University Press, 2007) and *Passage Through Hell: Modernist Descents, Medieval Underworlds* (Ithaca, NY: Cornell University Press, 1997) have also been invaluable guides for thinking about the underground.

CHAPTER ONE

1. Historians vary in their views of the length of time over which Agricola dominated the practice of mining. Rodman W. Paul, in "Mining, Metals," suggests an unbroken tradition of influence up to the nineteenth century in *The New Encyclopedia of the American West*, ed. Howard R. Lamar (New Haven, CT: Yale University Press, 1998), 702, whereas the Hoovers' introduction to their edition of *De Re Metallica* writes of two hundred years. Allan Sekula, by contrast, suggests, in "Photography between Labor and Capital," 212, that traditions of mining were carried by the miners themselves, not Agricola's text.
2. Patricia Limerick summarizes her position on the importance of mining in the West in chapter 5 of *Legacy of Conquest*, and in "The Gold Rush and the Shaping of the American West" in *Something in the Soil: Legacies and Reckonings in the New West* (New York: W. W. Norton & Company, 2001).
3. I am attempting to summarize an important strand of writing about western mining here, but, of course, the field of writing about nineteenth-century mining in the West is more complex than this. Historians of mining such as Richard E. Lingenfelter and Joseph E. King, for example, are of a very different school, and yet their histories of mining during this period are at least as condemnatory about technological change and finance in the industry as those of the New Western Historians. Likewise, not all histories of the mining West that have been published over the last decade or so are condemnatory at all. As historians have become more interested in attributing agency to the range of stakeholders in

mining, much more affirmative and nuanced accounts have appeared. Johnson's *Roaring Camp* and Elizabeth Jameson's *All That Glitters: Class, Conflict and Community in Cripple Creek* (Urbana and Chicago: University of Illinois Press, 1998) are obvious examples. For a useful historiography of western mining, see Mark Wyman, "Mining Frontiers," in *Hard Rock Epic: Western Miners and the Industrial Revolution, 1860-1910* (Berkeley: University of California Press, 1979).

4. Frank Norris sets out his view of Zola in "Zola as a Romantic Writer," *Wave* 15 (June 27, 1896). See also Donald Pizer's comments in his introduction to *The Literary Criticism of Frank Norris* (Austin: University of Texas Press, 1964), 69-70.

5. Accounts of Zola's investigative method are given in Colin Smethwick, *Zola: Germinal* (Glasgow: University of Glasgow French and German Publications, 1996), 10-16; and Colin Baguely, "*Germinal*: The Gathering Storm," in *The Cambridge Companion to Emile Zola*, ed. Brian Nelson (Cambridge: Cambridge University Press, 2007), 139-40.

6. Norris's enthusiastic support for the British is described in Joseph R. McElrath, Jr., and Jesse S. Crisler, *Frank Norris: A Life* (Urbana: University of Illinois Press, 2006), 189-91.

7. The complex situation of African workers in southern African mines receives a detailed and nuanced discussion in Elaine N. Katz, "Revisiting the Origins of the Industrial Color Bar in the Witwatersrand Gold Mining Industry," *Journal of South African Studies* 25, no. 1 (March 1999): 73-97, though, of course, the racialization of mining is discussed across the range of studies of southern African mining in the late nineteenth century. See, especially, Charles Van Onselon, *Studies in the Social and Economic History of the Witwatersrand, 1886-1914: New Babylon* (London: Longman, 1982), chap. 1.

8. From Frank Norris, "In the Compound of a Diamond Mine," *San Francisco Chronicle*, February 2, 1896, 10, quoted in McElrath and Crisler, *Frank Norris*, 186.

9. From Frank Norris, "In the Veldt of the Transvaal," *San Francisco Chronicle*, February 9, 1896, 1, quoted in McElrath and Crisler, *Frank Norris*, 186.

10. For example, there are newspaper reports of forced and enslaved labor being used in, for example, Burkina, Eritrea, and Sierra Leone.

11. The same observation is made in Ronald M. James, *The Roar and the Silence* (Reno: University of Nevada Press, 1998), 119; and by Wayne Franklin in his foreword to Richard V. Francaviglia's *Hard Places: Reading the Landscape of America's Historic Mining Districts* (Iowa City: University of Iowa Press, 1991), xi.

12. For a summarizing discussion of the German mining scene of the Renaissance, see Lynch, *Mining in World History*, 16-35. Paul's *Mining Lore* is threaded through with strands of history of the mines of the Harz Mountains and Freiberg.

13. The issue of the relative prosperity of miners by comparison with other workers has generated debate in various centers. See, for a single example, the arguments about Comstock Lode wages in James, *The Roar and the Silence*, 122ff; and Grant H. Smith, *The History of the Comstock Lode, 1850-1920* (Reno: Nevada State Bureau of Mines and the Mackay School of Mines, 1943), 241-43.

14. Within a complex and diffuse field, I have found studies of particular mining communities most helpful in evoking the varying relations between different ethnic groups. See, for example, Donald L. Hardesty, *The Archaeology of Mining and Miners: A View from the Silver State* (Pleasant Hill, CA: Society for Historical Archaeology, 1988); Johnson, *Roaring Camp*, chap. 4, 5, and 6; and Ralph E. Mann, *After the Gold Rush: Society in Grass Valley and Nevada City, 1849–1870* (Stanford, CA: Stanford University Press, 1982), 48–56, 142–51, 152–53, 168–79; as well as Elliot West's discussions in his expanded edition of Rodman W. Paul's *Mining Frontiers of the Far West, 1848–1880*, rev. ed. (1963; repr. Albuquerque: University of New Mexico Press, 2001); and Richard White, *It's Your Misfortune and None of My Own* (Norman: University of Oklahoma Press, 1993), chap. 11. Malcolm J. Rohrbough gives a useful transhistorical summary of North American mining by different ethnic communities in "Mining the Nineteenth Century American West," in *A Companion to the American West*, ed. William Deverell (Oxford: Blackwell, 2004), 113–29. As is well known (and traditional), associations amongst miners were often set up to combat a perceived threat of workers from elsewhere. See Lingenfelter, *Hardrock Miners*, and Mark Wyman, *Hard Rock Epic* (Berkeley: University of California Press, 1979) for a thorough discussion of the scene. For discussions of miners' radicalism, see David Emmons, *The Butte Irish: Class and Ethnicity in an American Mining Town* (Urbana and Chicago: University of Illinois Press, 1989); and Jameson, *All That Glitters*, chap. 6.

15. See also Joseph Campbell, *The Hero with a Thousand Faces* (Princeton, NJ: Princeton University Press, 1949), 80–101, for a further exposition of the mythological significance of the underground journey.

16. See Paul, *Mining Lore*, 323ff, for a discussion about the Reformation in relation to the German miners.

17. For a discussion of practices around "the last shift," see Wayland D. Hand, "Notes and Queries: The Fatal Last Shift etc.," *California Folklore Quarterly* 5, no. 2 (April 1946): 201–5.

18. For useful discussions of the relationship between literary writing and folklore, apart from those cited above, see Daniel R. Barnes, "Principles for Study of Folklore and Literature," in *Southern Folklore Quarterly* 43 (1979): 5–16; Preston, *Folklore, Literature and Critical Theory*; Rosenberg, *Folklore and Literature*; and Sandra K. D. Stahl, "Style in Oral and Written Narratives," *Southern Folklore Quarterly* 43 (1979): 29–62.

19. The story was collected in *Can Such Things Be?* (New York: Cassell, 1893). This is the version that appears in the *Collected Works* and that is used here. However, the story first appeared as "The Strange Night-Doings at Deadman's" in the *London Sketch-Book* in March 1874, and then in a slightly different form as "The Night-Doings as 'Deadman's'" in the *San Francisco Argonaut*, December 29, 1877.

20. Bierce published "The Night-Doings" during the rush to the Black Hills, and also as raids by local native nations continued. For the detail of events around 1877, see Watson Parker, *Gold in the Black Hills* (Lincoln: University of Nebraska Press,

1966), who explains that the placer gold rush reached its climax in 1877: "The Indians had been forced to sign away their title to the Hills, and the government had opened the area to settlement" (95).
21. Paul Fatout, *Ambrose Bierce and the Black Hills* (Norman: University of Oklahoma Press, 1956), 46.
22. This whole episode is the subject of Fatout, *Ambrose Bierce and the Black Hills*.
23. In fact, according to Madeline Yuan-yin Hsu, in *Dreaming of Gold, Dreaming of Home* (Stanford, CA: Stanford University Press, 2000), the practice of wearing a pigtail had a very different and highly political source: "Queues were the pigtails that Chinese men were forced to wear as symbols of their loyalty to the Quing (Dynasty). Cutting off one's queue . . . was a dramatic gesture of resistance to the Quing as was punishable by death. Any Chinese man who hoped to return to China had to retain his queue" (203).
24. Archie Green discusses the nationalist ardour that discouraged folklorists such as Emrich and Hand to collect lore that was unflattering to the fondly remembered "frontier" in *Only a Miner: Studies in Recorded Coal-Mining Songs* (Urbana: University of Illinois, 1972), 14ff.
25. This setting is described in detail in Richard O'Connor, *Ambrose Bierce: A Biography* (London: Victor Gollancz Ltd., 1968), 104–8.
26. In fact, in 1873, the year before Bierce first published his story, a Queue Ordinance was formulated in California, whereby Chinese men who were imprisoned were to have their queue cut off. The story was republished in San Francisco as the ordinance was enacted.
27. See http://www.thegeozone.com/treasure/colorado/tales/co019a.jsp for a series of stories about Deadman's Gulch in Colorado.
28. George MacDonald, *The Princess and Curdie* (1883; repr. Oxford: Oxford University Press, 1990), 175.

CHAPTER TWO

1. This episode is described in Richard A. Dwyer and Richard E. Lingenfelter, *Lying on the Eastern Slope: James Townsend's Comic Journalism on the Mining Frontier* (Miami: University Presses of Florida, 1984), chap. 12. James Townsend's work is discussed in chap. 5.
2. Franklin Walker gives a description of Mulford's strange life in the introduction to *Prentice Mulford's Californian Sketches* (San Francisco: Book Club of California, 1935). See also Walker's *San Francisco's Literary Frontier* (New York: A. A. Knopf, 1939), 70–73, 142–44, 204–6. See also Mulford's autobiography, *Life on Land and Sea* (New York: F. J. Needham, 1889).
3. J. Ross Browne's *A Peep at Washoe* (Balboa Island, CA: Paisano Press, 1959) was first published in *Harper's Monthly Magazine* in 1860–1861, and then appeared in book form as *Crusoe's Island, California and Washoe* (New York: Harper & Brothers, 1864).

4. Linda Diz Barnett's chapter "Writings about Bret Harte," in *Bret Harte: A Reference Guide* (Boston: G. K. Hall, 1980), gives the flavor of the arguments about integrity and shallowness that surrounded Harte from the start. I agree with Henry Seidel Canby in *The Short Story* (New York: Henry Holt and Company, 1902), that Harte's main problem, for his critics, lies in his being "incorrigibly mid-Victorian" (53). Some of the most useful criticism of Harte sets him within the literary setting of the era. See, for example, the chapters on Harte in Canby, *The Short Story*, 50–54; Fred Lewis Pattee, *Development of the American Short Story* (New York: Harper's, 1923); and, more recently in John Seelye, introduction to *Treasure Island*, by Robert Louis Stevenson (London: Penguin Books, 1999), xix–xx; and David Wyatt, introduction to in *Selected Stories and Sketches*, by Bret Harte (Oxford: Oxford University Press, 1995). Meanwhile, the research of Gary Scharnhorst provides a wealth of detail about and analysis of Harte's career: see, for example, "Bret Harte and the Literary Construction of the American West," in *A Companion to the Regional Literatures of America*, ed. Charles L. Crow (Oxford: Blackwell, 2003), 479–95; *Bret Harte: Opening the American Literary West* (Norman: University of Oklahoma Press, 2000); and *Selected Letters of Bret Harte* (Norman: University of Oklahoma Press, 1997).
5. Some critics have argued that Harte somehow obscured or even cut short the development of writing about California in a more truthful form. See, for example, Berkove and Kowalewski, "The Literature of the Mining Camps," 103; and Witschi, *Traces of Gold*, chap. 2.
6. This point is also drawn to our attention by Berkove and Kowalewski, "The Literature of the Mining Camps," 99; and developed in Kowalewski, "Romancing the Gold Rush," 208–10.
7. Interestingly, Twain's critics are quite accepting of the brevity of his western sojourn and of his mining of local sources for his first big success, "Jim Smiley and His Jumping Frog," *New York Saturday Press*, November 18, 1865. This perhaps has to do with the sense, on the part of critics, that, as a native of Missouri, he was, in any case, a frontiersman. Certainly, his contemporaries were barbed at times in their comments on Twain's disappearance from the West. See, for example, Dan De Quille's sarcastic comments quoted by Lawrence I. Berkove in *The Fighting Horse of the Stanislaus: Stories and Essays by Dan De Quille* (Iowa City: University of Iowa Press, 1990), 120–21. There is another issue here, of course, with respect to Harte's poor reputation as an artist of integrity: Mark Twain's extraordinary, obsessive, and lifelong campaign to discredit his former friend and mentor. This is described in Margaret Duckett's *Mark Twain and Bret Harte* (Norman: University of Oklahoma Press, 1964). The long-term impact of Twain's campaign is as difficult to divine as his motivation.
8. This story was actually first published in December 1860 as "The Work on Red Mountain," in the San Francisco *Golden Era*. Revised and lengthened, it was then published as "M'liss" in 1863, but it was the original version, now named "Mliss," that Harte included in *The Luck of Roaring Camp and Other Sketches* (Boston: Fields, Osgood and Co., 1870).

9. James J. Rawls, preface to *A Golden State: Mining and Economic Development in Gold-Rush California*, ed. James J. Rawls and Richard J. Orsi (Berkeley: University of California Press, 1999), 8.
10. See, in particular, the work of Margaret Duckett: "Bret Harte's Portrayal of Half Breeds," *American Literature* 2, no. 5 (May 1953): 193–212; "Bret Harte and the Indians of Northern California," *Huntington Library Quarterly* 18 (November 1954): 59–83; "Plain Language from Bret Harte," *Nineteenth-Century Fiction* 11 (March 1957): 241–60; and "The Crusade of a Nineteenth-Century Liberal," *Tennessee Studies in Literature* 4 (1959): 109–20. See also Loomis, "Bret Harte's Folklore," 20–22, for an argument about Harte's interest in Spanish-American lore.
11. Carl I. Wheat, introduction to *The Shirley Letters from the Californian Mines* (New York: Knopf, 1949), for example, argues that Harte "built upon [the letters] in several of his best stories" (xvi), whereas Blake Allmendinger, in *The Ten Most Wanted: The New Western Literature*, sees plagiarism of Clappe's work in Harte's stories (London and New York: Routledge, 1998), 65–66, 76–77.
12. My sources for information on Clappe's life are Wheat's introduction to his edition of the letters, and Rodman W. Paul's "In Search of Dame Shirley," *Pacific Historical Review* 33, no. 2 (May 1964): 127–64. On Clappe, see also Stephen Fender, *Plotting the Golden West* (Cambridge, MA: Cambridge University Press, 1981), 110–14, 117–20; and Brian Roberts, *American Alchemy* (Chapel Hill: University of North Carolina Press, 2000), 248–55.
13. I am indebted in this discussion of melodrama to Elaine Hadley's analysis of Dickens in chapter 3 of *Melodramatic Tactics: Theatricalized Dissent in the English Marketplace, 1800–1885* (Stanford, CA: Stanford University Press, 1995).
14. The response to Victor Hugo in America is discussed in Jeanne Rosselet, "First Reactions to *Les Misérables* in the US," *Modern Language Notes* 67, no. 1 (January 1952): 39–43; the quotations from the *New York Tribune* and the *Atlantic Monthly* are quoted on pp. 39–40.
15. For two contemporary reviews that demonstrate how exhilaratingly unconventional Harte was perceived to be, see William Dean Howells, "Reviews and Literary Notices," *Atlantic Monthly* 25 (May 1870): 633–35; and Thomas Hood's introduction to a British edition of *The Luck of Roaring Camp and Other Stories* (London: George Routledge, 1887).
16. Wallace Stegner, "History, Myth and the Western Writer," in *The Sound of Mountain Water* (Garden City, NY: Doubleday, 1969), 223; Pattee, *Development of the American Short Story*, 234; David Wyatt, introduction to *Selected Stories and Sketches*, xvi.
17. I have taken this list of national and ethnic groups from James J. Rawls's preface to *A Golden State*, 5.
18. See Limbaugh, "Making Old Tools Work Better," 27–31, for a discussion of the opportunities Californian mining offered people without prior knowledge and skills in mining; Malcolm J. Rohrbough, *Days of Gold: The California Gold Rush and the American Nation* (Berkeley: University of California Press, 1997), 123–34.

19. The processes used in California are described clearly and in detail in Limbaugh, "Making Old Tools Work Better," 24–51; and Rodman W. Paul, *California Gold* (Lincoln: University of Nebraska Press, 1947), chap. 5, especially 50–64.
20. George R. Stewart, *Bret Harte, Argonaut and Exile* (Boston: Houghton Mifflin, 1931), 164.
21. Review of "Tales of the Argonauts," *Saturday Review* 40 (December 25, 1875): 821.
22. See Linda Diz Barnett, *Bret Harte: A Reference Guide* (Boston: G. K. Hall, 1980), ix.
23. In fairness to Norris and Harte's other parodists—Mary Austin, for example—it must be said that part of what they were critiquing was the apparently mechanical repetition by Harte of the same content over the thirty years of his career.

CHAPTER THREE

1. I have taken the term "silver age" from Berkove, *The Sagebrush Anthology*. It has the virtue of conveying a complete episode in Nevadan history. On the other hand, the dramatic boom and bust history of the "age" actually falls into two parts, the first beginning with the first rush in 1859, peaking in 1861–1863, and ending with a slump around 1865; and the second framed with a massive strike in 1874 and an exodus in 1878, though historians vary in the precise dates with which they bracket the "age." The histories that I have found most useful in describing the whole episode are: James W. Hulse, *The Silver State* (Reno: University of Nevada Press, 1998), chap. 5; James, *The Roar and the Silence*, chap. 6; Eliot Lord, *Comstock Mining and Miners* (Washington, D.C.: Government Printing Office, 1883); Paul, *Mining Frontiers of the Far West*, 56–101; and Smith, *The History of the Comstock Lode*, 241–43.
2. The term "Sagebrush" was coined by Ella Sterling Cummins, in *The Story of the Files: A Review of Californian Writers and Literature* (San Francisco: Cooperative Printing Company, 1893), a study that gives exhaustive and invaluable lists of writers associated with this and other journalistic "schools." Cummins and others have wanted to associate these writers with the very particular landscape of Nevada, and have done so very evocatively; see, for example, Cummins, *The Story of the Files*, 102; Lawrence I. Berkove, "The Sagebrush School Revisited," in *A Companion to the Regional Literatures of America*, ed. Charles L. Crow (Oxford: Blackwell, 2003), 324; and Duncan Emrich, *Comstock Bonanza* (New York: Vanguard Press, 1950), xiv. I think that Berkove and Kowalewski in "The Literature of the Mining Camps" are probably right when they describe these writers' "intense love for the way of life that they tasted . . . [In] the years when the Old West hit its peak," and so I have used the name (112). At the same time, unsure as to how far these migrants had a feeling for the extraordinary landscape of the area, I find myself in greater sympathy with Lee Clark Mitchell, in "Verbally Roughing It: The West of Words," where he argues that these writers "attend[ed] more fully to language than landscapes," in *Nineteenth-Century Literature* 44, no. 1 (June 1989): 80.

3. For useful descriptions and discussions of Virginia City and its reputation, see, for example, Bernard De Voto, "Washoe," in *Mark Twain's America* (Boston: Houghton Mifflin, 1951); Paul Fatout, *Mark Twain in Virginia City* (Port Washington, NY: Kennikat Press, 1964), 8–19; James, *The Roar and the Silence*, especially the introduction; Lord, *Comstock Mining and Miners*, chap. 10; George D. Lyman, *Saga of the Comstock Lode*, Book Two (New York: Scribner, 1934); and Effie Mona Mack, *Mark Twain in Nevada* (New York: Charles Scribner's Sons, 1947), chap. 3.
4. The claim comes from a letter to an unidentified person, printed in *Mark Twain's Letters*, vol. 2, ed. Albert Bigelow Paine (New York: Harper & Brothers, 1917), 541–43.
5. For discussions of the Sagebrushers in these scholars' work, see especially Berkove, "The Sagebrush School Revisited"; Berkove and Kowalewski, "The Literature of the Mining Camps," 106–13; and Dwyer and Lingenfelter, *Lying on the Eastern Slope*, 1–6. These discussions do not necessarily deal with the same writers, and, indeed, it is not easy to decide whom to include. It seems to me, however, that the most characteristic writing of the group was produced by those who arrived in Nevada as young men, and devoted their efforts to mining or writing for mining newspapers in the heyday of the "flush times." In consequence I have not considered a number of the figures to whom Berkove gives attention.
6. The exception is the commentary of Witschi in *Traces of Gold*, whose response to the writing collected in Berkove's *Sagebrush Anthology* is to describe it as "the literature from the new industrial blast furnace," a response to which I shall return later in the chapter (88).
7. Berkove, "The Sagebrush School Reviewed," 324, 330; and Dwyer and Lingenfelter, *Lying on the Eastern Slope*, 2. Dwyer and Lingenfelter, in *Lying on the Eastern Slope*, give highly evocative accounts of the newspaper culture of Nevada, including its rivalries, squabbles, and apparently ceaseless changes of personnel. Other discussions evoking the print culture of the region, and especially the *Territorial Enterprise*, include: Lucius M. Beebe, *Comstock Commotion: The Story of the Territorial Enterprise and the Virginia City News* (Stanford, CA: Stanford University Press, 1954); James E. Caron, *Mark Twain: Unsanctified Reporter* (Columbia: University of Missouri Press, 2008), 99–101; Oscar Lewis, *The Life and Times of the Virginia City Territorial Enterprise* (Ashland, OR: L. Osborne, 1971); Henry Nash Smith, *Mark Twain of the Enterprise* (Berkeley: University of California Press, 1957), 5–7; Oscar Lewis, introduction to *The Big Bonanza*, by Dan De Quille (New York: Alfred Knopf, 1947), x–xi; and Albert Bigelow Paine, *Mark Twain, a Biography: The Personal and Literary Life of Samuel Langhorne Clemens*, vol. 1 (New York: Harper & Brothers, 1912), x–xi.
8. "Pungent" is Berkove's well-chosen term in "The Sagebrush School Reviewed," 333. Arguments about the rejection of Eastern culture in these writers' work have long been rehearsed. See, for example, Mitchell, "Verbally Roughing It," 77; and Smith, *Mark Twain of the Enterprise*, 3–4.

9. The determination of Anglo-Americans to dominate and pacify Nevada is described in Hulse, *The Silver State*, chap. 5 and 6; Robert M. Utley, *The Indian Frontier of the American West* (Albuquerque: University of New Mexico Press, 1984), 37–52, 70–72, and 93–102.
10. In making this generalization I think that I am doing Dan De Quille a particular injustice. His first western writing, collected in *Washoe Rambles* (Los Angeles: Westernlore Press, 1963), is full of interesting discussion of native men and women. See, for example, chap. 2 and 3.
11. Townsend, Twain, and Denis MacCarthy, the co-owner with Goodman of the *Territorial Enterprise*, had experience as printers. Rollin Daggett, Joe Goodman, and Denis MacCarthy had worked on the San Francisco *Golden Era*. Lewis, *The Life and Times of the Virginia City Territorial Enterprise*, which consists of the reminiscences of five Comstock journalists, gives a comparatively unvarnished and unedited picture of the relations between different journalists.
12. This information on Hart derives from Berkove, *The Sagebrush Anthology*, 303. See also Beebe, *Comstock Commotion*, 53–54; and Alf Doten, "Early Journalism in Nevada," in Lawrence I. Berkove, *The Sagebrush Anthology: Literature from the Silver Age of the Old West* (Columbia: University of Missouri Press, 2006), 270–71.
13. The *Territorial Enterprise* has been the subject of some wonderful description. See, for example: Edgar Marquess Branch, *The Literary Apprenticeship of Mark Twain* (Urbana: University of Illinois Press, 1950), 61–83; and Caron, *Mark Twain: Unsanctified Reporter*, 85–160. Lyman, *The Saga of the Comstock Lode*, is also full of anecdote.
14. Quoting Townsend is a problematic matter, famous as he was for lying and practical joking. What his words convey, at least, is the symbiotic relationship between the mining business and the newspapers, even in a situation where, as was the case with the *Territorial Enterprise*, the newspaper was not owned by mining companies.
15. Berkove provides a brief summary of Goodman's career in *The Sagebrush Anthology*, 10–11. As he notes, "The TRUMPET comes to Pickeye" is "one of the few Sagebrush stories that has been kept current by occasional reprintings," but he gives no date or place for its first appearance (15).
16. Goodman was clearly politically engaged. See, for example, the episodes cited by Berkove in *The Sagebrush Anthology*, 10 and 283. See also the reminiscences of him in Lewis, *The Life and Times of the Virginia City Territorial Enterprise*, 18–22, 32–33.
17. I say relatively because there are numerous accounts of the increasing stratification of Virginia City. Francaviglia, *Hard Places*, 104–8, is excellent on this point. See also James, *The Roar and the Silence*, chap. 10; and Richard H. Peterson's preface to the second edition of *The Bonanza Kings: The Social Origins and Business Behavior of Western Mining Entrepreneurs, 1870–1900* (Norman: University of Oklahoma Press, 1991). Stephen Fender gives an interesting account of Twain's and De Quille's engagement with the comparatively genteel aspects of Virginia City in *Plotting the Golden West* (Cambridge: Cambridge University Press, 1981), 141–55.

18. "Torture Unutterable" was published in the *Territorial Enterprise*, October 14, 1877, and is reprinted in Berkove, *The Fighting Horse of the Stanislaus*, 25–30.
19. This report is reprinted in Branch, *The Literary Apprenticeship of Mark Twain*, 75, from the *Cedar Falls Gazette*, July 10, 1863. Branch surmises that it was written by Twain in the absence of De Quille (285n50).
20. Dave Kennedy, "The Frontier in South African History," *Journal of the West* 34, no. 4 (October 1995): 23.
21. Christopher Saunders and Iain R. Smith, "Southern Africa, 1795–1910," in *The Oxford History of the British Empire*, vol. 3, ed. Andrew Porter (Oxford: Oxford University Press, 1999), 263.
22. Keith Beavon, *Johannesburg: The Making and Shaping of the City* (Pretoria: University of South Africa Press, 2004), 6.
23. See Lewis, introduction to *The Big Bonanza*, xiii–xiv.
24. This is certainly not a fair summary of Witschi's argument in *Traces of Gold*, which is that the Sagebrush writers are expressing anxiety and rage at "a culture wherein the value of material goods is constantly at issue and, as a result, terribly unstable" (32). For Witschi, the hoaxes of the Sagebrush writers both represent and erase the "physical trauma of mining" (33).
25. Dwyer and Lingenfelter, *Lying on the Eastern Slope*, 76.
26. This is, of course, a much discussed piece. For a range of examples of interesting discussions, see Fatout, *Mark Twain in Virginia City*, 99–112; Randall Knofer, *Acting Naturally: Mark Twain in the Culture of Performance* (Berkeley: University of California Press, 1995), 38–39; Lyman, *Saga of the Comstock Lode*, 246–50; Bruce Michelson, *Printer's Devil: Mark Twain and the American Publishing Revolution* (Berkeley: University of California Press, 2006), 69–75; Witschi, *Traces of Gold*, 32–36; and, on another of Twain's hoaxes, Kerry Driscoll, "The Fluid Identity of 'Petrified Man,'" *American Literary Realism* 43, no. 3 (Spring 1990): 214–31.
27. The term "luck hunters" comes from Hannah Arendt, *Origins of Totalitarianism* (London: Secker and Warburg, 1951), 105. Her comments on the "new type of social individual" who appeared at the mines in southern Africa are suggestive as far as Nevada is concerned. See, especially 105, 198–99.

CHAPTER FOUR

1. The quotation in the title of this chapter may be found in Raymond E. Dumett, *El Dorado in West Africa: The Gold-Mining Frontier, African Labor and Colonial Capitalism in the Gold Coast, 1875–1900* (Athens: Ohio University Press, 1998), 8.
2. The argument about the West as a "plundered province" is summarized in William G. Robbins, "The Plundered Province Thesis," *Pacific Historical Review* 55, no. 4 (November, 1986): 577–97. For related arguments, see, for example, Bryant, "Entering the Global Economy," 195–235; see also William Cronon, George Miles, and Jay Gitlin, "Becoming West: Toward a New Meaning for Western History," in *Under an Open Sky: Rethinking America's Western Past* (New York: W. W. Norton & Company, 1992), 3–27; and Clark C. Spence, *British Investment and the American Mining Frontier, 1860–1901* (Ithaca, NY: Cornell University Press, 1958).

3. See William G. Robbins, "Western History: A Dialectic on the Modern Condition," *Western Historical Quarterly* 2, no. 4 (November 1989): 429–50, especially 439; and *Colony and Empire: The Capitalist Transformation of the American West* (Lawrence: University Press of Kansas, 1994), ix–xi.
4. See the opening discussion in Hardesty, *Archaeology of Mining and Miners*, 1–3; as well as David Hamer, *New Towns in the New World* (New York: Columbia University Press, 1990), chap. 5; and Paul, *Mining Frontiers of the Far West*, 37.
5. The best discussion of "instant cities" is in Gunther Barth, *Instant Cities: Urbanization and the Rise of San Francisco and Denver* (New York and Oxford: Oxford University Press, 1975). Barth's study is focused on San Francisco and Denver, but his discussion of the origins of the instant city the introduction has a broad sweep.
6. The best summary, in my reading, of Leadville's development as an urban settlement is in Vivian H. Wurz, "The Leadville Camp: A Colorado Mining Community, 1876–1883" (MA thesis, University of Colorado, May 1941), and the financing and development of the mines are dealt with in detail in Joseph E. King, *A Mine to Make a Mine: Financing the Colorado Mining Industry, 1859–1902* (College Station: Texas A&M University Press, 1977). See also Don L. Griswold and Jean Harvey Griswold, *The Carbonate Camp Called Leadville* (Denver, CO: University of Denver Press, 1951) and *History of Leadville and Lake County*. The following more popular histories are also helpful: Edward Blair, *Leadville: Colorado's Magic City* (Boulder, CO: Pruett Publishing, 1980); and Ed B. Larsh and Robert Nichols, *Leadville, U.S.A.* (Boulder, CO: Johnson Books, 1951).
7. Robert B. Westbrook, "Leadville," in *The New Encyclopedia of the American West*, ed. Howard R. Lamar (New Haven, CT: Yale University Press, 1998), 623.
8. Wilde's account was not a report of what actually happened on his visit to Leadville. For the newspaper record and some interesting local responses, see Griswold and Griswold, *History of Leadville and Lake County Colorado*, vol. 1, 954–57.
9. Elliott West's *The Contested Plains: Indians, Goldseekers, and the Rush to Colorado* (Lawrence: University Press of Kansas, 1998) offers an approach to the whole subject of relationships between different groups in the region that I aspire to follow. Studies of the circumstances of particular rushes that I have found especially instructive are: the work of Julie Cruikshank in *Life Lived Like a Story: Life Stories of Three Yukon Native Elders* (Lincoln: University of Nebraska Press, 1990) on the impact of the Klondike rush on Tagish and Tlingit nations; Ferol Egan, *Sand in a Whirlwind* (Reno: University of Nevada Press, 1972), on the Pyramid Lake War; and Albert L. Hurtado, *Indian Survival on the California Frontier* (New Haven, CT: Yale University Press, 1990). Utley, *The Indian Frontier of the American West*, has also been useful.
10. Jameson, *All That Glitters*, 24.

11. Hamlin Garland's research is discussed briefly in *A Daughter of the Middle Border* (New York: The Macmillan Company, 1921), 256–59. The quotation comes from Thomas K. Urdahl, introduction to *The Cripple Creek Strike of 1893*, by B. M. Rastall (Colorado Springs: Colorado College Studies, 1905), i. The conflict that he described is discussed in B. M. Rastall, *The Cripple Creek Strike of 1893* (Colorado Springs: Colorado College Studies, 1905), and analyzed in Jameson, *All That Glitters*, especially chapter 2.
12. Stevenson's articles ran in *Scribner's Monthly* 27, no. 1 (November 1883): 27–40; no. 2, 182–92. He added new material for *The Silverado Squatters* (London: Chatto and Windus, 1883), from which I am quoting here.
13. The history of Silverado is summarized in Anne Roller Issler, *Our Mountain Heritage: Silverado and Robert Louis Stevenson* (Stanford, CA: Stanford University Press, 1950), 76–84. See also James D. Hart, introduction to *From Scotland to Silverado*, by Robert Louis Stevenson (Cambridge, MA: Belknap Press of Harvard University Press, 1966).
14. For the complex and disparate uses made by Stevenson of his Silverado experience, see Hart, introduction to *From Scotland to Silverado*, xliii–li.
15. The discussions of this form that I have found most useful, apart from Gillian Beer, *The Romance* (London: Methuen, 1970) are: Peter Brooks, *The Melodramatic Imagination: Balzac, Henry James and the Mode of Excess* (New Haven, CT: Yale University Press, 1995), 154–57, 173–75; and Richard Chase, *The American Novel and Its Tradition* (New York: Doubleday, 1957).
16. William Dean Howells, "The Editor's Study," *Harper's Monthly* 72, no. 432 (May 1886): 973; and Charles Dudley Warner, "Modern Fiction," *Atlantic Monthly* 51, no. 306 (April 1883): 469.
17. Beer, *Romance*, 3.
18. Recent discussions and definitions of legend are usefully examined in Timothy R. Tangherlini, "'It Happened Not Too Far From Here,'" *Western Folklore* 49, no. 4 (October 1990): 371–90. See also Robert A. Georges, "The General Concept of Legend," in *American Folk Legend: A Symposium*, ed. Wayland D. Hand (Berkeley: University of California Press, 1971).
19. The speech is printed in Paul, *Mining Lore*, 595.
20. Reprinted in B. A. Botkin, *A Treasury of American Folklore: Stories, Ballads and Traditions of the People* (New York: Crown Publishers, 1944), 630.
21. John A. McClure, *Late Imperial Romance* (London: Verso, 1994), 9. For discussions of imperial romance, see also, for example, Linda Dryden, *Joseph Conrad and the Imperial Romance* (New York: St. Martin's Press, 1999); Wendy Katz, *Rider Haggard and the Fiction of Empire: A Critical Study of British Imperial Fiction* (Cambridge: Cambridge University Press, 1987), chap. 2; and Amy Kaplan, "Romancing the Empire: The Embodiment of American Masculinity in the Popular Historical Novel of the 1890s," *American Literary History* 2, no. 4 (Winter 1990): 659–90.

22. The case on which *The Led-Horse Claim* was based, a case in which Foote and her husband, Arthur Foote, were involved (and which precipitated their departure from Leadville) is described in detail in Griswold and Griswold, *History of Leadville and Lake County, Colorado*, vol. 1, 693–94. The Griswolds compare the events with Foote's account.
23. Mining law of the period and the difficulties produced by the Apex Law are summarized in Rodman W. Paul, "Mining Law," in *The New Encyclopedia of the American West*, ed. Howard R. Lamar (New Haven, CT: Yale University Press, 1998), 707–8. For an extended discussion of mining litigation, see Malcolm J. Rohrbough, *Aspen: The History of a Silver-Mining Town, 1879–1893*, (Boulder: University Press of Colorado, 2000), chap. 7. See also Caroline Bancroft, "Folklore of the Central City District, Colorado," *California Folklore Quarterly* 4, no. 4 (October 1945): 327.
24. According to D. W. Brunton's "Technical Reminiscences," in *Mining Engineering in Colorado* (San Francisco: n.p., 1915), "Conditions in Leadville during its early days are so truthfully and graphically portrayed in Mary Hallock Foote's most interesting novels ... that it would be a waste of time to describe them here" (251).
25. See, for example, Melody Graulich, "Legacy Profile: Mary Hallock Foote," *Legacy* 3, no. 2 (Fall 1986): 46–48; Lee Ann Johnson, *Mary Hallock Foote* (Boston: Twayne, 1980), 155–58; Darlis A. Miller, *Mary Hallock Foote: Author-Illustrator of the American West* (Norman: University of Oklahoma Press, 2002), 267–70; and Rodman W. Paul, introduction to *A Victorian Gentlewoman in the Far West: The Reminisces of Mary Hallock Foote*, by Mary Hallock Foote, ed. Rodman W. Paul (San Marino, CA: Huntington Library, 1992). Ironically Wallace Stegner, whose *Angle of Repose* (Harmondsworth, UK: Penguin, 1992) virtually erased the career of his fictionalized Foote, is more wholehearted than most in recognizing the value of Foote's portrait of the mining West, in *Selected American Prose, 1841–1900: The Realistic Movement* (New York: Rinehart, 1958), xi. See also the broad-ranging discussion of Foote in Richard W. Etulain, *Re-Imagining the Modern American West: A Century of Fiction, History and Art* (Tucson: University of Arizona Press, 1996).
26. See T. A. Rickard, "A. de Witt Foote," in *Interviews with Mining Engineers* (San Francisco: Mining and Scientific Press, 1922), 175–76. For a discussion of Foote's early background, most illuminating are Miller, *Mary Hallock Foote*, and Paul's edition of Foote's autobiographical writings in *A Victorian Gentlewoman in the Far West*. The Pre-Raphaelite attraction to the frontier is suggested in Roger B. Stein, *Ruskin and Aesthetic Thought in America* (Cambridge, MA: Harvard University Press, 1967), 108.
27. For a discussion of Foote's artistic training, see Janet Floyd, "A Sympathetic Misunderstanding," *Frontiers: A Journal of Women's Studies* 22, no. 3 (Special Issue: Women's West, 2001): 148–67.
28. Foote refers to her lifelong love of Tennyson in Paul, ed., *A Victorian Gentlewoman in the Far West*, 60, 93, and 382.

29. See, for example, Foote's use of the term in "In Exile," *Atlantic Monthly* 48 (August and September 1881): 330.
30. It is difficult to know how much Foote knew about the history of native nations, and whether she deliberately chose the name of a nation that had not traditionally occupied the area around Leadville. Certainly, by the time she was in Colorado, some Shoshone were indeed drifting into the area. It is interesting to note that, while in Leadville, Foote was visited by Helen Hunt Jackson in 1879, though Jackson's *Century of Dishonor* (New York: Harper & Brothers, 1881) did not appear until 1881. Certainly the naming of a mine for a native nation was not a matter of chance. In Foote's *John Bodewin's testimony* (Boston: Ticknor and Company, 1886), the name of the mine owned by the public scoundrel and private gentleman is the Uinta.
31. Tristram does not appear in Tennyson's *Idylls*, in *Poems* (London: Edward Moxon & Co., 1857), but in other Victorian texts, for example, Swinburne's *Tristram of Lyonesse and Other Poems* (London: Chatto and Windus 1882); and Richard Wagner's opera, *Tristan Und Isolde*, first performed in 1865 (New York: Dover, 1973).
32. Foote, *John Bodewin's testimony*, 344.
33. Davis's novel is critiqued in this way in Kaplan, "Romancing the Empire." John Seelye, *War Games* (Amherst: University of Massachusetts Press, 2003), though broadly in agreement with Kaplan, gives a detailed, nuanced account of Davis's outlook.

CHAPTER FIVE

1. The starting points for my discussion of mining, gender, and sexuality in this chapter have been Eliade, *The Forge and the Crucible*, chap. 3, and three discussions of mining that foreground negotiations of gender and sexuality: James Ferguson, *Expectations of Modernity: Myths and Meanings of Urban Life in the Zambian Copperbelt* (Berkeley: University of California Press, 1999); Janet L. Finn, *Tracing the Veins of Copper, Culture and Community from Butte to Chuquicamata* (Berkeley: University of California Press, 1998); and Thomas M. Klubock, "Working-Class Masculinity," *Journal of Social History* 30, no. 2 (Winter 1996): 435–63.
2. In thinking of the camps and mining towns as spaces for improvisations of gender and sexuality, I have used David Goodman, *Gold Seeking: Victoria and California in the 1850s* (Stanford, CA: Stanford University Press, 1994); Johnson, *Roaring Camp*; and Roberts, *American Alchemy*, as my starting point, with their emphasis on the contestedness of categories of gender generally, as well as their sense of the mining camps and towns as places of negotiation of those categories. At the same time, I have found the arguments about gender, sexuality, and imperialism in broader studies of the nineteenth century suggestive, especially in the summarizing arguments of R. W. Connell, "Masculinities and Globalization,"

Men and Masculinities 1, no. 1 (July 1998): 3–23; Richard Phillips, "Histories of Sexuality and Imperialism: What's the Use?," *History Workshop Journal* 63, no. 1 (Spring 2007): 136–53; and Ann Laura Stoler, "Tense and Tender Ties," *Journal of American History* 88, no. 3 (December 2001): 829–65.

3. On the significance of the visibility of "marginal" sexualities at the imperial center, I am indebted to a paper given by Frank Bongiorno, "Aspects of the History of Sexuality in Early Colonial Australia," delivered at the Menzies Centre at King's College London, April 28, 2010.

4. I have chosen to use the term "prostitute" rather than "sex worker," despite the grim associations of the former term. Although the latter term seems to restore a sense of agency and choice to the work that is altogether appropriate to the setting of the mining camps and towns, the argument that all work is sex work, that is, all work is always conducted in a setting where sexuality is critical, seems to me more powerful still. For the arguments around the different names, see the introduction to Sheila Jeffreys, *The Idea of Prostitution* (North Melbourne, Victoria: Spinifex Press, 2008), vii–xii; and Joanna Brewis and Stephen Linstead, *Sex, Work and Sex Work: Eroticizing Organization* (New York and London: Routledge, 2000), 226–31. Brewis and Linstead's study is devoted to questions of how sex and work intersect.

5. For the developing discussion of Chinese prostitution in the mining West, and indeed of the limits of the stereotype to which I refer, see Lucie Cheng Hirata, "Free, Indentured, Enslaved," *Signs* 5, no. 1 (Autumn 1979): 3–29; and Annette White-Parks, "Beyond the Stereotypes," in *Writing the Range: Race, Class and Culture in the Women's West*, ed. Elizabeth Jameson and Susan Armitage (Norman: University of Oklahoma Press, 1997), 258–73. See also Alexy Simmons, "Ladies of the Night," in *Social Approaches to an Industrial Past: The Archaeology and Anthropology of Mining*, ed. A. Bernard Knapp, Vincent C. Pigott, and Eugenia W. Herbert (London and New York: Routledge, 1998), 59–79, for a suggestive discussion of ethnicity and prostitution.

6. Apart from Julia Ann Laite's survey of the field in "Historical Perspectives," *Historical Journal* 52, no. 3 (September 2009): 739–61; and, of course, Anne M. Butler's groundbreaking work, I have found the following studies most fruitful in combining a theoretical perspective on prostitution with empirical study: Ferguson, *Expectations of Modernity*, chap. 5; Paula Petrik, *No Step Backward* (Helena: Montana Historical Society Press, 1987), chap. 2; and Simmons, "Ladies of the Night," 59–79.

7. Marion S. Goldman, *Gold Diggers and Silver Miners* (Ann Arbor: University of Michigan Press, 1981), 31.

8. Arthur Wing Pinero's *The Second Mrs. Tanqueray* (London: Heinemann, 1895); and George Bernard Shaw's *Mrs. Warren's Profession* (London: Grant Richards, 1902), which opened in London in 1893 and 1902, respectively, opened in the United States during the same period as *The Golden Girl*.

9. This point is thoroughly examined in Jaclyn J. Gier and Laurie Mercier's introduction to *Mining Women: Gender in the Development of Global Industry, 1670–2005* (New York: Palgrave Macmillan, 2006).
10. Gier and Mercier summarize the process in broad terms. See also Anne McClintock, *Imperial Leather* (New York and London: Routledge, 1995), 112–18, for a discussion of Victorian attitudes to women and mining. A useful general discussion of the exclusion of women both from particular forms of work and from whole industries appears in Stephanie Coontz, *The Social Origins of Private Life: American Families, 1600–1900* (London: Verso, 1988), chap. 8.
11. For examples, see Gier and Mercier, introduction to *Mining Women*, 15. The Women in Mining website, www.womeninmining.net, is an interesting source on this point.
12. For detailed discussions of women's work in Gold Rush mines, see Johnson, *Roaring Camp*, 30–31, 62, 222–23. Sally Zanjani's observations in *A Mine of Her Own* (Lincoln: University of Nebraska Press, 2000), introduction and chap. 1, are an excellent starting point for thinking about women prospectors in general. For discussions of the emphasis on women servicing a working husband in the home, see the discussions in Gier and Mercier, *Mining Women*, 89–90, 171–73; and Jameson, *All That Glitters*, chap. 3.
13. See, for examples within a large field, Frances Backhouse, *Women of the Klondike* (Vancouver: Whitecap Books, 1995); Cynthia B. Driscoll, *One Woman's Gold Rush* (Kalamazoo, MI: Oak Woods Media, 1996); Mary E. Hitchcock, *Two Women in the Klondike* (New York: G. P. Putnam's Sons, 1899); Melanie J. Mayer, *Klondike Women* (Athens: Swallow Press / Ohio University Press, 1989); Clare Murphy, *Gold Rush Women* (Anchorage: Alaska North-West Books, 1997); and Zanjani, *A Mine of Her Own*.
14. The point is gracefully made in, for example, Fender, *Plotting the Golden West*, 60–63, and updated and expanded in Goodman, *Gold Seeking*, 149–67.
15. This point is approached from another direction in Johnson, *Roaring Camp*, 138 and 141–42, where Johnson examines the common trope in which miners are pictured missing the presence of women.
16. Working-class homes were not, of course, shaped by a "cult of domesticity." Women of different ethnicities interpreted their relationship to home and work in ways that were at odds with the Anglo-American concept of domesticity. See Coontz, *The Social Origins of Private Life*, for a survey of different domesticities.
17. On this point, see Pascale Absi, "Lifting the Layers of the Mountain's Petticoats," in Gier and Mercier, *Mining Women*, 58–61; and Wayland D. Hand, "Californian Miners' Folklore: Below Ground," *California Folklore Quarterly* 1, no. 2 (April 1942): 127–53; and Paul, *Mining Lore*, 502ff. See also Mara Lou Hawse, "Superstitions about the Mines," suite101.com, June 18, 1999.
18. The poem from which the quotation comes is "The Miner's Morning Melody," in *The New Rush and Other Poems and Songs*, by J. Rogers (Melbourne: n.p., 1864), 54–56.

19. Here Finn is actually quoting Jorge Alvear Urrutia, *Chile, Nuestro Cobre* (Santiago: Editorial Lastra, 1975), 65–66.
20. Interestingly, the classic studies of American miners' folklore do draw beliefs deriving from miners of different ethnicities into the discussion. In the work of Hand, for example, the folklorist sees common beliefs inflected by miners' different ethnic origins rather than these origins producing distinct sets of beliefs.
21. The strains of work (such as mining) that are demanding and destructive of the body are discussed in Mike Donaldson, *Time of Our Lives* (Sidney: Allen & Unwin, 1991), 15–28.
22. The formation of a "hardline masculine fundamentalism" in imperial settings is situated and analyzed in Connell, "Masculinities and Globalization," 17.
23. The term "conquest mentality" is Albert L. Hurtado's in "When Strangers Met," in *Writing the Range: Race, Class and Culture in the Women's West*, ed. Elizabeth Jameson and Susan Armitage (Norman: University of Oklahoma Press, 1997), 136. The impact of demographic imbalance is often stated, but disparities are often not differentiated between areas and indeed over time. For useful snapshots of the variable imbalance in mining populations between men and women, see, for example, Mann, *After the Gold Rush*, 224; Elliott West, "Five Idaho Mining Towns," *Pacific Northwest Quarterly* 73, no. 3 (July 1982): 108–20; and Duane A. Smith, "The San Juaner," *Colorado Magazine* 52 (Spring 1975): 137–52.
24. There were, of course, women writers at work in this context, especially in San Francisco, though they are rarely mentioned. The best source for information on their lost work is Cummins, *The Story of the Files*, though Ida Rae Egli, *No Rooms of Their Own* (Berkeley, CA: Heyday, 1997), is a good source of texts.
25. For an authoritative discussion of the Western tradition of linking mining with rape, see Carolyn Merchant, *The Death of Nature*, 39–41.
26. See Frances Fuller Victor, "The New Penelope," "How Jack Hastings Sold His Mine," and "Mr. Ela's Story," in *The New Penelope and Other Stories and Poems* (San Francisco: Bancroft and Co., 1877).
27. Joaquin Miller's life is crisply summarized in James Folsom, "Joaquin Miller," in *The New Encyclopedia of the American West*, ed. Howard R. Lamar (New Haven, CT: Yale University Press, 1998), 701–2. Details of his work and his writing may be found at www.joaquinmiller.com.
28. Henry Adams, *Education of Henry Adams* (Boston: Houghton Mifflin, 1918), 1071. Adams's comment and its treatment by Harte's later critics receive an interesting discussion in Jeffrey F. Thomas, "Bret Harte and the Power of Sex," *Western American Literature* 8, no. 3 (Fall 1973): 91–92.
29. For discussions of homosociality and same-sex love between men in the camps see, for example, Johnson, *Roaring Camp*, especially 170–75; Rohrbough, *Days of Gold*, 78–80; and Peter Stoneley, "Rewriting the Gold Rush," *Journal of American Studies* 30, no. 2 (August 1996): 189–209.

30. For suggestive discussions of relations between men underground with their implications for male/female relations, see, for example, Finn, *Tracing the Veins*, 140-41; and T. Dunbar Moodie, *Going for Gold: Men, Mines and Migration* (Berkeley: University of California Press, 1994), 15-20.
31. Narjot's life and work is discussed in Harvey L. Jones, "Souvenirs of the Mother Lode" and "Sentiment and Nostalgia," in *Art of the Gold Rush*, ed. Janice T. Driesbach, Harvey L. Jones, and Katherine Church Holland (Berkeley: Oakland Museum of California, Crocker Art Museum, and University of California Press, 1998), 65-66, 105-9.
32. For a discussion of Nahl's life and work, see Harvey L. Jones, "The Hessian Party" and "Sentiment and Nostalgia" 47-49, 100-105.
33. The quotations are from Rohrbough's discussion of partners, *Days of Gold*, 78.
34. The classic expression of the idea of the mate and mateship is in Russell Ward, *The Australian Legend* (Melbourne: Oxford University Press, 1978), 109-10, but see also T. Inglis Moore, *Social Patterns* (Sidney: Angus and Robertson, 1971), 220-37.
35. For the most extensive comparative discussion of the two rushes, see Goodman, *Gold Seeking*. See also Douglas Fetherling, *The Gold Crusades: A Social History of the Gold Rushes, 1849-1929* (Toronto: University of Toronto Press, 1997); and Morrell, *The Gold Rushes*, for discussions of both rushes that are essentially comparative in character.
36. Ward, in *The Australian Legend*, quotes a wonderful song that, as he says, "reflects nicely the mingled admiration and irritation which the Yankees inspired in Colonial breasts" (125).
37. Moore, *Social Patterns*, 221; and Goodman, *Gold Seeking*, 8.
38. For descriptions of the fighting that resulted from these impositions, see Fetherling, *The Gold Crusades*, 50; and Morrell, *The Gold Rushes*, chap. 7.
39. For a commentary on the exhibition of "savage" women in the context of a discussion about sexualizations of colonized peoples, see Phillipa Levine, "Sexuality and Empire," in *At Home with the Empire: Metropolitan Culture in the Imperial World*, ed. Catherine Hall and Sonya O. Rose (Cambridge: Cambridge University Press, 2006), 127-29; and Yvette Abrahams, "Images of Sara Bartram: Sexuality, Race and Gender in Early Nineteenth-Century Britain," in *Nation, Empire, Colony: Historicizing Gender and Race*, ed. Ruth R. Pierson, Nupur Chaudhuri, and Beth McAuley (Bloomington: Indiana University Press, 1998), 220-36.

CHAPTER SIX

1. The quotation is from Garland, quoted in Franklin Walker, *Jack London and the Klondike* (London: Bodley Head, 1966), 14. For examples of discussions of the Klondike's significance, see Kenneth S. Coates, introduction to *The Klondike Stampede*, by Tappan Adney (1900; repr., Vancouver: University of British

Columbia Press, 1994), xv–xvii; Morrell, *The Gold Rushes*, 374–410; Kathryn Taylor Morse, introduction to *The Nature of Gold: An Environmental History of the Klondike Gold Rush* (Seattle: University of Washington Press, 2003); and David Wharton, *The Alaska Gold Rush* (Bloomington: Indiana University Press, 1972), 1. Discussions of the cultural significance of the landscape and position of the North may be found in Coates, introduction to *The Klondike Stampede*, xvii; Susan Kollin, *Nature's State: Imagining Alaska as the Last Frontier* (Chapel Hill: University of North Carolina Press, 2001), 61–64; Joseph Ladue, *Klondyke Nuggets* (New York: American Technical Book Co., 1897), 12–13; Morse, *The Nature of Gold*, 17–18; and Wharton, *The Alaska Gold Rush*, 1. "Talking Klondike" is Leroy S. Townsend's term, in *Alaska Gold Rush Letters and Photographs* (Murphy, OR: Castle Peak Editions, 1999), 31.

2. The significance of the economic depression in the United States is discussed most extensively in Lisa Mighetto and Marica Montgomery, *Hard Drive to the Klondike: Promoting Seattle during the Gold Rush* (Seattle: University of Washington Press, 2002), 9–11; while Morse, in *The Nature of Gold*, chap. 1, explores the broader context of money and value during this period. For discussions of the Klondike as a poor man's rush, see Bolotin, *A Klondike Scrapbook*, xx; Julie Cruikshank, "Images of Society in Klondike Gold Rush Narratives: Skookum Jim, and the Discovery of Gold," *Ethnohistory* 39, no. 1 (Winter 1992): 57–84; and William S. Greever, *The Bonanza West: The Story of the Western Mining Rushes, 1848–1900* (Norman: University of Oklahoma Press, 1963), 346ff. The complex social makeup of the migrants is discussed in Charlene Porsild, *Gamblers and Dreamers: Women, Men and Community in the Klondike* (Vancouver: University of British Columbia Press, 1998), 71.

3. This assessment is given in Porsild, *Gamblers and Dreamers*, 18.

4. The ethnicity of the Klondikers is discussed in Wharton, *The Alaska Gold Rush*, 6–9; while the regional mix of U.S. Klondikers is mentioned in Ron T. Bailey, *Frozen in Silver: The Life and Frontier Photography of P. E. Larson* (Athens: Swallow Press / Ohio University Press, 1998), 82.

5. The experience of both groups receives illuminating discussion in Kenneth S. Coates, *Best Left as Indians: Native-White Relations in the Yukon Territory, 1840–1975* (Montreal: McGill-Queen's Press, 1991), and Julie Cruikshank, "Discovery of Gold on the Klondike," in *Reading Beyond Worlds: Contexts for Native History*, ed. Jennifer S. H. Brown and Elizabeth Vibert (Peterborough, Ontario: Broadview, 1996).

6. The imperial dimension of the Klondike Rush is discussed in Cruikshank, "Images of Society," 25; and Kollin, *Nature's State*, 61–64.

7. In this chapter I do not discuss the particularities of the experience of the many women who journeyed to the Klondike, not because they are not historically significant—on the contrary—but because neither the writing of the Klondike as the experience of every man, nor the writing of the working-class voice admits

the significance of that presence. Studies of the women who came to the region in search of gold have been the object of energetic scholarly recovery. See chapter 5, note 12. Equally, the representation of the Klondike in writing in English does little justice to the ethnic mix amongst the Klondikers. Those accounts of the Klondike that do greatest justice to differences on grounds of class and ethnicity in the experience of the Klondike are Cruikshank, "Images of Society," especially 22–27; and Kenneth S. Coates and William R. Morrison, *Land of the Midnight Sun: A History of the Yukon* (Edmonton, Alberta: Hurtig Publishers, 1988), chap. 4.

8. Pierre Berton, in *Klondike: The Life and Death of the Last Great Gold Rush* (London: W. H. Allen, 1960), gives the following numbers: 100,000 set out for the Klondike, 30,000 to 40,000 made it to Dawson City (the town nearest the diggings), and then 15,000 to 20,000 worked the gold fields (47). Porsild, *Gamblers and Dreamers*, gives the higher number of 50,000 for numbers at the diggings (8–23).

9. The availability of facilities to ease the journey for those who could afford them are described in Morse, *The Nature of Gold*, 40–44; and Greever, *Bonanza West*, 346.

10. The medical condition of poor Klondikers is most fully discussed in the diary of a young doctor: Townsend, *Gold Rush Letters and Photographs*, 14 and 19ff, from which the quotation derives (19).

11. The quotation comes from a famous contemporary account of the Chilkoot climb in Edward S. Curtis, "The Rush to the Klondike," *The Century Magazine* 55, no. 5 (March 1898): 697. The presence and activities of the many photographers of the Klondike are discussed in Bailey, *Frozen in Silver*, 42–46, 55, and 81. Bailey's book is a study of the work of Hegg and P. E. Larson. Bolotin, *Klondike Scrapbook*, 4, is also useful on these points, as is Richard Frederick, "Asahel Curtis," *Alaska Journal* 13, no. 2 (Spring 1983): 115 and passim.

12. Quoted in McElrath and Crisler, *Frank Norris*, 54.

13. Townsend, *Gold Rush Letters and Photographs*, 52; and William Shape, *Faith of Fools: A Journal of the Klondike Rush* (Pullman: Washington State University Press, 1998), 1.

14. For discussions of this point, see Coates and Morrison, *Land of the Midnight Sun*, 87; and Greever, *Bonanza West*, 333.

15. *The Sunday Gleaner* 1, no. 10, September 24, 1899, 1.

16. The story is related in Rev. R. M. Dickey, *Gold Fever: A Narrative of the Great Klondike Gold Rush, 1897–1899* (Murphy, OR: Castle Peak Editions, 1997), 47.

17. See Coates and Morrison, *Land of the Midnight Sun*, 98–100, for these details. The quotation given appeared in the *Report of the North-West Mounted Police* (Ottawa: King's Printer, 1898), 309.

18. Fred Baker, letter written from Dawson, May 1897, quoted in Alfred Page, *Klondike Day and Yukon Travel in 1898* (Phoenix, AZ: Ruby Wine Sheldon, 2006), 19.

19. Dickey, *Gold Fever*, 230.

20. Helen Rowland Kelly's introduction to *Letters from the Klondike*, by Volney Rowland (Sacramento, CA: Yukon Publications, 2002), 6–7, describes her grandfather's background.
21. The working regime in the Klondike diggings is described in Morrell, *The Gold Rushes*, 377–95; Morse, *The Nature of Gold*, chap. 4; and Porsild, *Gamblers and Dreamers*, 74–76.
22. See, for a succinct discussion of Service's background, James Mackay, *Vagabond of Verse: Robert Service: A Biography*. (Edinburgh and London: Mainstream Publishing, 1995), 21–27.
23. See also Coates and Morrison, *Land of the Midnight Sun*, 145, 149–50, for a discussion of Dawson during this period.
24. Service's devotion to the amateur theatricals of Whitehorse and Dawson is described in Mackay, *Vagabond of Verse*, 141, 161, and 171.
25. This statement is quoted in John W. Garvin, *Canadian Poets* (Toronto: McLelland and Stewart, 1916), 360–61.
26. Mackay, *Vagabond of Verse*, 81, 91.
27. Details of the local reaction to Service's published verses, and about his sense of audience, are given in Mackay, *Vagabond of Verse*, 165–67, 170–72. On his fondness for Kipling, see ibid., 141, 164.
28. The reaction to Service in Dawson is described in Mackay, *Vagabond of Verse*, 171; and Carl F. Klinck, "Robert Service," in *Dictionary of Literary Biography: Canadian Writers, 1890–1920*, ed. Carl F. Klinck and W. H. New (Detroit, MI: Gale, 1990), 345.
29. See Klinck, "Robert Service," 344.
30. "Just from Dawson," *Klondike Nugget*, June 23, 1898, and reprinted in Murray Morgan, *One Man's Gold Rush: A Klondike Album* (Seattle: University of Washington Press, 1995), 19–20.
31. "The Sour Dough's Lament," *Klondike Nugget: Special Souvenir Edition*, November 1, 1899, 22.
32. See Coates, *Best Left as Indians*, xxi–xxii, 36–46; Cruikshank, *Life Lived Like a Story*, 8–11; and Wharton, *The Alaska Gold Rush*, 1–5.
33. This story, or set of stories, is set out in Cruikshank, "Images of Society," 25–27.
34. The most helpful source on London's Klondike experience is Walker, *Jack London and the Klondike*. London's comment on getting a "breathing space" is quoted in Walker, 14.
35. London's class background and his engagements with working-class culture as a young man are discussed in Joan D. Hedrick, *Solitary Comrade: Jack London and His Work* (Chapel Hill: University of North Carolina Press, 1982), 3–13.
36. The first Klondike story, "To the Man on the Trail," was published by the *Overland Monthly* in January 1899. "The White Silence" appeared in the February issue.
37. See Walker, *Jack London and the Klondike*, 100–104, 183–89.
38. See Cruikshank, "Discovery of Gold on the Klondike," 443–44.

39. See Walker, *Jack London and the Klondike*, 185–89, especially 186–87.

AFTERWORD

1. Jason Rhoades's installation was shown at the David Zwirmer Gallery, New York, in 2000.

Selected Bibliography

Abrahams, Yvette. "Images of Sara Bartram: Sexuality, Race and Gender in Early Nineteenth-Century Britain." In *Nation, Empire, Colony: Historicizing Gender and Race*. Edited by Ruth R. Pierson, Nupur Chaudhuri, and Beth McAuley, 220–36. Bloomington: Indiana University Press, 1998.

Absi, Pascale. "Lifting the Layers of the Mountain's Petticoats: Mining and Gender in Potosi's Pachamama." Translated by Michele A. May. In *Mining Women: Gender in the Development of a Global Industry, 1670–2005*. Edited by Jaclyn J. Gier and Laurie Mercier, 58–70. New York: Palgrave Macmillan, 2006.

Adams, Henry. *The Education of Henry Adams*. 1918. Boston: Houghton Mifflin. In *Novels, Mont Saint Michel, The Education*, 715–1192. Reprint, New York: Library of America, 1983.

Adney, Tappan. *The Klondike Stampede*. New York: Harper & Brothers, 1900.

Agricola, Georgius. *De Re Metallica*. Translated by Herbert Clark and Lou Henry Hoover. New York: Dover Publications, 1950.

Aldington, Richard. *Portrait of a Rebel: The Life and Work of Robert Louis Stevenson*. London: Evans, 1957.

Allende, Isabel. *Daughter of Fortune*. Translated by Margaret Sayers Peden. New York: Harper, 1999.

Allmendinger, Blake. *The Ten Most Wanted: The New Western Literature*. London and New York: Routledge, 1998.

Altman, Robert. *McCabe and Mrs. Miller*. Directed by Robert Altman. Burbank, CA: Warner Brothers, 1971.

Anderson, Frederick. *Mark Twain: The Literary Heritage*. London: Routledge and Kegan Paul, 1971.

Arendt, Hannah. *The Origins of Totalitarianism*. London: Secker and Warburg, 1951.
Armstrong, Isabel. *Victorian Poetry*. London and New York: Routledge, 1993.
Auerbach, Jonathan. Introduction to *Northland Stories*, by Jack London, vii–xxiii. London and New York: Penguin, 1997.
Backhouse, Frances. *Women of the Klondike*. Vancouver: Whitecap Books, 1995.
Bacon, Francis. *De Augmentis. Complete Works 4*. Edited by J. Spedding, Robert Leslie Ellis, and Douglas Denon. London: Longmans, 1875.
Baguely, Colin. "*Germinal*: The Gathering Storm." In *The Cambridge Companion to Emile Zola*. Edited by Brian Nelson, 137–51. Cambridge: Cambridge University Press, 2007.
Bailey, Ron T. *Frozen in Silver: The Life and Frontier Photography of P. E. Larson*. Athens: Swallow Press / University of Ohio Press, 1998.
Bancroft, Caroline. "Folklore of the Central City District, Colorado." *California Folklore Quarterly* 4, no. 4 (October 1945): 315–42.
Bancroft, Hubert Howe. *California Inter Pocula: A Review of Some Classical Abnormities*. San Francisco: The Historical Company, 1888.
Barman, Jean. "Taming Aboriginal Sexuality: Gender, Power and Race in British Columbia, 1850–1900." In *Women and Gender in the American West*. Edited by Mary Ann Irwin and James F. Brooks, 210–34. Albuquerque: University of New Mexico Press, 2004.
Barnes, Daniel R. "Towards the Establishment of Principles for the Study of Folklore and Literature." *Southern Folklore Quarterly* 43 (1979): 5–16.
Barnett, Linda Diz. *Bret Harte: A Reference Guide*. Boston: G. K. Hall, 1980.
Barth, Gunther. *Instant Cities: Urbanization and the Rise of San Francisco and Denver*. New York and Oxford: Oxford University Press, 1975.
Bauman, Zygmunt. *Wasted Lives: Modernity and its Outcasts*. Cambridge: Polity Press, 2004.
Beavon, Keith. *Johannesburg: The Making and Shaping of the City*. Pretoria: University of South Africa, 2004.
Beebe, Lucius M. *Comstock Commotion: The Story of the Territorial Enterprise and the Virginia City News*. Stanford, CA: Stanford University Press, 1954.
Beer, Gillian. *The Romance*. London: Methuen, 1970.
Belasco, David. *The Girl of the Golden West: A Play in Four Acts*. 1905. Reprint, New York: Samuel French, 1933.
Bell, Peter. "The Fabric and Structure of Australian Mining Settlements." In *Social Approaches to an Industrial Past: The Archaeology and Anthropology of Mining*. Edited by A. Bernard Knapp, Vincent C. Pigott, and Eugenia W. Herbert, 27–38. London and New York: Routledge, 1994.
Berkove, Lawrence I. *The Fighting Horse of the Stanislaus: Stories and Essays by Dan De Quille*. Iowa City: University of Iowa Press, 1990.
———. "The Sagebrush School Reviewed." In *A Companion to the Regional Literatures of America*. Edited by Charles L. Crow, 324–43. Oxford: Blackwell, 2003.

———. *The Sagebrush Anthology: Literature from the Silver Age of the Old West.* Columbus: University of Missouri Press, 2006.
Berkove, Lawrence I., and Michael Kowalewski. "The Literature of the Mining Camps." In *Updating the Literary West.* Edited by Thomas J. Lyon et al., 99–114. Fort Worth: Texas Christian University Press, 1998.
Bernstein, Marvin D. *The Mexican Mining Industry, 1890–1950.* New York: SUNY Press, 1964.
Bersani, Leo. *A Future for Astyanax: Character and Desire in Literature.* Boston: Little, Brown and Co., 1984.
Berton, Pierre. *Klondike: The Life and Death of the Last Great Gold Rush.* London: W. H. Allen, 1960.
Bierce, Ambrose. "The Night-Doings at 'Deadman's.'" 1877. In *The Collected Works of Ambrose Bierce 3.* Reprint, New York and Washington: The Neale Publishing Co., 1910.
Blair, Edward. *Leadville: Colorado's Magic City.* Boulder, CO: Pruett Publishing, 1980.
Bolotin, Norman. *Klondike Lost: A Decade of Photographs by Kinsey and Kinsey.* Anchorage: Alaska Northwest Publishing Company, 1980.
———. *A Klondike Scrapbook: Ordinary People, Extraordinary Times.* Vancouver: Raincoast Books, 1987.
Botkin, B. A. *A Treasury of American Folklore: Stories, Ballads and Traditions of the People.* New York: Crown Publishers, 1944.
Branch, Edgar Marquess. *The Literary Apprenticeship of Mark Twain.* Urbana: University of Illinois Press, 1950.
Brechin, Gary. *Imperial San Francisco: Urban Power, Earthly Ruin.* Berkeley: University of California Press, 2006.
Brewis, Joanna, and Stephen Linstead. *Sex, Work and Sex Work: Eroticizing Organization.* London and New York: Routledge, 2000.
Brooks, Peter. *The Melodramatic Imagination: Balzac, Henry James and the Mode of Excess.* New Haven, CT: Yale University Press, 1995.
Brown, Ronald C. *Hard-Rock Miners: The Inter-Mountain West, 1860–1920.* College Station: Texas A&M University Press, 1979.
Browne, J. Ross. *A Peep at Washoe.* 1860. Reprint, Balboa Island, CA: Paisano Press, 1959.
Brunton, D. W. *Mining Engineering in Colorado.* San Francisco: n.p., 1915.
Bryant, Keith L. "Entering the Global Economy." In *The Oxford History of the American West.* Edited by Clyde A. Milner II, Carol A. O'Connor, and Martha A. Sandweiss, 195–235. New York and Oxford: Oxford University Press, 1994.
Bryden, Inga. *Reinventing King Arthur: The Arthurian Legends in Victorian Culture.* Aldershot, UK: Ashgate, 2009.
Butler, Anne M. *Daughters of Joy, Sisters of Misery: Prostitutes in the American West, 1865–90.* Urbana and Chicago: University of Illinois Press, 1985.
Campbell, Joseph. *The Hero with a Thousand Faces.* Princeton, NJ: Princeton University Press, 1949.

Canby, Henry Seidel. *The Short Story*. New York: Henry Holt, 1913.
Caron, James E. *Mark Twain: Unsanctified Reporter*. Columbus: University of Missouri Press, 2008.
Chan, Loren B. "The Chinese in Nevada: An Historical Survey, 1856-1970." *Nevada Historical Society Quarterly* 25, no. 4 (Winter 1982): 266-314.
Chase, Richard. *The American Novel and Its Tradition*. New York: Doubleday, 1957.
Clappe, Louise [pseud. Dame Shirley]. *The Shirley Letters from the California Mines, 1851-1852*. New York: Alfred Knopf, 1949.
Coates, Kenneth S. *Best Left as Indians: Native-White Relations in the Yukon Territory, 1840-1975*. Montreal: McGill-Queen's University Press, 1991.
———. Introduction to *The Klondike Stampede*, by Tappan Adney, xv-xxii. 1900. New York: Harper & Brothers. Reprint, Vancouver: University of British Columbia Press, 1994.
———, and William R. Morrison. *Land of the Midnight Sun: A History of the Yukon*. Edmonton, Alberta: Hurtig Publishers, 1988.
Connell, R. W. "Masculinities and Globalization." *Men and Masculinities* 1, no. 1 (July 1998): 3-23.
Conrad, Joseph. *Nostromo*. London: Harper & Brothers, 1904.
Conrad, Peter. *Imagining America*. London: Routledge, 1980.
Coontz, Stephanie. *The Social Origins of Private Life: American Families, 1600-1900*. London: Verso, 1988.
Cooper, Frederick. *Colonialism in Question: Theory, Knowledge, History*. Berkeley: University of California Press, 2005.
Cornford, Daniel. "'We all live more like brutes than miners': Labor and Capital in the Gold Rush." In *A Golden State: Mining and Economic Development in Gold-Rush California*. Edited by James J. Rawls and Richard J. Orsi, 78-104. Berkeley: University of California Press, 1999.
Crampton, Frank A. *Deep Enough: A Working Stiff in the Western Mine Camps*. Norman: University of Oklahoma Press, 1956.
Cronon, William. "Foreword: All That Glitters." In *The Nature of Gold: An Environmental History of the Klondike Gold Rush*, by Kathryn Morse, ix-xiii. Seattle: University of Washington Press, 2003.
———, George Miles, and Jay Gitlin. "Becoming West: Toward a New Meaning for Western History." In *Under an Open Sky: Rethinking America's Western Past*. Edited by William Cronon, George Miles, and Jay Gitlin, 3-27. New York: W. W. Norton & Company, 1992.
Cruikshank, Julie. "Images of Society in Klondike Gold Rush Narratives: Skookum Jim, and the Discovery of Gold." *Ethnohistory* 39, no. 1 (1992): 57-84.
———. "Discovery of Gold on the Klondike: Perspectives from Oral Tradition." In *Reading Beyond Worlds: Contexts for Native History*. Edited by Jennifer S. H. Brown and Elizabeth Vibert, 435-58. Peterborough, Ontario: Broadview, 1996.
———, with Angela Sidney, Kitty Smith, and Angela Ned. *Life Lived Like a Story: Life Stories of Three Yukon Native Elders*. Lincoln: University of Nebraska Press, 1990.

Cummins, Ella Sterling. *The Story of the Files: A Review of Californian Writers and Literature*. San Francisco: Cooperative Printing, 1893.

Curtis, Edward S. "The Rush to the Klondike over the Mountain Passes." *The Century Magazine* 55, no. 5 (March 1898): 692–97.

Dane, G. Ezra. Foreword to *Pen-Knife Sketches or Chips of the Old Block*, by Alonzo Delano, v–xiii. San Francisco: Grabhorn Press, 1934.

Davis, Richard Harding. *The West from a Car-Window*. New York: Harper & Brothers, 1892.

———. *Soldiers of Fortune*. 1897. New York: Charles Scribner's. Reprint, Toronto: Broadview, 2006.

Deadwood. Directed by David Milch. HBO/Paramount Television. New York: 2004–2006.

De Caro, Frank, and Rosan Augusta Jordan, eds. *Re-Situating Folklore: Folk Contexts and Twentieth Century Literature and Art*. Knoxville: University of Tennessee Press, 2004.

De Quille, Dan. *The Big Bonanza*. 1876. Hartford, CT: American Publishing Company. Reprint, New York: Alfred A. Knopf, 1947.

———. "Eyeless Fish That Live in Hot Water." *Territorial Enterprise*, February 19, 1876. In *The Fighting Horse of the Stanislaus: Stories and Essays by Dan De Quille*. Edited by Lawrence I. Berkove, 20. Reprint, Iowa City: University of Iowa Press, 1990.

———. "Jones' Opinion." *Cedar Falls Gazette*, January 17, 1862. In *The Fighting Horse of the Stanislaus: Stories and Essays by Dan De Quille*. Edited by Lawrence I. Berkove, 83. Reprint, Iowa City: University of Iowa Press, 1990.

———. "Letter from Dan De Quille." *Cedar Falls Gazette*, January 17, 1862. In *The Fighting Horse of the Stanislaus: Stories and Essays by Dan De Quille*. Edited by Lawrence I. Berkove, 83. Reprint, Iowa City: University of Iowa Press, 1990.

———. "Old Johnny Ranchero." *Territorial Enterprise*, November 18, 1877. In *The Fighting Horse of the Stanislaus: Stories and Essays by Dan De Quille*. Edited by Lawrence I. Berkove, 66–68. Reprint, Iowa City: University of Iowa Press, 1990.

———. "A Strange Monomania." *Territorial Enterprise*, September 13, 1874. In *The Fighting Horse of the Stanislaus: Stories and Essays by Dan De Quille*. Edited by Lawrence I. Berkove, 84–89. Reprint, Iowa City: University of Iowa Press, 1990.

———. "Torture Unutterable." *Territorial Enterprise*, October 14, 1877. In *The Fighting Horse of the Stanislaus: Stories and Essays by Dan De Quille*. Edited by Lawrence I. Berkove, 25–30. Reprint, Iowa City: University of Iowa Press, 1990.

———. *Washoe Rambles*. 1861. Reprint, Los Angeles: Westernlore Press, 1963.

De Voto, Bernard. *Mark Twain's America*. Boston: Houghton Mifflin, 1931.

Delano, Alonzo. *Pen Knife Sketches or Chips of the Old Block: A Series of Original Illustrated Letters Written by One of California's Pioneer Miners*. Sacramento, CA: Sacramento Daily Union Office, 1853.

———. *A Live Woman in the Mines*. 1857. New York: Samuel French. In *California Gold-Rush Plays*. Edited by Glenn Loney, 65–101. Reprint, New York: Performing Arts Journal Publications, 1983.

Desai, Anita. *The Zigzag Way*. London: Chatto and Windus, 2004.
Dickey, Rev. R. M. *Gold Fever: A Narrative of the Great Klondike Gold Rush, 1897–1899*. Murphy, OR: Castle Peak Editions, 1997.
Donaldson, Mike. *Time of Our Lives*. Sydney: Allen and Unwin, 1991.
Dorson, Richard M. *American Folklore and the Historian*. Chicago: University of Chicago Press, 1971.
Driscoll, Cynthia B. *One Woman's Gold Rush*. Kalamazoo, MI: Oakwoods Media, 1996.
Driscoll, Kerry. "The Fluid Identity of the 'Petrified Man.'" *American Literary Realism* 43, no. 3 (Spring 1990): 214–31.
Dryden, Linda. *Joseph Conrad and the Imperial Romance*. New York: St. Martin's Press, 1999.
Duckett, Margaret. "Bret Harte and the Indians of Northern California." *Huntington Library Quarterly* 18 (1954): 59–83.
———. "Bret Harte's Portrayal of Half Breeds." *American Literature* 2, no. 5 (May 1953): 193–212.
———. "The 'Crusade' of a Nineteenth-Century Liberal." *Tennessee Studies in Literature* 4 (1959): 109–20.
———. "Plain Language from Bret Harte." *Nineteenth-Century Fiction* 11 (March 1957): 241–60.
———. *Mark Twain and Bret Harte*. Norman: University of Oklahoma Press, 1964.
Dumett, Raymond E. *El Dorado in West Africa: The Gold-Mining Frontier, African Labor and Colonial Capitalism in the Gold Coast, 1875–1900*. Athens: Ohio University Press, 1998.
Dwyer, Richard A. and Richard E. Lingenfelter. *Lying on the Eastern Slope: James Townsend's Comic Journalism on the Mining Frontier*. Miami: University Press of Florida, 1984.
———. *Dan De Quille, the Washoe Giant: A Biography and Anthology*. Western Literature Series. Reno: University of Nevada Press, 1990.
Eagleton, Terry. *Exiles and Émigrés: Studies in Modern Literature*. London: Chatto and Windus, 1970.
Egan, Ferol. *Sand in a Whirlwind*. Reno: University of Nevada Press, 1972.
Ehrlich, Lea Kajati. "A Corking Adventure: Eugene Allen and the *Klondike Nugget*." *Alaska Journal* 13, no. 4 (Autumn 1983): 8–15.
Eliade, Mircea. *The Forge and the Crucible*. Translated by Stephen Corrin. London: Rider and Co., 1962.
Ellis, Anne. *The Life of an Ordinary Woman*. 1929. Boston: Houghton Mifflin. Reprint, Lincoln: University of Nebraska Press, 1980.
Emerson, Ralph Waldo. *The Conduct of Life*. Boston: Ticknor and Fields, 1860.
Emmons, David. *The Butte Irish: Class and Ethnicity in an American Mining Town*. Urbana and Chicago: University of Illinois Press, 1989.
Emrich, Duncan. *Comstock Bonanza*. New York: Vanguard Press, 1950.
Etulain, Richard W. *Re-Imagining the Modern American West: A Century of Fiction, History and Art*. Tucson: University of Arizona Press, 1996.

Fatout, Paul. *Ambrose Bierce in the Black Hills*. Norman: University of Oklahoma Press, 1956.

———. *Mark Twain in Virginia City*. Port Washington, NY: Kennikat Press, 1964.

Fender, Stephen. *Plotting the Golden West*. Cambridge: Cambridge University Press, 1981.

Ferguson, James. *Expectations of Modernity: Myths and Meanings of Urban Life in the Zambian Copperbelt*. Berkeley: University of California Press, 1999.

Fetherling, Douglas. *The Gold Crusades: A Social History of the Gold Rushes, 1849–1929*. Rev. ed. Toronto: University of Toronto Press, 1997.

Finn, Janet L. *Tracing the Veins of Copper, Culture and Community from Butte to Chuquicamata*. Berkeley: University of California Press, 1998.

Floyd, Janet. "A Sympathetic Misunderstanding? Mary Hallock Foote's Mining West." *Frontiers: A Journal of Women's Studies* 22, no. 3 (Special Issue: Women's West, 2001): 148–67.

Folsom, James. "Joaquin Miller." In *The New Encyclopedia of the American West*. Edited by Howard R. Lamar, 701–2. New Haven, CT: Yale University Press, 1998.

Foote, Mary Hallock. "In Exile." *Atlantic Monthly* 48 (August and September 1881): 184–92, 322–30.

———. *John Bodewin's testimony*. Boston: Ticknor & Co., 1886.

———. *The Last Assembly Ball and The Fate of a Voice*. Boston: Houghton Mifflin Company, 1889.

———. *The Led-Horse Claim*. Boston: Houghton Mifflin Company, 1883. Reprint, Upper Saddle River, NJ: Gregg Press, 1968.

Foucault, Michel. *The History of Sexuality I*. Translated by Robert Hurley. London: Allen Lane, 1978.

Francaviglia, Richard V. *Hard Places: Reading the Landscape of America's Historic Mining Districts*. Iowa City: University of Iowa Press, 1991.

Franklin, Wayne. Foreword to *Hard Places: Reading the Landscape of America's Historic Mining Districts*, by Richard V. Francaviglia, xvii–xx. Iowa City: University of Iowa Press, 1991.

Frederick, Richard. "Asahel Curtis and the Klondike Stampede." *Alaska Journal* 13, no. 2 (Spring 1983): 113–21.

Friedman, Albert B. "Folklore and Medieval Literature: A Look at Mythological Considerations." *Southern Folklore Quarterly* 43 (1979): 135–48.

Gair, Christopher. "The 'American Dickens': Mark Twain and Charles Dickens." In *A Companion to Mark Twain*. Edited by Louis J. Budd and Peter Messent, 141–56. Oxford: Blackwell, 2005.

Gally, James W. "Spirits." In *Comstock Bonanza*. Edited by Duncan Emrich, 149–57. New York: Vanguard Press, 1950.

Gardner, Joseph H. "Bret Harte and the Dickensian Mode in America." *Canadian Review of American Studies* 2, no. 2 (Fall 1971): 89–101.

Garland, Hamlin. *A Daughter of the Middle Border*. London: John Lane, 1921.

———. *Hesper*. New York: Harper, 1904.

———. *The Trail of the Goldseekers: A Record of Travel in Prose and Verse.* New York: MacMillan, 1899.
Garvin, John W. "Robert W. Service." In *Canadian Poets.* Toronto: McLelland and Stewart, 1916.
Georges, Robert A. "The General Concept of Legend: Some Assumptions to be Reexamined and Reassessed." In *American Folk Legend: A Symposium.* Edited by Wayland D. Hand, 1–20. Berkeley: University of California Press, 1971.
Gier, Jaclyn J., and Laurie Mercier. *Mining Women: Gender in the Development of a Global Industry, 1670–2005.* New York: Palgrave Macmillan, 2006.
Goldman, Marion S. *Gold Diggers and Silver Miners.* Ann Arbor: University of Michigan Press, 1981.
Gonzalez, Michael J. "My Brother's Keeper: Mexicans and the Hunt for Prosperity in California, 1848–2000." In *Riches for All: The California Gold Rush and the World.* Edited by Kenneth N. Owens, 118–41. Lincoln: University of Nebraska Press, 2002.
Goodman, David. "The 'El Dorados.'" *Journal of the West* 43, no.1 (Winter 2004): 14–20.
———. *Gold Seeking: Victoria and California in the 1850s.* Stanford, CA: Stanford University Press, 1994.
Goodman, Joseph. "The TRUMPET comes to Pickeye." 1939. San Francisco: Book Club of California. In *The Sagebrush Anthology: Literature from the Silver Age of the Old West.* Edited by Lawrence I. Berkove, 97–106. Reprint, Columbia: University of Missouri Press, 2006.
Graulich, Melody. "Legacy Profile: Mary Hallock Foote." *Legacy* 3, no. 2 (Fall 1986): 43–52.
Green, Archie. *Only a Miner: Studies in Recorded Coal-Mining Songs.* Urbana: University of Illinois Press, 1972.
Greenwald, Maggie. *The Ballad of Little Jo.* Directed by Maggie Greenwald. Los Angeles: New Line Cinema/Polygram, 1993.
Greever, William S. *The Bonanza West: The Story of the Western Mining Rushes, 1848–1900.* Norman: University of Oklahoma Press, 1963.
Griswold, Don L., and Jean Harvey Griswold. *The Carbonate Camp Called Leadville.* Denver: University of Denver Press, 1951.
———. *History of Leadville and Lake County, Colorado.* 2 vols. Denver: Colorado Historical Society and University Press of Colorado, 1996.
Gurian, Jay. "Literary Convention and the Mining Romance." *Journal of the West* 5, no. 1 (1966): 106–14.
Hadley, Elaine. *Melodramatic Tactics: Theatricalized Dissent in the English Marketplace, 1800–1885.* Stanford, CA: Stanford University Press, 1995.
Haggard, H. Rider. *King Solomon's Mines.* London: Cassell & Co., 1881.
Hamer, David. *New Towns in the New World: Images and Perceptions of the Nineteenth-Century Urban Frontier.* New York: Columbia University Press, 1990.
Hand, Wayland D. "California Miners' Folklore: Below Ground." *California Folklore Quarterly* 1, no. 2 (April 1942): 127–53.
———. "Notes and Queries: The Fatal Last Shift etc." *California Folklore Quarterly* 5, no. 2 (April 1946): 201–5.

Hardesty, Donald L. *The Archaeology of Mining and Miners: A View from the Silver State*. Special Publication Series No. 6. Pleasant Hill, CA: Society for Historical Archaeology, 1988.

———. "Power and the Industrial Mining Community in the American West." In *Social Approaches to an Industrial Past: The Archaeology and Anthropology of Mining*. Edited by A. Bernard Knapp, Vincent C. Pigott, and Eugenia W. Herbert, 81–96. London and New York: Routledge, 1998.

Hart, Fred. H. *The Sazerac Lying Club: A Nevada Book*. San Francisco: Henry Keller & Co., 1878.

Hart, James D. Introduction to *From Scotland to Silverado*, by Robert Louis Stevenson. Cambridge, MA: Belknap Press of Harvard University Press, 1966.

Harte, Bret. *Condensed Novels and Other Papers*. New York: Carleton and Co., 1867.

———. "The Idyl at Red Gulch." *Overland Monthly* 3, no. 6 (December 1869). Reprint, *Selected Stories and Sketches*, 50–59. Oxford: Oxford World's Classics, 1995.

———. "Miggles." *Overland Monthly* 2, no. 6 (June 1869). Reprint, *Selected Stories and Sketches*, 29–39. Oxford: Oxford World's Classics, 1995.

———. "Mliss." *The Luck of Roaring Camp and Other Sketches*. 1870. Boston: Fields, Osgood and Co. *Selected Stories and Sketches*. Reprint, Oxford: Oxford World's Classics, 1995.

———. *Mrs Skaggs's Husbands and Other Stories*. London: Routledge, 1873.

———. "The Outcasts of Poker Flat." *Overland Monthly* (January 1869). Reprint, *Selected Stories and Sketches*, 18–28. Oxford: Oxford World's Classics, 1995.

———. "Plain Language from Truthful James." *Overland Monthly* 5, no. 3 (September 1870): 287–88.

———. "The Rise of the Short Story." *Cornhill Magazine* 15 (July 1899), 1–8.

———. "Tennessee's Partner." *Overland Monthly* 3, no. 4 (October 1869). Reprint, *Selected Stories and Sketches*, 40–49. Oxford: Oxford World's Classics, 1995.

Hawthorne, Nathaniel. *The Scarlet Letter*. 1850. Boston: Ticknor, Reed and Fields. Reprint, Boston: James R. Osgood and Co., 1876.

Hayes, A. A. "Grubstakes and Millions." *Harper's New Monthly Magazine* 60, no. 358 (February 1880): 380–97.

Hays, John Hammond. *The Autobiography of John Hays Hammond*. New York: Farrar and Rinehart Inc., 1935.

Hedrick, Joan D. *Solitary Comrade: Jack London and His Work*. Chapel Hill: University of North Carolina Press, 1982.

Herbert, Eugenia V. "Mining as a Microcosm in Pre-colonial Sub-Saharan Africa: An Overview." In *Social Approaches to an Industrial Past: The Archaeology and Anthropology of Mining*. Edited by A. Bernard Knapp, Vincent C. Pigott, and Eugenia W. Herbert, 138–54. London and New York: Routledge, 1998.

Herzog, Werner. *Fitzcarraldo*. Directed by Werner Herzog. Vienna, Austria: Herzog Filmproducktion/ZDF, 1982.

Hirata, Lucie Cheng. "Free, Indentured, Enslaved: Chinese Prostitutes in the Nineteenth-Century America." *Signs* 5, no. 1 (Autumn 1979): 3–29.

Hitchcock, Mary E. *Two Women in the Klondike*. New York: Putnam, 1899.
Hood, Thomas. Introduction to *The Luck of Roaring Camp and Other Stories*, by Bret Harte, i–xix. London: George Routledge, 1887.
Houston, James D. "The Far West: Introduction." In *A Literary History of the American West*. Compiled by the Western Literature Association, 326–38. Fort Worth: Texas Christian University Press, 1987.
Howells, William Dean. "Reviews and Literary Notices." *Atlantic Monthly* 25 (May 1870): 633–35.
———. "Editor's Study." *Harper's Monthly* 72, no. 432 (May 1886): 972–76.
———. "Mark Twain: An Inquiry." *North American Review* (February 1901). In *William D. Howells as Critic*. Edited by Edwin Cady. 337–51. London and Boston: Routledge and Kegan Paul, 1973.
Hughes, Langston. "In the Johannesburg Mines." 1928. In *The Collected Poems of Langston Hughes*. Edited by Arnold Rampersand, 43. New York: Vintage Books, 1994.
Hulse, James W. *The Silver State*. 2nd ed. Reno: University of Nevada Press, 1991.
Hurtado, Albert L. *Indian Survival on the Californian Frontier*. New Haven, CT: Yale University Press, 1988.
———. "When Strangers Met: Sex and Gender on Three Frontiers." In *Writing the Range: Race, Class and Culture in the Women's West*. Edited by Elizabeth Jameson and Susan Armitage, 122–42. Norman: University of Oklahoma Press, 1997.
Ibsen, Henrik. *John Gabriel Borkman*. Translated by William Archer. London: Heinemann, 1897.
Ingersoll, Ernest. "The Camp of Carbonates." *Scribner's Monthly* 18, no. 6 (October 1879): 801–24.
———. *The Silver Caves: A Mining Story*. New York: Dodd, Mead and Company, 1890.
Issler, Anne Roller. *Our Mountain Heritage: Silverado and Robert Louis Stevenson*. Stanford, CA: Stanford University Press, 1950.
Jackson, Helen Hunt. *Bits of Travel at Home*. Boston: Roberts Brothers, 1878.
———. *A Century of Dishonor*. New York: Harper & Brothers, 1881.
James, Ronald M. *The Roar and the Silence*. Reno: University of Nevada Press, 1998.
Jameson, Elizabeth. *All That Glitters: Class, Conflict and Community in Cripple Creek*. Bloomington: University of Illinois Press, 1998.
Jeffreys, Sheila. *The Idea of Prostitution*. North Melbourne, Victoria: Spinifex Press, 2008.
Johnson, Lee Ann. *Mary Hallock Foote*. Boston: Twayne, 1980.
Johnson, Susan Lee. *Roaring Camp: The Social World of the Californian Gold Rush*. New York: W. W. Norton & Company, 2000.
Jones, Harvey L. "The Hessian Party." In *Art of the Gold Rush*. Edited by Janice T. Driesbach, Harvey L. Jones, and Katherine Church Holland, 47–64. Berkeley: Oakland Museum of California, Crocker Art Museum, and University of California Press, 1998.
———. "Sentiment and Nostalgia." In *Art of the Gold Rush*. Edited by Janice T. Driesbach, Harvey L. Jones, and Katherine Church Holland, 101–16. Berkeley: Oakland Museum of California, Crocker Art Museum, and University of California Press, 1998.

———. "Souvenirs of the Mother Lode." In *Art of the Gold Rush*. Edited by Janice T. Driesbach, Harvey L. Jones, and Katherine Church Holland, 65–76. Berkeley: Oakland Museum of California, Crocker Art Museum, and University of California Press, 1998.

Josephy, Alvin M. *The Civil War in the American West*. New York: Knopf, 1991.

Kaplan, Amy. "Nation, Region and Empire." In *The Columbia History of the American Novel*. Edited by Emory Elliott, 240–66. New York: Columbia University Press, 1991.

———. "Romancing the Empire: The Embodiment of American Masculinity in the Popular Historical Novel of the 1890s." *American Literary History* 2, no. 4 (Winter 1990): 659–90.

Katz, Elaine N. "Revisiting the Origins of the Industrial Color Bar in the Witwatersrand Gold Mining Industry, 1891–1899." *Journal of South African Studies* 25, no. 1 (March 1999): 73–97.

Katz, Wendy. *Rider Haggard and the Fiction of Empire: A Critical Study of British Imperial Fiction*. Cambridge: Cambridge University Press, 1987.

Kennedy, Dave. "The Frontier in South African History." *Journal of the West* 34, no. 4 (October 1995): 23–31.

Kernan, Alvin B. "Aggression and Satire: Art Considered as a Form of Biological Adaptation." In *Literary Theory and Structure: Essays in Honor of William K. Wimsatt*. Edited by Frank Brady, John Palmer, and Martin Price, 115–29. New Haven, CT: Yale University Press, 1973.

Killick, David. "On the Value of Mixed Methods in Studying Mining Communities." In *Social Approaches to an Industrial Past: The Archaeology and Anthropology of Mining*. Edited by A. Bernard Knapp, Vincent C. Pigott, and Eugenia W. Herbert, 279–90. London and New York: Routledge, 1998.

King, Clarence. *Mountaineering in the Sierra Nevada*. 1872. Reprint, New York: Charles Scribner's Sons, 1901.

King, Joseph E. *A Mine to Make a Mine: Financing the Colorado Mining Industry, 1859–1902*. College Station: Texas A&M University Press, 1977.

Klein, Barbro. "Folklore." In *Folklore: An Encyclopedia of Beliefs, Customs, Tales, Music and Art 1*. Edited by Thomas A. Green, 331–37. Santa Barbara, CA: ABC-CLIO, 1997.

Klinck, Carl F. *Robert Service: A Biography*. New York: Dodd, Mead and Company, 1976.

———. "Robert Service." In *Dictionary of Literary Biography: Canadian Writers, 1890–1920*. Edited by Carl F. Klinck and W. H. New, 343–48. Detroit, MI: Gale, 1990.

Klubock, Thomas M. "Working-Class Masculinity, Middle-Class Morality, and Labor Politics in the Chilean Copper Mines." *Journal of Social History* 30, no. 2 (Winter 1996): 435–63.

Knofer, Randall. *Acting Naturally: Mark Twain in the Culture of Performance*. Berkeley: University of California Press, 1995.

Kollin, Susan. *Nature's State: Imagining Alaska as the Last Frontier*. Chapel Hill: University of North Carolina, 2001.
Kowalewski, Michael, ed. *Gold Rush: A Literary Exploration*. Berkeley, CA: Heyday Books, 1997.
———. "Romancing the Gold Rush: The Literature of the California Frontier." *California History* 79, no. 2 (Summer 2000): 204–25.
Ladue, Joseph. *Klondyke Nuggets*. New York: American Technical Book Company, 1897.
Laite, Julia Ann. "Historical Perspectives on Industrial Development, Mining and Prostitution." *Historical Journal* 52, no. 3 (September 2009): 739–61.
Larsh, Ed B., and Robert Nichols. *Leadville, U.S.A.* Boulder, CO: Johnson Books, 1951.
Law, John. "After Action Network Theory: Complexity, Naming and Topology." In *Actor Network Theory and After*. Edited by John Law and John Hassard, 1–14. Oxford: Blackwell, 1999.
Lawrence, Susan. "Gender and Community Structure on Australian Colonial Goldfields." In *Social Approaches to an Industrial Past: The Archaeology and Anthropology of Mining*. Edited by A. Bernard Knapp, Vincent C. Pigott, and Eugenia W. Herbert, 39–58. London and New York: Routledge, 1998.
Lawson, Henry. "An Old Mate of Your Father's." 1889. *The Penguin Henry Lawson*. Reprint, Harmondsworth, UK: Penguin, 1986.
Levine, Phillipa. "Sexuality and Empire." In *At Home with the Empire: Metropolitan Culture in the Imperial World*. Edited by Catherine Hall and Sonya O. Rose, 122–42. Cambridge: Cambridge University Press, 2006.
Lewis, Marvin. "Humor of the Western Regions." *Western Folklore* 14, no. 2 (April 1955): 92–97.
Lewis, Oscar. Introduction to *The Big Bonanza*, by Dan De Quille, vii–xli. New York: Alfred Knopf, 1947.
———. *The Life and Times of the Virginia City Enterprise*. Ashland, OR: L. Osborne, 1971.
Lillard, Richard G. "Dan De Quille: Comstock Reporter and Humorist." *Pacific Historical Review* 13 (1944): 251–59.
Limbaugh, Ronald H. "Making Old Tools Work Better: Pragmatic Adaptation and Innovation in Gold-Rush Technology." In *A Golden State: Mining and Economic Development in Gold-Rush California*. Edited by James J. Rawls and Richard J. Orsi, 24–51. Berkeley: University of California Press, 1999.
Limerick, Patricia Nelson. "The Gold Rush and the Shaping of the American West." *Something in the Soil: Legacies and Reckonings in the New West*. New York: W. W. Norton & Company, 2001.
———. *The Legacy of Conquest*. New York: Norton, 1987.
Lingenfelter, Richard E. *The Hardrock Miners: A History of the Mining Labor Movement in the American West, 1863–1893*. Berkeley: University of California Press, 1974.
London, Jack. "The White Silence." *Overland Monthly* 33, no. 194 (February 1899): 138–42. Reprint, *Northland Stories*, 1–10. London: Penguin Books, 1997.

———. "To the Man on the Trail." *Overland Monthly* 33, no. 193 (January 1899): 36–40. Reprint, *Northland Stories*, 43–51. London: Penguin Books, 1997.
Loomis, C. Grant. "Bret Harte's Folklore." *Western Folklore* 15, no. 1 (Winter 1956): 19–22.
Lord, Eliot. *Comstock Mines and Miners*. Washington, D.C.: Government Printing Office, 1883.
Lyman, George D. *The Saga of the Comstock Lode*. New York: Scribner's, 1934.
Lynch, Martin. *Mining in World History*. London: Reaktion Books, 2004.
MacDonald, George. *The Princess and Curdie*. London: Chatto and Windus, 1883. Reprint, Oxford: Oxford World Classics, 1990.
Mack, Effie Mona. *Mark Twain in Nevada*. New York: Scribner's, 1947.
Mackay, James. *Vagabond of Verse: Robert Service: A Biography*. Edinburgh and London: Mainstream Publishing, 1995.
Mann, Ralph E. *After the Gold Rush: Society in Grass Valley and Nevada City, 1849–1870*. Stanford, CA: Stanford University Press, 1982.
Marks, Paula Mitchell. *Precious Dust: The American Gold Rush Era*. New York: William Morrow, 1994.
Mayer, Melanie J. *Klondike Women*. Athens, OH: Swallow Press, 1989.
McCarl, Robert. "Occupational Folklife/Folklore." In *Folklore: An Encyclopedia of Beliefs, Customs, Tales, Music and Art*. Edited by Thomas A. Green, 596–604. 2 vols. Santa Barbara, CA: ABC-CLIO, 1997.
McClintock, Anne. *Imperial Leather: Race, Gender and Sexuality in the Colonial Context*. New York and London: Routledge, 1995.
McClure, John A. *Late Imperial Romance*. London: Verso, 1994.
McCullough, Joseph B. *Hamlin Garland*. Boston: G. K. Hall, 1978.
McElrath, Joseph R., Jr., and Jesse S. Crisler. *Frank Norris: A Life*. Urbana: University of Illinois Press, 2006.
Melville, Herman. *Moby-Dick, or The Whale*. 1851. New York: Harper & Brothers. Reprint, London: Constable and Co, 1922.
Merchant, Carolyn. *The Death of Nature: Women, Ecology and the Scientific Movement*. San Francisco: Harper and Row, 1980.
Michelson, Bruce. *Printer's Devil: Mark Twain and the American Publishing Revolution*. Berkeley: University of California Press, 2006.
Mighetto, Lisa, and Marica Montgomery. *Hard Drive to the Klondike: Promoting Seattle during the Gold Rush*. Seattle: University of Washington Press, 2002.
Miller, Darlis A. *Mary Hallock Foote: Author-Illustrator of the American West*. Norman: University of Oklahoma Press, 2002.
Miller, Joaquin. *First Fam'lies in the Sierras*. Chicago: McClurg and Co., 1876.
Milton, John R. *The Novel of the American West*. Lincoln: University of Nebraska Press, 1980.
Mitchell, Lee Clark. "Verbally Roughing It: The West of Words." *Nineteenth-Century Literature* 44, no. 1 (June 1989): 67–92.
Moehring, Eugene P. "The Civil War and Town Founding in the Inter-Mountain West." *Western Historical Quarterly* 28 (Autumn 1997): 317–41.

———. *Urbanism and Empire in the Far West, 1840–1890*. Reno: University of Nevada Press, 2004.
Moodie, T. Dunbar. *Going for Gold: Men, Mines and Migration*. Berkeley: University of California Press, 1994.
Moore, T. Inglis. *Social Patterns in Australian Literature*. Sydney: Angus and Robertson, 1971.
Morgan, Murray. *One Man's Gold Rush: A Klondike Album*. Seattle: University of Washington Press, 1995.
Morrell, William P. *The Gold Rushes*. London: Adam and Charles Black, 1940.
Morrow, Patrick D. *Bret Harte, Literary Critic*. Bowling Green, OH: Bowling Green State University Popular Press, 1979.
Morse, Kathryn. *The Nature of Gold: An Environmental History of the Klondike Gold Rush*. Seattle: University of Washington Press, 2003.
Muir, John. *The Mountains of California*. In *Nature Writings*. New York: Library of America, 1992.
Mulford, Prentice. "Justifiable Fiction." *Overland Monthly* 11, no. 1 (July 1873): 39–42.
———. "Peleg Cowcopper." *The Californian*, August 17, 1867. Reprint, *Prentice Mulford's California Sketches*, 8–14. San Francisco: Book Club of California, 1935.
———. *Prentice Mulford's California Sketches*. Edited with an introduction by Franklin Walker. San Francisco: Book Club of California, 1935.
———. *Prentice Mulford's Story: Life on Land and Sea*. New York: F. J. Needham, 1889.
Mumford, Lewis. *Technics and Civilization*. New York: Harcourt, Brace and Co., 1934.
Murphy, Clare. *Gold Rush Women*. Anchorage: Alaska North-West Books, 1997.
Murray, Jean. *Music of the Alaska-Klondike Gold Rush: Songs and History*. Fairbanks: University of Alaska Press, 1999.
Nash Smith, Henry, ed. *Mark Twain of the Enterprise*. Berkeley: University of California Press, 1957.
Norris, Frank. "A Hero of Tomato Can. By B—T H—TE." *Wave* 16 (December 18, 1897), 5–7. In *The Literary Criticism of Frank Norris*. Edited by Donald Pizer, 174–76. Reprint, Austin: University of Texas Press, 1964.
———. *McTeague: A Story of San Francisco*. New York: Doubleday and McClure Co., 1899.
———. 1896. "Zola as a Romantic Writer." *Wave* 15. In *The Literary Criticism of Frank Norris*. Edited by Donald Pizer, 71–72. Reprint, Austin: University of Texas, 1964.
O'Connor, Richard. *Ambrose Bierce: A Biography*. London: Victor Gollancz, 1968.
Onion, Rebecca. "Sled Dogs of the Arctic North: On Masculinity, Whiteness and Human Freedom." In *Animals and Agency: An Interdisciplinary Exploration*. Edited by Sarah E. MacFarland and Ryan Hediger, 129–55. Leiden and Boston: Brill, 2009.
Page, Alfred. *Klondike Days and Yukon Travel in 1898*. 1898. Reprint, Phoenix: Ruby Wine Sheldon, 2006.
Paine, Albert Bigelow. *Mark Twain, A Biography: The Personal and Literary Life of Samuel Langhorne Clemens*. Vol. 1. New York: Harper & Brothers, 1912.
Palmer, Louise M. "How We Live in Nevada." *Overland Monthly* 2, no. 5 (May 1869): 457–62.

Parker, Watson. *Gold in the Black Hills.* 1966. Lincoln: University of Nebraska Press. Reprint, Lincoln: Bison Books, 1982.
Pattee, Fred Lewis. *The Development of the Short Story.* New York: Harper's 1923.
Paul, Rodman W. *California Gold: The Beginning of Mining in the Far West.* Cambridge, MA: Harvard University Press, 1947.
———. "Gold and Silver Rushes." In *The New Encyclopedia of the American West.* Edited by Howard R. Lamar, 433–37. New Haven, CT: Yale University Press, 1998.
———. Introduction to *A Victorian Gentlewoman in the Far West: The Reminiscences of Mary Hallock Foote.* San Marino, CA: Huntington Library, 1972.
———. *Mining Frontiers of the Far West, 1848–1880.* 1963. Rev. ed. Reprint, Albuquerque: University of New Mexico Press, 2001.
———. "Mining Law." In *The New Encyclopedia of the American West.* Edited by Howard R. Lamar, 707–8. New Haven, CT: Yale University Press, 1998.
———. "Mining, Metals." In *The New Encyclopedia of the American West.* Edited by Howard R. Lamar, 702–7. New Haven, CT: Yale University Press, 1998.
———. "In Search of 'Dame Shirley.'" *Pacific Historical Review* 33, no. 2 (May 1964): 127–64.
Paul, Wolfgang. *Mining Lore: An Illustrated Composition and Documentary Compilation with an Emphasis on the Spirit and History of Mining.* Portland, OR: Morris Print Co., 1970.
Peck, Gunther. "Manly Gambles: The Politics of Risk on the Comstock Lode, 1860–1880." In *Across the Great Divide: Cultures of Manhood in the American West.* Edited by Matthew Basso, Laura McCall, and Dee Garceau, 73–96. New York and London: Routledge, 2001.
Peterson, Richard H. *The Bonanza Kings: The Social Origins and Business Behavior of Western Mining Entrepreneurs, 1870–1900.* 2nd ed. Norman: University of Oklahoma Press, 1991.
Petrik, Paula. *No Step Backward: Women and Family on the Rocky Mountain Frontier, Helena Montana, 1865–1900.* Helena: Montana Historical Society Press, 1987.
Pfaffenberger, Bryan. "Mining Communities, Chaînes Opératoires and Sociotechnical Systems." In *Social Approaches to an Industrial Past: The Archaeology and Anthropology of Mining.* Edited by A. Bernard Knapp, Vincent C. Pigott, and Eugenia W. Herbert, 291–300. London and New York: Routledge, 1998.
Phillips, Richard. "Histories of Sexuality and Imperialism: What's the Use?" *History Workshop Journal* 63, no. 1 (Spring 2007): 136–53.
Pike, David. *Metropolis on the Styx: The Underworlds of Modern Urban Culture, 1880–2001.* Ithaca, NY: Cornell University Press, 2007.
———. *Passage Through Hell: Modernist Descents, Medieval Underworlds.* Ithaca, NY: Cornell University Press, 1997.
Pizer, Donald. Introduction to *The Literary Criticism of Frank Norris*, i–xxvi. Austin: University of Texas Press, 1964.

Poggie, John J., Jr., and Carl Gersuny. "Risk and Ritual: An Interpretation of Fisherman's Folklore in a New England Community." *Journal of American Folklore* 85, no. 335 (1972): 66–72.
Polanski, Roman, and Gerard Brach. *Tess*. Directed by Roman Polanski. New York: Penn Productions, 1979.
Porsild, Charlene. *Gamblers and Dreamers: Women, Men and Community in the Klondike*. Vancouver: University of British Columbia Press, 1998.
Preston, Cathy Lynn, ed. *Folklore, Literature and Cultural Theory: Collected Essays*. New York: Garland, 1995.
Pykett, Lynne. "Reading the Periodical Press: Text and Context." In *Investigating Victorian Journalism*. Edited by Laurel Brake, Aled Jones, and Lionel Madden, 3–18. Basingstoke, UK: MacMillan, 1990.
Rastall, B. M. *The Cripple Creek Strike of 1893*. Colorado Springs: Colorado College Studies, 1905.
Rawls, James J. Preface to *A Golden State: Mining and Economic Development in Gold-Rush California*. Edited by James J. Rawls and Richard J. Orsi, 1–23. Berkeley: University of California Press, 1999.
Rawls, James J., and Richard J. Orsi, eds. *A Golden State: Mining and Economic Development in Gold-Rush California*. Berkeley: University of California Press, 1999.
Rickard, T. A. *Interviews with Mining Engineers*. San Francisco: Mining and Scientific Press, 1922.
Ridge, John Rollin [Yellow Bird]. *The Life and Adventures of Joaquin Murieta: The Celebrated Californian Bandit*. 1854. San Francisco: W. B. Cooke. Reprint, Norman: University of Oklahoma Press, 1955.
Robbins, William G. *Colony and Empire: The Capitalist Transformation of the American West*. Lawrence: University Press of Kansas, 1994.
———. "The Plundered Province Thesis." *Pacific Historical Review* 55, no. 4 (November 1986): 577–97.
———. "Western History: A Dialectic on the Modern Condition." *Western Historical Quarterly* 2, no. 4 (November 1989): 429–50.
Roberts, Brian. *American Alchemy: The Gold Rush and Middle-Class Culture*. Chapel Hill: University of North Carolina Press, 2000.
Rogers, J. *The New Rush and Other Poems and Songs*. Melbourne: Wilson and McKinnon, 1864.
Rohrbough, Malcolm J. *Aspen: The History of a Silver Mining Town, 1879–93*. New York and Oxford: Oxford University Press, 1986.
———. *Days of Gold: The California Gold Rush and the American Nation*. Berkeley: University of California Press, 1997.
———. "Mining the Nineteenth Century American West." In *A Companion to the American West*. Edited by William Deverell, 113–29. Oxford: Blackwell, 2004.

Rosenberg, Bruce A. *Folklore and Literature: Sibling Rivals*. Knoxville: University of Tennessee Press, 1991.

Rosselet, Jeanne. "First Reactions to *Les Misérables* in the US." *Modern Language Notes* 67, no. 1 (January 1952): 39–43.

"Roughing It or The Innocents at Home." *Manchester Guardian*. 1872. In *Mark Twain: The Critical Heritage*. Edited by Frederick Anderson, 46–47. Reprint, London: Routledge and Kegan Paul, 1971.

Rowland, Volney. *Letters from the Klondike*. Edited by Helen Rowland Kelly and Kathryn Graves Yoder. Sacramento, CA: Yukon Publications, 2002.

Saunders, Christopher, and Iain R. Smith. "Southern Africa, 1795–1910." In *The Oxford History of the British Empire*, vol. 3. Edited by Andrew Porter, 597–623. Oxford: Oxford University Press, 1999.

Scharnhorst, Gary. *Bret Harte*. New York: Twayne, 1992.

———. *Bret Harte: Opening the Literary West*. Norman: University of Oklahoma Press, 2000.

———. "Bret Harte and the Literary Construction of the American West." In *A Companion to the Regional Literatures of America*. Edited by Charles L. Crow, 479–95. Oxford: Blackwell, 2003.

———. *Selected Letters of Bret Harte*. Norman: University of Oklahoma Press, 1997.

Seelye, John. Introduction to *Treasure Island*, by Robert Louis Stevenson, vii–xxvi. London: Penguin Books, 1999.

———. *War Games: Richard Harding Davis and the New Imperialism*. Amherst: University of Massachusetts Press, 2003.

Seidel, Michael. *The Satiric Inheritance*. Princeton, NJ: Princeton University Press, 1979.

Sekula, Allan. "Photography between Labor and Capital." In *Mining Photographs and Other Pictures, 1948–1968*. Edited by Benjamin H. D. Buchloh and Robert Wilkie, 193–268. Halifax, Nova Scotia: The Press of Nova Scotia College, 1983.

Service, Robert W. *Songs of a Sourdough*. Toronto: William Briggs, 1907.

Shape, William. *Faith of Fools: A Journal of the Klondike Rush*. Pullman: Washington State University Press, 1998.

Shinn, Charles Howard. *Mining Camps: A Study in American Frontier Government*. 1884. New York: Scribner's. Reprint, New York: Harper and Row, 1965.

Simmons, Alexy. "Ladies of the Night and Men of the Day." In *Social Approaches to an Industrial Past: The Archaeology and Anthropology of Mining*. Edited by A. Bernard Knapp, Vincent C. Pigott, and Eugenia W. Herbert, 59–79. London and New York: Routledge, 1998.

Smethwick, Colin. *Zola: Germinal*. Glasgow: University of Glasgow French and German Publications, 1996.

Smith, Duane A. "Colorado's Urban-Mining Safety Valve." *Colorado Magazine* 48 (1971): 299–318.

———. *Mining America: The Industry and the Environment, 1800–1980*. Lawrence: University Press of Kansas, 1987.

———. *Rocky Mountain Mining Camps: The Urban Frontier*. Niwot: University Press of Colorado, 1992.

———. "The San Juaner: A Computerized Portrait." *Colorado Magazine* 52, no. 2 (Spring 1975): 137–52.
Smith, Grant H. "The History of the Comstock Lode, 1850–1920." *University of Nevada Bulletin* 37, no. 3 (Geology and Mining Series, July 1943): 241–43.
Snyder, Gary. "Milton by Firelight." 1955. *Riprap and Cold Mountain Poems*. San Francisco: Four Seasons Foundation, 1965.
Spence, Clark C. *British Investment and the American Mining Frontier, 1860–1901*. Ithaca, NY: Cornell University Press, 1958.
Stahl, Sandra K. D. "Style in Oral and Written Narratives." *Southern Folklore Quarterly* 43 (1979): 29–62.
Starr, Kevin. *Americans and the California Dream, 1850–1915*. New York: Oxford University Press, 1973.
Stegner, Wallace. *Angle of Repose*. 1971. Harmondsworth, UK: Penguin, 1992.
———. "History, Myth and the Western Writer." In *The Sound of Mountain Water*, 188–230. Garden City, NY: Doubleday, 1969.
———, ed. *Selected American Prose, 1841–1900: The Realistic Movement*. New York: Holt, Rinehart and Winston, 1958.
Stein, Roger B. *Ruskin and Aesthetic Thought in America, 1840–1900*. Cambridge, MA: Harvard University Press, 1967.
Steinberg, Mark B. *Proletarian Imagination: Self, Modernity and the Sacred in Russia, 1910–1925*. Ithaca, NY: Cornell University Press, 2002.
Stevenson, Robert Louis. *From Scotland to Silverado*. Edited by James D. Hard. Cambridge, MA: Belknap Press of Harvard University Press, 1966.
———. *The Silverado Squatters*. London and Boston: Chatto & Windus and Roberts Bros., 1884.
———. *Treasure Island*. London: Cassell, 1883.
Stewart, George R. *Bret Harte: Argonaut and Exile*. Boston: Houghton Mifflin, 1931.
Stoler, Ann Laura. "Tense and Tender Ties: The Politics of Comparison." *Journal of American History* 88, no. 3 (December 2001): 829–65.
Stoneley, Peter. "Rewriting the Gold Rush: Twain, Harte and Homosociality." *Journal of American Studies* 30, no. 2 (August 1996): 189–209.
Tangherlini, Timothy R. "'It Happened Not Too Far From Here': A Survey of Legend Theory and Characterization." *Western Folklore* 49, no. 4 (October 1990): 371–90.
Tenfelde, Klaus. "The Miners' Community and the Community of Mining Historians." In *Towards a Social History of Mining in the Nineteenth and Twentieth Centuries*. Edited by Klaus Tenfelde, 1201–15. Papers presented to the International Mining History Congress, Bochum, September 3–7, 1989. München: Beck, 1992.
Tennyson, Alfred. "The Lotos-Eaters." In *Poems*. London: E. Moxon, 1832.
Thelan, David. "Of Audiences, Borderlands, and Comparisons: Toward the Internationalization of American History." *Journal of American History* 79, no. 2 (September 1992): 432–62.
Thomas, Jeffrey F. "Bret Harte and the Power of Sex." *Western American Literature* 8, no. 3 (Fall 1973): 91–109.

Townsend, Leroy S. *The Alaska Gold Rush Letters and Photographs of Leroy S. Townsend, 1898-99*. Edited by Peggy Jean Townsend, Patricia Roppel, and Art Peterson. Murphy, OR: Castle Peak, 1999.

Trachtenberg, Alan. *Reading American Photographs: Images as History, Mathew Brady to Walker Evans*. New York: Hill and Wang, 1989.

Tremain, Rose. *The Colour*. London: Chatto and Windus, 2003.

Twain, Mark. "A Bloody Massacre near Carson." *Territorial Enterprise*, October 28, 1863. In *The Sagebrush Anthology: Literature from the Silver Age of the Old West*. Edited by Lawrence I. Berkove, 20-22. Reprint, Columbia: University of Missouri Press, 2006.

———. *The Celebrated Jumping Frog of Calaveras County and Other Sketches*. New York: C. H. Webb, 1867.

———. *Roughing It*. New York: Harper & Brothers, 1872.

Urdahl, Thomas K. Introduction to *The Cripple Creek Strike of 1893*, by B. M. Rastall, i–ii. Colorado Springs: Colorado College Studies, 1905.

Utley, Robert M. *The Indian Frontier of the American West, 1846-90*. Albuquerque: University of New Mexico Press, 1984.

Van Onselon, Charles. *Studies in the Social and Economic History of the Witwatersrand, 1886-1914: New Babylon*. London: Longman, 1982.

Victor, Frances Fuller. *The New Penelope and Other Stories and Poems*. San Francisco: Bancroft and Co., 1877.

Walker, Franklin. *Frank Norris: A Biography*. New York: Doubleday, 1932.

———. Introduction to *Prentice Mulford's California Sketches*, vi–xxii. San Francisco: Book Club of California, 1935.

———. *Jack London and the Klondike: the Genesis of an American Writer*. London: Bodley Head, 1966.

———. *San Francisco's Literary Frontier*. New York: Alfred A. Knopf, 1939.

Ward, Russell. *The Australian Legend*. Melbourne: Oxford University Press, 1958.

Warner, Charles Dudley. "Modern Fiction." *Atlantic Monthly* 51, no. 306 (April 1883): 464-74.

West, Elliot. *The Contested Plains: Indians, Goldseekers, and the Rush to Colorado*. Lawrence: University Press of Kansas, 1998.

———. "Five Idaho Mining Towns: A Computerized Profile." *Pacific Northwest Quarterly* 73 no. 3 (July 1982): 108-20.

———. Discussions in *Mining Frontiers of the Far West, 1848-1880*, by Rodman Paul. Rev. ed. Albuquerque: University of New Mexico Press, 2001.

———. *The Saloon on the Rocky Mountain Frontier*. Lincoln: University of Nebraska Press, 1979.

Westbrook, Robert B. "Leadville." In *The New Encyclopedia of the American West*. Edited by Howard R. Lamar, 632-33. New Haven, CT: Yale University Press, 1998.

Western Literature Association. *Updating the Literary West*. Fort Worth: Texas Christian University Press, 1997.

Wharton, David. *The Alaska Gold Rush*. Bloomington: Indiana University Press, 1972.
Wheat, Carl I. Introduction to *The Shirley Letters from the Californian Mines*, ix–xxix. New York: Knopf, 1949.
Whipple-Haslam, Mrs. Lee. *Early Days in California*. Jamestown, CA: Mother Lode Magnet, 1925.
White-Parks, Annette. "Beyond the Stereotypes: Chinese Pioneer Woman in the American West." In *Writing the Range: Race, Class and Culture in the Women's West*. Edited by Elizabeth Jameson and Susan Armitage, 258–73. Norman: University of Oklahoma Press, 1997.
White, Richard. *"It's Your Misfortune and None of My Own": A New History of the American West*. Norman: University of Oklahoma Press, 1991.
Wilde, Oscar. *Impressions of America*. Sunderland: Keystone Press, 1906.
Williams, Rosalind. *Notes on the Underground: An Essay on Technology, Society and the Imagination*. Cambridge, MA: MIT Press, 1990.
Williams, Stanley T. *The Spanish Background of American Literature*. New Haven, CT: Yale University Press, 1955.
Winterbottom, Michael. *The Claim*. Directed by Michael Winterbottom. Los Angeles: United Artists, 2000.
Wister, Owen. *The Virginian: A Horseman of the Plains*. 1902. New York: MacMillan. Reprint, Lincoln: University of Nebraska Press, 1992.
Witschi, Nicolas S. *Alonzo 'Old Block' Delano*. Western Writers Series. Boise, ID: Boise State University English Department, 2006.
——. Review of *The Sagebrush Anthology*, edited by Lawrence I. Berkove. *American Literary Realism* 41, no. 1 (Fall 2008): 87–89.
——. *Traces of Gold: California's Natural Resources and the Claim to Realism in Western American Literature*. Tuscaloosa: University of Alabama Press, 2002.
Wurz, Vivian Helen. "The Leadville Camp: A Colorado Mining Community, 1876–1883." MA thesis, University of Colorado, May 1941.
Wyatt, David. Introduction to *Selected Stories and Sketches*, by Bret Harte, vii–xxvii. Oxford: Oxford University Press, 1995.
Wyman, Mark. *Hard Rock Epic: Western Miners and the Industrial Revolution, 1860–1910*. Berkeley: University of California Press, 1979.
——. "Mining Frontiers." In *The American Frontier and Western Issues: A Historiographical Review*. Edited by Roger L. Nichols, 109–30. New York and Westport, CT: Greenwood Press, 1986.
Young, Otis E. *Black Powder and Steel: Miners and Machines in the Old Western Frontier*. Norman: University of Oklahoma Press, 1975.
Yuan-yin Hsu, Madeline. *Dreaming of Gold, Dreaming of Home: Transnationalism and Migration between the US and China, 1882–1943*. Stanford, CA: Stanford University Press, 2000.
Zanjani, Sally. *A Mine of Her Own*. Lincoln: University of Nebraska Press, 1997.
Zola, Émile. *Germinal*. Paris: G. Charpentier et Co., 1885.

Index

accidents in mining, 2, 19, 65, 94; mining disasters, 2
Adams, Henry, 103
Agricola, Georgius, 16, 138n1
Allende, Isabel, 131–32
Apex Law, 84
Arthurianism, 84, 87, 130

Bacon, Francis, 33
Ballad of Little Jo, The, 131
Bancroft, H. H., 13
Barman, Jean, 101
Bauman, Zygmunt, 17
Belasco, David, 10, 94–95
Berkove, Lawrence I., 6, 42, 55–56, 65, 144n2
Bierce, Ambrose, 9, 26; engagement with miners' lore, 27–29; "The Night-Doings at 'Deadman's,'" 9, 26–29, 140n20; view of anti-Chinese sentiment, 26–27
Big Bonanza, The, 15–16, 66, 67
Branch, Edgar M., 69
Browne, J. Ross, 33, 36–37, 52, 141n3

Californian Gold Rush, 26–27, 33, 51; anti-Chinese sentiment, 26–27; ethnic hostilities, 41; placer mining in, 50; population, 48; writing of, 33–53 *passim*
Chilkoot Pass, 112–13; in photographs, 114–15, 116, 117, 127
Chinese miners, 48, 141n23, 141n26; anti-Chinese sentiment, 24, 26–27, 130, 131
Civil War, 70
Claim, The, 133–34
Clappe, Louise, 9, 42–45, 52; compared with Bret Harte, 44–48
communities, mining, 18, 22, 55, 76–77, 78, 99; non-normative behaviors in, 97, 101–2, 104–5, 107
Conrad, Joseph, 83, 86
Crampton, Frank A., 23
Cripple Creek War, 23, 78–79
Cronon, William, 110
Cruikshank, Julie, 126, 127

"Dame Shirley." *See* Louise Clappe
Davis, Richard Harding, 18; *Soldiers of Fortune*, 89–90, 132; *The West from a Car Window*, 77
Deadwood, 131–32, 133
Delano, Alonzo, 9, 52; *A Live Woman in the Mines*, 10, 108–9; *Pen-Knife Sketches*, 41–42

INDEX

De Quille, Dan, 10, 54, 55, 57–58, 66–70, 146n10; *The Big Bonanza*, 15–16, 66, 67; "Eyeless Fish That Live in Hot Water," 68; "Letter" to *Cedar Falls Gazette*, 100–101; "Old Johnny Ranchero," 67–68; "Torture Unutterable," 59, 60, 70
Desai, Anita, 134
destruction in mining, 16–18, 19–20, 93; environmental damage, 8, 78, 101, 112, 114; mining as rape, 101
De Voto, Bernard, 54, 68–69
documentary representation of mining, 3, 5, 6, 130, 137n15
Dumett, Raymond E., 96
Dwyer, Richard A., 55, 58

earth: agency of, 29; represented in literature, 30–31; reproductive powers, 97–98; sexualization of, 98. *See also* underground
Eliade, Mircea, 29–30, 97–98
Ellis, Anne, 99–100
Emerson, Ralph Waldo, 13
Emrich, Duncan, 55, 141n24

Fender, Stephen, 51, 56, 146n17
Fenn, G. Manville, 115–16
Ferguson, James, 92
First Fam'lies in the Sierras, 102–3
Foote, Mary Hallock, 4, 10, 83–84, 133; art training, 84–85; critical reputation, 84; "In Exile," 85; *John Bodewin's testimony*, 83, 84, 86–87, 132; Leadville portrayed by, 4, 83–84; *The Led-Horse Claim*, 83, 84, 85–86, 88–89, 150n22; love of Tennyson, 85; view of native nations, 151n30
Foucault, Michel, 91
Francaviglia, Richard V., 2

Gally, James, 54; "Spirits," 61

Garland, Hamlin, 10, 90, 110; *Hesper*, 78–79, 80, 86, 88; research on Cripple Creek War, 79; *The Trail of the Goldseekers*, 113–14, 133
gender and mining, 91, 93, 97; multiethnic gender relations, 99, 101. *See also* women and mining
Germinal, 18–19
Girl of the Golden West, The, 10, 94–95
Goodman, David, 32, 106, 146n11, 151n2
Goodman, Joe, 54, 58–59
Green, Archie, 2, 141n24

Hadley, Elaine, 47
Haggard, H. Rider, 7–8, 18, 82
Hand, Wayland D., 24, 76, 88, 97, 141n24, 154n20
Hardesty, Donald L., 76, 92
hard rock mining, 5, 50; in Nevada, 65–66, 68
Hart, Fred H., 10, 54, 57; "High Fever," 61; *The Sazerac Lying Club*, 64–65
Harte, Bret, 4, 6, 9, 33; career, 38–39, 52; compared with Louise Clappe, 42–48; critical reputation, 5, 6, 33, 37–38, 48–49, 51–52, 142n4; eroticism in, 10, 103; fondness for French writers, 47; "The Idyl at Red Gulch," 103, 104, 106; impact of, 77, 106, 130; Mark Twain on, 54–55; melodrama in the writing of, 42–43, 46–47; "Miggles," 47–48, 52; "Mliss," 40, 132, 142n8; "Mrs. Skaggs's Husbands," 40, 51; "The Outcasts at Poker Flat," 45–47, 51; parodied, 52–53; portrait of California, 39–41, 47–48, 51, 52; "Tennessee's Partner," 105, 106
Harz mining stories, 27–28, 81
Hayden, Asa Thurston, 4
Hayes, A. A., 77–78
Hesper, 78–79, 80, 86, 88
homosociality, 103–8. *See also* mateship; partners

Hughes, Langston, 2–3, 4
Hunt Jackson, Helen, 28, 30
Hurtado, Albert L., 99, 108

Ibsen, Henrik, 30
imperialism, 7–8, 13, 15, 17–18, 31, 59, 77–78, 89; in romance, 74, 82–83
industrialism, 17, 19. *See also* destruction in mining; hard rock mining; technologization of mining
instant cities, 8, 10, 76, 77, 78

Johannesburg, 2, 62; depicted by Langston Hughes, 2; print culture of, 63–64
John Bodewin's testimony, 83, 84, 86–87, 132
John Gabriel Borkman, 30
Johnson, Susan L., 101

King, Clarence, 30–31
King Solomon's Mines, 8, 18, 82, 83
Kinsey and Kinsey, 3–4
Klondike Gold Rush, 1, 3, 10; ballads of, 121–22; dogs in, 115, 116–17; journey to the diggings, 112–19; as the last rush, 1, 110, 127; newspapers in, 116, 120–22; photography of, 114–15, 116, 117; as a poor man's rush, 111–22. *See also* Chilkoot Pass
Klondike Nugget, The, 120–22
Kowalewski, Michael, 3, 6, 33, 42, 144n2

Laite, Julia A., 93
Law, John, 14, 31
Leadville, 5, 76–77; depicted by Mary Hallock Foote, 4, 83–84; journalistic response to, 77–78; Oscar Wilde in, 77
Led-Horse Claim, The, 83, 84, 85–86, 88–89, 150n22
Life and Adventures of Joaquin Murieta, The, 40–41, 42
Limerick, Patricia, 17, 136n12
Lingenfelter, Richard E., 55, 58, 66

London, Jack, 6, 10, 111, 124; Klondike experiences of, 123; "To the Man on the Trail," 123–25, 126; "The White Silence," 125–27; as worker author, 127
Loomis, C. Grant, 25
Lord, Eliot, 66

MacDonald, George, 30
mateship, 105–7
McCabe and Mrs. Miller, 133
McTeague, 9, 18–21, 29
migration, 1, 57, 75, 97; in grand narratives of mining rushes, 13; within the Klondike journey, 112–19
Miller, Joaquin, 102–3
miners' lore, 3, 6, 7, 23–25, 29–30; in conversation with romance, 81–82; "the last shift," 24; literary writing of, 26–29; magic men, 24–25; response to danger, 24–25, 99; women in mines, 97–98. *See also* Harz mining stories; mythology
miners' work, 2, 4–5, 21–23, 31; craft skill and traditions of, 5, 22–23; Mumford on, 17, 22; as slavery, 21, 31; as toil, 16, 17; uniqueness of, 21–22. *See also* hard rock mining; placer mining
mines: invisibility of, 2; remoteness of, 1, 129. *See also* destruction in mining; industrialism; miners' work; technologization of mining
mining industry: antipathy toward, 2, 6; grand narratives of, 13–18, 76; within national development, 77–78; spatial and temporal complexity of, 74–76, 87; transnationalism of, 6–7, 7–8, 14, 75–76, 130. *See also* imperialism; industrialism; violence; war
Mitchell, Lee Clark, 59, 144n2
Moby-Dick, 49
Moehring, Eugene P., 14, 65, 70
Moodie, T. Dunbar, 98, 99
Moore, T. Inglis, 106

www.ingramcontent.com/pod-product-compliance
Lightning Source LLC
Chambersburg PA
CBHW020934230426
43666CB00008B/1679